MW00834740

Luban Jing
Chinese Grimoire of Magic
and Esoteric Feng Shui

By Jason E. Read

Dedicated to my soulmate
and Priestess of Hu Xian, Vicky Yun

© Jason Read 2023

First Edition

All rights reserved. No part of this work may be reproduced, stored in a retrieval system, or transmitted in any form or by any means, electronic, mechanical, photocopying, recording or otherwise without the prior permission of the publisher.

The methodologies in this book stem from the author's own experiences. The Reader must not regard the information as an alternative to medical advice, which he should obtain from a qualified professional. The Reader who thinks he might be suffering from a medical condition should seek medical advice immediately. The Reader who is already in receipt of medical treatment should not discontinue or delay this treatment or disregard medical advice as a consequence of having read the information in this book. The author and the publishers cannot accept legal responsibility for any problem arising out of experimenting with the methods described.

© Jason Read 2023
First Edition

All rights reserved. No part of this work may be reproduced, stored in a retrieval system, or transmitted in any form or by any means, electronic, mechanical, photocopying, recording or otherwise without the prior permission of the publisher.

The methodologies in this book stem from the author's own experiences. The Reader must not regard the information as an alternative to medical advice, which he should obtain from a qualified professional. The Reader who thinks he might be suffering from a medical condition should seek medical advice immediately. The Reader who is already in receipt of medical treatment should not discontinue or delay this treatment or disregard medical advice as a consequence of having read the information in this book. The author and the publishers cannot accept legal responsibility for any problem arising out of experimenting with the methods described.

Contents

Acknowledgements and Preface

The book you now hold in your hands is a training book for a real Taoist School somewhat unknown in the West and misunderstood in Asia.

In the West, academics tend to focus on either philosophical Taoism or its manifestation in a distant historical past. In actuality Taoism has moved with the times and has a new vocabulary of which the academic scholar has no inkling. Yet, all Taoism is rooted in over 5000 years of history. One may read an academic text on Tang Dynasty rituals and terminology and think that is how modern Taoists work, which mostly, just isn't the case. Taoism in Asia has developed and evolved.

This is particularly true in folk Taoism which is as far removed from Taoist orthodoxy as much as say Gnosticism is from the Catholic Church.

After my studies with teachers in China and Malaysia and having returned to the United Kingdom, I looked for books on the subject in English, I found not many at all. Academic works were highly impractical and focused on the past or the Daoist Canon. Most other works were the usual texts on Qigong, alchemy and very westernised approaches to Taoism. There was very little actual material on real Taoist magic, and those that were published were either mostly guesswork or so unwieldy as to be impractical. In other words there was a deficit of actual workable material for those who want a way in. Thus the idea of this series of books was born.

The main focus of this volume is to introduce the reader to the real training methods, theory and spells used by the Chinese schools of magic. It is not an academic study nor a piece of missionary work from some Buddhistic-Taoist mix, such as Quanzhen or other orthodox Taoist 'churches'.

Here you will meet the methods of the Chinese schools of magic, their Gods, their methods and their way of working. If you are wondering why there is no bibliography, that's because the sources are an oral tradition and currently not in print.

I hope it opens the door for you and takes you beyond what you imagined Taoism to be.

I would like to thank my teacher Dr. Liang, now in his 90s yet seemingly ever young.

To my beautiful partner in crime, Vicky Yun.

To my publishers Mogg Morgan and Diti Morgan for their patience and support.

Jason Read

2023 UK

Introduction

The Luban Shu or the 'Book of Luban' or even the 'Luban Classic' is well known to the Chinese speaking occult community. The book has the same or similar reputation as the Key of Solomon among western practitioners of magic, and at one time nearly every village had a local magician, a 'fangshi' who was skilled in the Luban technique, and everyone, in older times, had a tale to tell about the Luban.

The Luban was, and is, both loved and dreaded by the Chinese. Luban is at first appearance a collection of spells gathered into one volume along with information about the magical aspects of feng shui.

Obviously the text was meant for the well educated magus as some of the spells concern complex notions of chinese astrology and geometry as well as the procedures of magic in itself.

The origin of the text is shrouded in mystery and a number of versions circulated throughout China.

What makes the Luban so attractive is that it is free of the dogma of orthodox religious Daoism, Confucianism and Buddhism. And yet it relies on their principles in a certain folk manner, much in the same way the grimoires of the West implied a Christian or Judaic worldview.

The Luban thus represents a means for the individual sorcerer to seek a pathway to power within a personal context and without having to limit themselves to the orthodox temples. This was a book for the outsider, the sorcerer who was also a scholar of the deepest and most profound mysteries of magic.

Another attractive element was that there was no need for

rare and exotic ingredients that are impossible to access and have lost their meaning to the modern mind. The Luban Shu is ancient but a LIVING tradition. Its gods and spirits are not only alive and well, throughout millions of Temples and shrines in Asia, but are part of the land, the rocks, the trees, the running waters and so forth.

It is not a speculative tradition which tries to piece together fragments from long lost practices that exist in broken papyri, and attempt at a working tradition. Side by side with the text there is also an oral tradition of transmitted knowledge. We do not need to resort to often subjective reconstructionism to attempt a revival of a lost tradition.

In this text therefore, we give not only the text itself with notes on obscure terms, but actual oral teachings from my own teacher Dr. Liang. For scholars it will be an interesting cultural source for the sorcerous magic outside of the main Dao stream. And for many it will be a teacher of a definite Way. If you choose this practical side, we urge you to follow all the oral advice and taboos and make a careful study of the initiation into the Luban Pai.

In the Luban system you must first enter its stream before it can work for you. The spells in the Luban must also be carefully cultivated. It is a myth that one can pick a random spell and hey presto it works. On average a spell must be PRACTISED many times before it can actually work. You will also see in the oral commentary there is inner work to do, some of which will be familiar to practitioners of more profound schools of neigong, as opposed to qigong.

Jason Read 2022, Year of the Tiger.

Finding A Moon Beyond
A Finger Pointing

Even before I was a teenager, I was interested in what is generally known as the occult. I found this to be a common situation with others who study esotericism, the occult or magic.

I had a number of what would be called 'paranormal' experiences as a child, including spontaneous OBEs, dreaming true and encounters with entities. This also seems to be a common factor in those who choose to pursue this path.

Two experiences in particular stick in mind. One because it was beautiful and another because it was terrifying.

To give the bad news first, the terrible experience was thus.

I was around eleven years old and jumped into bed. Like many a child, sleep seemed to be a surrender of life so I was then in the habit of using a torch to read under the bed covers. Finally, my fight against the natural tendency to sleep began to wane, and I prepared to sleep.

It was then I had the distinct impression that there was a shift of weight at the end of my bed. It was unmistakable in its reality. Looking, I saw a hunched dwarf-like creature that seemed ideally designed to terrify. It was almost monotone in earthy greys and browns, with a terrifying, mocking and leering face. Naturally, I screamed out and my mother came rushing in and rationalised it as a 'bad dream'. Yet, I knew it was some kind of objective reality. The shift of weight on the bed had been too real and the image too detailed and I had been fully awake to experience it. I was not in some in-between state conducive to 'sleep paralysis' or other such commonly offered explanations. I had, when I screamed, felt the weight again suddenly shift as the creature seemed to spring off the bed.

The other experience was beautiful. In a similar position, and a little older, I heard a tinkling sound, rather like tiny silver bells, and there floated before me three luminous spheres about the size of tennis balls. There they were drifting across my bedroom. The feeling was beautiful and I felt a surge of lovely calm and joy. As suddenly as they appeared they disappeared with an apparently audible popping sound.

It was not long after these experiences as I headed towards my teens that I began to study the occult more seriously.

At first I read popular books on the subject. My first experiments were in British witchcraft. I can still remember one of my first experiments taken from Doreen Valiente's *Witchcraft for Tomorrow*. And it wasn't long before I was familiarising myself with popular books such as Colin Wilson's *The Occult*, Lyall Watson's *Supernature* and so on.

It was Dion Fortune who gave me my first introduction to the nature of western magic. Who can forget their first reading of *The Mystical Qabalah* and *Psychic Self Defence*?

Over the years I got more and more serious with my studies and practice. It wasn't long before I was studying The Golden Dawn and then Crowley. By 19 I was a member of the OTO and in an encampment studying Saturnal Magic.

It was in this era that I first came across the works of the Typhonian OTO written by Kenneth Grant and its references to Chinese magic. Firstly there was a description of a ritual with an anonymous Chinese Priestess conducting strange 'Rites of Ku', in the Limehouse District of London. It was then something deep inside me resonated.

Perhaps the resonation rang louder because I was also a practitioner of Chinese martial arts and was 'tuned in' to the Asian current.

Unfortunately at that time, apart from Qigong and Tai Chi there wasn't much known about Chinese magical practice and certainly no resources for the same.

Most of what you could find in print was just speculation or wholly made up, for example the magical use of the I Ching by Crowley, Bertiaux and others. Or a truly awful book that I shall not name that was merely Southern United States Hoodoo with the label 'Taoist'.

Much closer to the mark was the scholarly work of Michael Saso which had a real description of Chinese ritual magic. It was the hints of Kenneth Grant and of Michael Saso that finally, and eventually lead me to realise that I must actually go to Asia to find any real magic of the type I was looking for.

After leaving a period of service in the Royal Navy and with some money saved I decided to travel to China to search for true magic of the kind I had read about. Perhaps it was a naive decision when I look back on it now.

Westerners tend to have a vision of China skewed by the media, and mine certainly was. Either we view China as a kind of oppressive Maoist regime full of drones and soldiers in Mao caps singing 'Shining Red Star' or a paradise with tall cloud wrapped mountains full of dragons and temples and a 200 year old sage on every peak.

Both views are wrong.

In 2007 with not much more than a traveller's backpack, a

passport and a pile of cash I took the plane to China, headed for Beijing.

It was a surprisingly short flight. My first impression is how modern China is and how cold Beijing was.

I had secured a small part time job in the city of Henyang in Hunan Province teaching English, to ensure I had enough money to survive, and a place to stay, since accommodation was part of the package. Henyang seemed a good choice as it was big enough to be a city and small enough to be less conditioned by the political modernisation of Chinese communism. Also nearby was a major centre of Taoism on the Southern holy mountain of Mount Heng.

Now with Henyang as my base I first decided to go to the various Temples…with some disappointment. I won't go into any details but the temples were largely controlled by certain government agencies and controlling bodies. I include most of the well known ones including Wudang, the primary focus for western students adventuring to China to learn Tai Chi and Qigong. Nothing but a tourist trap and a money making machine for the Chinese government.

As well as taking lessons in Chinese, I began to apply myself to Chinese Social media to look for and search for the Chinese 'underground' occult scene.

I should explain here that technically, occultism and the mystical arts are illegal in China. So social media tends to use a lot of camouflage to hide as best they can their identity.

However it was not long before I found several threads on Chinese occultism and even a healthy trade in manuscripts of ancient Chinese magic that belonged to family traditions rather than government sanctioned temples.

Right before my eyes there was a whole subculture of

Chinese magic and folk Daoism that kept itself hidden from the main flow of Chinese society.

However, the difficulty was winning the trust of some of these individuals.

Strangely enough it was I being a foreigner, that allowed me to win the trust of several prominent writers on these forums, some of whom spoke about learning in small groups or societies in private village or house temples.

One of these was, as it turned out, a girl living in nearby Yueyang. After some months of back and forth communication we not only shared an interest in occultism but became romantically involved.

That's when I met Vikki and she described how her grandfather was a believer and practitioner of a particular folk tradition called Maoshan. I had at this stage only had a cursory knowledge of it from the work of Michael Saso, but looking back the comparison is slight as they are entirely different manifestations.

In time me and Vikki married and won the trust of the family, I became a student of Mr. Liang.

This series of books represents some of those teachings received by me and others in that period from Liang.

I did not learn some cleaned up Daoism sanctioned by the government as 'acceptable' to the people's republic, but a tradition with both light and dark aspects given as they were meant to. Nor did I learn in some temples by stuffy priests with more book learning and tai chi moves than actual power.

Often the lessons were in a humble house with chinese tea and a mother and daughters preparing in a nearby kitchen Hunan and Malaysian foods, since Dr Liang had studied and worked for some time abroad in Kuala Lumpur.

Sometimes the lessons were more of a practical nature. Sitting in with clients or attending the small household temple annexed to the Liang family house.

J. E. Read 2022 Southampton,UK

The Origins Of The Principles
Of Chinese Magic

To truly understand Chinese magic we need to have a small survey of the history and archeology of Chinese religion and magic.

This is an important task because more recent publications tend to term Chinese magical, medical and mystical practices as 'Taoist', when clearly this is not entirely true.

Many of the fundamental beliefs and practices we think of as Taoist were crystallised at a much earlier time and only later were viewed and coloured through the lens of Taoist culture.

Beliefs in the Bagua, Yin and Yang and the Five Elements are clearly pre-Taoist. The Yi Jing was considered old before Taoists looked at it. Feng shui, a belief in the power of peachwood, the Gods, the Big Dipper, the basics of Chinese medicine are all older than the concept of Taoism. So it is, in conclusion, a mistake to contextualise all that is magical and mystical in China as Taoist.

The great schools of Chinese philosophy were not really developed until the Spring and Autumn Period with the Hundred Schools of Thought (諸子百家) that included Confucianism, Mohism and Taoism.

Generally Confucianism developed a philosophy that centred on the role of the individual within the confines of society. Taoism focused on the role of the individual in relation to Nature.

Yet both these philosophies were built on, and drew upon

much older beliefs that were embedded and taken for granted in Chinese society.

An immediate precursor to Taoism as we know it was the Yin and Yang School of Zou Yun that sought to explain all phenomena through the principles of polarity. Yet, even Zou Yun expanded upon and codified far more ancient conceptualisations that are found as far back as at least the pre-Confucian and pre-Taoist I ching, and possibly even further back to the Shang Dynasty Oracles.

To really understand 'Taoist' magic before it was codified and even force-fitted into monkish rigidity, we must go downstream to the sources. Furthermore we find that a much more 'pure' stream of Chinese magic is not found so much in conventional texts of Temple traditions, but in the less known folk magic traditions of China, Mongolia and Malaysia.

Neolithic Indications Of Magical Belief

Unfortunately we can only rely on archaeological evidence and speculate on the remains of cultures long-gone to come to some tentative conclusions as to the earliest beliefs of Chinese magic and religious belief.

The way people buried their dead gives us clues. As elsewhere red ochre was used in graves and on bones of the dead to apparently give life-blood to the dead. More unique to China was the use of cinnabar or vermillion for the same purpose.

Cinnabar has been found to be used not only on bones but objects such as pots and other grave goods. We can assume that cinnabar was a symbol of life and of the blood the dead no longer possessed, and its use was to irrigate the bones with the strength of life.

For example excavations in the Shao site have vestiges of cinnabar use in graves as does Baoji and sites in Huaxian.

To this day vermilion and cinnabar have a prominent place in the world of Chinese magic as we shall see, as a Yang power with life-giving and exorcistic properties.

Judging by the evidence, religion and magic seemed to have taken a great leap forward during the Neolithic period, perhaps hand in hand with the development of agriculture.

There was a great attention on where and how the dead were buried, and there seems to be a lore associated with the burial of the dead. Such lore would of course be the basis of much lore such as Yin House Feng Shui, that is the feng shui of the Houses of the dead.

Evidence suggests certain modes of burials. The most primitive favoured the burial of the dead in or near the family home to express the continuity of the family. Later the dead were buried at roads or in cemeteries outside the village. There are examples of posturing the bodies, either in the familiar and universal crouch burial or a supine position. Evidence suggests animal sacrifices, pigs and dogs being popular.

Pigs were, in Chinese thought, a symbol of wealth and prosperity and still are, and Neolithic burials show how ancient this idea is.

Dog's blood, especially the blood of a black dog, is still ubiquitous in Chinese sorcery.

Naturally grave goods were included in most burials. In some burials the objects were clearly broken on purpose, perhaps 'transforming' their nature for use by the dead in the afterlife.

Naturally, in Chinese magic and folk tradition we still see this practice in the form of joss money and paper objects burned for use by the dead.

Outsiders and criminals seem to have been buried differently to the 'normal' dead. We can see the logic of this in later texts.

With time many of the key ideas that filtered into magical texts such as the Luban were crystallised.

Initially China was a primal religious culture with a fear and dread and yet a seemingly contradictory reverence for nature and especially the dead.

As is typical of most developing societies a class of people who could act as intermediaries between the world of the Unseen and the world of man and visible nature arose and became increasingly more sophisticated in their practices and philosophies. This brings us to the next stage, that of the 'professional' sorcerer.

Wu: The Tribal Wizard Becomes The Civic Official

In Chinese there is a term, JUE DI TIAN TONG, meaning that the affairs of heaven should be kept apart from the normal life of the folk. The declared aim was to keep a balance between ordinary life of folk on earth and Heaven, that is the world of spirits.

In essence this was a political move to put spirituality into the hands of a few people who in turn served the rulers of kingdoms and city states.

At first these few elected civic wizards were chosen for their propensity towards a spiritual life, their unique mystical talents and sometimes even their unusual physical appearance. It seems lame people in particular were favoured candidates. In later Daoism there are various lame or crippled saints, and to this day when we walk the Big Dipper one foot is always dragged to simulate the crippled leg of the legendary bear shaman Yu the Great.

Such professional wizards were exempt from the common labour of the folk and were all at once doctors, advisors, diviners and so forth to rulers, warlords and generals.

It would have been rare for a general to embark on war without his magician by his side. One famous example is Zhuge Liang, the morally ambiguous wizard and advisor of the War of the Three Nations.

Skills of these wizards included reading the state of qi in certain areas to ascertain if conditions were suitable for certain undertakings. An art that perhaps went on to form the basis of Qimen Dunjia, a divination system that originated in the application of military magic.

Dream interpretation, reading the cracks in bones which had been heated, healing and exorcism were all arts that were practised by these Wu shamans.

Another of their responsibilities was the reading of the stars to interpret the will of heaven.

As time passed these wu shamans began to grow rich and highly educated. They would record history as a byproduct of their divinations. Indeed the first real evidence of writing and Chinese characters are on the oracle bones and turtle plastrons on which they recorded their observations.

It could be argued that the basis of the trigrams and

hexagrams of the Yi Jing were inspired by the complete or broken lines on such bones. To this day the turtle is strongly associated with the Yi Jing.

The Three Doctrines

With the development of Confucianism and Daoism in China the old teachings became more codified into various systems of belief. Confucianism stressed class and family and the ideal family of the nation as a fatherly Emperor who overlooked the family of scholars, officials, warriors, tradesmen and ancestors. This world view was seen as a reflection of the Order of Heaven that could be the ideal model for the running of the kingdom.

It is worth pointing out that while China has many nature gods and spirits, just as many, if not more, are in fact revered ancestors of the great, gifted or mighty who somehow 'ascended' to immortality and divine status.

Daoism concerned itself more with tuning into and becoming one with the eternal essence from which nature flows. Though in practice this was also a struggle that seemed to go against nature to conquer even death itself.

Buddhism brought even more elements to the magical mix. Practically speaking the idea of karma and rebirth as well as mantra and mudra became common in Daoist mystical practice.

Magic itself was developed in this context of the Three Doctrines and had both an inner and an outer spiritual component.

By inner, we mean the magician himself went through a period of self discipline and cultivation with diet, breath control and alchemy to 'celestify' the body or rather create a new spiritual body that was active and immortal in a spiritual and magical context.

The outer practices were communication with the spirit world in all its aspects, including a kind of possession called shen gong. This communication and possession was believed to also cause changes within the magician by exposure to a kind of 'occult radiation' and by residual memory left behind in the magician by the superior spiritual being that had possessed him or her.

In time the cultivated wizard could order commands of lower spirits by virtue of his cultivation and 'good report' with the spiritual entities with which he had intercourse with.

Thus the use of paper talismans that figure heavily in most Chinese speaking magical practices. Not only are they orders and commands that a general or emperor might issue, but they are living beings in their own right.

Such paper talismans are often burned to transform their exterior form and become a magical essence in the spirit realm.

The ashes or 'salt' of these talismans can be drunk in water for healing or increasing magical power, sometimes they are secreted in certain places or carried as a beacon for spirits or to work by 'occult radiation'... or both.

One may also notice that in the spells of the Luban (and in Chinese magic in general) the identification between the magician and the being becomes increasingly less separated until at the climax they become one. This is an important point if you choose to work with the material. The self conscious ego identifying mortal that you are melts into the deity or spirit with which you are working until there is no difference between the invoker and the invoked. A process called Bian Shen in

Chinese occult terminology and means, change body or change life.

The Luban Method sometimes known as the Witchcraft of the Carpenter has a long and esteemed history at first associated with the building trade.

This connection at first may not seem obvious to the reader. In most societies trade people such as blacksmiths, millers and builders have long held to have their own trade secrets and also their magical ones.

The carpenter had a deep knowledge not only of trees and mountains, the source of his materials, but also of times and seasons, the auspicious and inauspicious times to build or cut down trees or hew stones. He knew sacred measurement and proportion and was skilled in temple and tomb building that had to encode certain spiritual ideas to ably perform their respective functions.

He built houses at the correct time and place with the correct rituals to ensure they were places of happiness and prosperity.

Yet there was a dark side too, for this knowledge could be manipulated not only for good but also towards certain less noble aims ... revenge, seduction and even magical warfare. Let us not forget that Luban was also a patron of military engineering.

There are in fact records of this occurring in various anecdotes in the annals of China.

Shortly after the Tang Dynasty it was a popular custom of builders to place small figures in secret places in newly built houses and ships. These would either bring blessings or the residents of the house would find themselves infected with strange diseases and the family's fortunes floundered.

In the Northern Song Dynasty text *Northern Dreams and Words*, Volume 9, we read that in the Tang Dynasty, a certain gentleman would walk into the home of the Lu family and see a mysterious and beautiful maiden and fall ill. A suspicious and alert Daoist priest named Wu Shou Yuan soon realised that something magical was afoot. He searched the house and found hidden in the interior of a wooden pillar the carved figure of a maiden with the words 'Hong Ying' (Red Flower) written on its back. The priest burned the wooden doll and the magically generated phantom maiden was extinguished.

A major component of this earlier Luban tradition was thus the hiding of objects of a 'fierce' nature or the manufacture of 'artificial ghosts' that attack the Qi of the inhabitants of the targeted house.

The magic of the Luban remained well hidden until the Ming and Qing dynasties. All woodworkers and stone masons were considered to have mastery of witchcraft.

There are frequent warnings in books of the day of unscrupulous craftsmen placing objects in a house and in hushed tones spoke about the generations of passed on know-how in craftsmen families.

In the Caotang Biji (*Notes from a Thatched Hut*) by Yun Ji Yun, the author discusses the case of a certain Mo family who every night were disturbed by the sounds of apparent fighting, tumbling, footsteps and so forth … in other words classic poltergeist activity. On searching the house they found two wooden dolls in grooves made in the crossbeams of the house.

In another example from the same text, a family was anxious to find the cause of why the women of their family over three generations were deeply depressed. One day, when repairs on this house were made they found a wooden female doll surrounded by several wooden male dolls in obscene positions with the female doll.

The ghost charm is one of the most famous magical methods of the Luban. Another case is reported in the Xu Zi Buyu (*Sons Do Not Speak*). In this collection of stories, Yuan Mei shares the story of the scholar Gao Ming who flourished in the Ming Dynasty.

Gao Ming, tired from his duties, laid down to rest and fell soundly asleep. Suddenly there was a whisper in his ears that sounded like 'Lei Lei'. He bolted upright in his bed and saw a child-like figure around a foot tall before his bed. The terrified Gao Ming reached for his sword and attempted to stab the menacing imp but it vanished before his eyes.

Again, wooden puppets were found in the house, dressed in red clothes and strangling each other.

Other tales as found in the Jiang Du Jiao Xun *Book of Reminisces* describes how in 1697 repairers found in a house an odd painting of a green judge and next to him a small ghost in chains, a curse on the family who had lost child after child.

However we should not leave the reader with the impression that Luban was entirely a system of black magic. Indeed much of it is about healing, protection and prosperity and the tales that survive are those that make the best spooky story!

Luban Shu
An Introduction

Where are we to begin in introducing you to the Luban Shu? Perhaps by relating some of the well known anecdotes of the Luban itself, those interesting little pieces of folk gossip that both entertain and enlighten. Some of these folk anecdotes draw on the actual spells found in the Luban itself and give a hint of the power of its masters.

The Fixed To The Root Method

This method is not to be confused with the 'Body Fixing Method'. The Body Fixing Method was used to paralyse a person to the spot, while the Root-Fixing Method was to make a person do the same action over and over again.

One popular story of this method occurred in the 1970s. There was an old man who was known as a 'Luban wizard'.

A local teased the old man about his study of the Luban and made a wager with him that he could not work any provable magic. The wizard took him up on it. Seeing a girl combing her hair, he muttered some words under his breath without looking back. The sceptic jeered that nothing happened ... until some five hours later, the girl, apparently in a dream-like trance, was still combing her hair! The doubting Thomas, realising what he was seeing, immediately bowed and gave the wizard his wager.

With a few words the girl suddenly 'woke up' startled. When the people asked her why she was combing her hair for so long, she just said she seemed to go into a dream but couldn't explain it herself.

The Snow Mountain Method

The Snow Mountain Method is a technique used by all schools of Daoist magic. It works with the yin cold quality usually for curing fever or freezing things. A more macabre use was to stop corpses of the dead oozing fluids in a wooden coffin, so they wouldn't slop around in their own organic goo. A less friendly use was the Snow Mountain Palm Attack.

In this little folk ditty there was an old man, also known as a Luban practitioner who lived in the village and was both respected and feared.

One day a popular man of the village invited his village to a large feast at his house. The nature of the celebration is not recorded. However, he made the mistake of not inviting the wizard. Another fellow, sensing trouble quickly reminded the host that he had forgotten to invite the old man to the feast. The worried host quickly saw to it that the wizard was invited and sent off a messenger to get him.

However, before the old man arrived no cooking could be done. No matter how much wood was added to the stove it could not be lit.

It is said the wiley old wizard used the Snow Mountain Spell.

According to legend the Luban Method of Magic was created by Luban, a master of the ancient state of Lu.

Luban was a carpenter, builder and engineer somewhat in

the mould of Daedalus in Greek mythology. He was also a Master of Taoism.

The techniques of magic used in the Luban seem to originate in the area of the Sichuan Plateau. Most Luban works until recently were hand written and passed from generation to generation, some with beautiful diagrams and illustrations.

The practitioner was exhorted to have noble virtues and a compassionate heart. The Luban Shu is sometimes known as the Luban Jing, or Luban Classic or Luban Sutra.

Another common title is the Lesser Wood Metal Sutra. Quite why it has his name is something of a mystery, but it may be a reference to one of the key legendary Masters who passed down the text to various disciples, named Mu Jing Xianshi, or Wood Metal Immortal Master.

It is the most infamous of the magical books in China. Where it came from is uncertain.

Luban, is the name of an ancestral master craftsman of the Song Dynasty. He was praised as a great wood crafter and engineer. He was credited with numerous inventions such as the curved ruler, the wood saw, the ink line … a device for drawing straight lines and for numerous engineered war technology such as the cloud ladder, a ladder with hooks used to clamber over walls.

According to popular Chinese history Luban was a native of the Lu Nation during the Spring and Autumn period, and his traditional years of birth and death are given as 507-444 BC.

In one legend, Luban went into the mountains to cut down trees, but in climbing the dangerous slopes of that region, slipped and fell. He saw he was bleeding and found the cause to be a leaf with a serrated edge. That leaf inspired him to invent the saw.

Luban is in reality the Chinese Daedalus, an engineer of mythic status with a large collection of legends that have gathered around him.

In one legend for example, Luban made a wooden magpie that flew for three days non-stop.

The legend and reputation of the Luban Jing even lead to a popular horror novel called 'The Curse of Luban'

Legends state that to become a practitioner of Luban magic one must accept that it is a 'Lack a Door' method, that is you must give up something to successfully practise it. One must sacrifice or give up a long life, sight, health, riches, marriage and children and so on. Another superstition is that one goes blind after reading it.

At least one version is known as the 'Orphan Recension', as it was traditionally passed to the orphan or the poor.

One legend states that Luban married his beautiful wife, but soon after had to leave her to travel to a distant province for work. Missing her he made a wooden flying device, some say, a type of kite so they could meet more quickly.

One day, his curious wife attempted to fly the contraption. She attached herself to the machine and said the spell and soared upwards. However, she was menstruating and her yin blood touched the wood of the machine. Immediately, the blood 'contaminated' the spell, the machine crashed down to earth and she was killed. From then on the grieving Luban cursed anyone who read or attempted the spells in his work.

Thus in popular culture the curse of Luban is perhaps the best known legend concerning the text presented in this book.

What are we to make of it? In reality it is just that, a folk legend or urban myth that has grown with the book's reputation and not one taken seriously by any magical practitioner.

Such legends also sprung up in the western magical tradition, for example with the Petit Albert and in more modern times the *Book of the Sacred Magic of Abramelin*.

Traditionally there are ten major spells that are prominent in Wuxi in Jiangsu Province where the Luban tradition is strong, and these are emphasised in the local folklore, with only one having been learned by the better known Zhuge Liang, the Sage of the Three Kingdoms.

1. HOUSE BUILDING

Are the skills of not only physical construction, but the selection of auspicious days, taboos such as the Three Evil Positions.

2. FENG SHUI

When and where to build a house or tomb, to construct and place altars and so on.

3. FIX ROOT METHOD

A method of fixing a person to the spot. In one legend a Lord yelled at Luban angrily, so Luban just pointed at him and he was fixed to the spot.

4. HARMONY WATER

It was a magical method of seduction in which a lady or gentleman, would unawares, step over a specially charged bowl of water and fall in love with the one who placed it there.

5. INVISIBILITY METHOD

This was a way to hide the bodily form, usually by the help of the five elements, trees, rocks, mountains and so forth. In local Wuxi lore there was a scoundrel who used the method to spy on over 380 women but was finally arrested by the law after ten years. A variant has him being burned alive by Five Thunder Fire, another spell in Luban.

6. LIFE EXTENSION METHOD

Is to lengthen the life when your life is coming to an end, and this can be read in the Romance of the Three Kingdoms.

7. DRIVING ROCKS

Was a magical method of moving objects.

8. GIANT'S STRENGTH

Was a temporary method of increasing personal strength to lift over a thousand pounds.

9. HAIR STRANDS

Was a method of lifting heavy objects with one's own (long) hair.

10. SERPENT MASTER SPELL.

A certain spell was said and snakes gathered and even built a home.

There are in fact several versions of the Luban, but most of them share a certain corpus of spells.

The Orphan Version as was mentioned was apparently only allowed to be given to orphans, a term however that extends to the poor and the childless.

The most famous is the so-called Greater Wood Luban, which is a veritable encyclopaedia of Chinese sorcery.

This book combines the three versions of the Luban to give a complete Book of Luban, and consists of:

1. The Lesser Wood Metal Classic.
2. The Greater Wood Metal Classic.
3. The Orphan Edition.
4. Oral notes given by a Master of the Luban Tradition.

No one can be quite sure when the 'grimoires' of Luban surfaced in China, but the most likely dates are the Ming Dynasty judging by literal style and content.

The Nature Of The Texts

The texts themselves are largely hand written in traditional right to left columns with traditional ink and brush. Some are beautifully written with wonderful illustrations, while others are rather crude with barely legible cursive handwriting. Most seem to date from the Early to Late Ming Dynasty.

The content of the Luban Sutras focus on practical magic and serve as a practical handbook of magic for the wizard.

The spells range from self cultivation and healing such as drinking talisman empowered water, healing methods such as staunching bleeding and curing a bone stuck in the throat and protecting a pregnant woman and so on.

This idea of cultivation before employing spells is an important distinction in Chinese style grimoires. Neigong (internal alchemy), the practice of the Golden Light, drinking special empowered water to enhance Fali (internal power that can be directed towards magical goals) is prominent in the

Luban but is either implicit or missing entirely in say the Papyrus Magicae Graecae hereafter called PGM for example, though there surely must have been some now largely lost cultivation methodology in that tradition beyond uttering names and burning kyphi.

Another class of spells are those that are focused on the magic of the place. In Chinese culture the breaking of soil, the cutting of trees and stone, the construction or repair of houses has long been considered a vulnerable time. One could easily offend the Gods, especially local spirits and the like. Therefore certain rituals were practised to offset such misfortunes.

The Luban also deals with funeral rituals, another vulnerable, liminal period where spirits and the like can interfere with the smooth transition of a soul from this world to another. On a more prosaic level the Luban practitioner would be called in to deal with matters such as the ripening of corpses and the ensuing stench.

Disturbingly, the Luban offers methods to punish wrong-doers such as purposely causing the body to rapidly rot and stink or the coffin to become so heavy that mourners cannot lift it.

Another concern for the Luban is battling 'evil masters', that is dealing with those who cast evil spells. Various methods are given to shut down and even physically kill witches and black magicians.

Miscellaneous spells deal with matters that have long been the concern of folk traditions worldwide such as revealing and punishing thieves, healing, fighting and even killing black magicians and witches who seek to harm a community, stopping bleeding, protecting a house, destroying demons and such matters.

There are uniquely Chinese ideas however. Such as the Feng Shui magic of building, the willow doll for communicating with spirits, changing appearance, neutralising violations against the order of the flow of the Dao and so forth, all of which are dealt with in this translation.

The spells themselves cannot be simply read from the text. Explanations in the Luban itself explain how they must be cultivated on certain hours, days and in total secrecy over a period of time before they become effective.

The spells seem to come from a variety of traditions, but notably Maoshan and Lei Fa (Thunder Method). Glyphs and symbols of the Lei Fa Method are on almost every page. We can therefore assume the Luban wizard would have had some

Wuxi, Jiangsu Province where the Luban Magic flourishes to this day

cultivation in Thunder cultivation.

As to the Maoshan influence, we are here talking about the various Maoshan Factions of Southern and Western China, and not the cultivation based Shanqing on Mao Mountain that many writers confuse it with.

Indeed some of the very same spells found in the Luban are also to be found stock spells of popular Maoshan Sects such as True Heart Maoshan and others.

It does beg the question who had them first? Did the Maoshan masters draw on the folk tradition of the Luban, or did the Luban draw on the Maoshan folk tradition? Perhaps we will never know.

I personally rather suspect there is a quite consistent reservoir of spells circulating in the folk traditions of Southern and Western China that perhaps both drew upon, and the labels Luban and Maoshan are merely accidental in the Aristotelian sense. What was important to the Luban, Maoshan or Meishan folk magicians was the essence.

Methods In The Luban

Luban indicates by internal evidence that the reader has some level of cultivation in the Taoist arts and would be familiar with many of the processes as well as having developed a certain amount of internal magical power often referred to as having 'Fa li' which can be translated as Method Power or Dharma Power.

This would have involved the reading of scriptures, meditation and internal alchemy, as well as factors such as the daily cultivation of his or her relationship with the Gods and spirits.

Reading the Luban we ascertain several methods:

1. Use of talismans.
2. Use of spells and mantras.
3. Use of water.
4. Self transformation.
5. Use of hand seals.

The talismans are usually drawn on yellow paper and with cinnabar ink and represent commands to the Immortals and Gods who the wizard has communed with.

Sometimes they merely embody the intention of the spell itself.

Those that embody the spell's intention are written in the Yu-Gui or Rain Ghost configuration. That is the character of rain, representing the powers of nature and in particular, Heaven forms a kind of 'canopy' over the character of ghost, representing spiritual power. Within the body of the ghost character is written a word representing the spell's intention.

Usually when writing these Rain Ghost Character Spells the wizard verbally says Yu and Gui and then the character of the spell intention. See diagram page 45.

Spells and mantras are also usually employed. These fall into two classes.
1. In the first class there is a direct appeal to Gods or Immortals to assist the wizard working the spell.
2. In the second class there is both an appeal but also an idea that the wizard himself becomes the God or Immortal in question. There is a unity between the invoker and the

invoked.

Quite often there is colourful imagery associated with the spells, for example "rising and scintillating fires of the vajra thunderbolt".

Or the spell dictates the actions desired in a far simpler narration. Occasionally certain power words are used. These can include:

1. Sanskrit-like mantras with no discernible meaning.
2. Sounds that are onomatopoeia in nature such as thunder cracking, hissing and so on.
3. Appeals to astrological ideas such as the Bing Ding to represent fire and Ren-Gui to represent water, to the Five Elements, Yin and Yang, and to the spiritual essences of the year, month, days and hours of time.
4. The names of Gods, Immortals, Masters and of course various Tongzi (Spiritual Boys). Tongzi represent angelic beings of a pure, virgin and yang nature who often serve definite functions. For example there is a Tongzi for healing, a Tongzi for witchcraft and so on.

Spiritual Troops are frequently summoned. It is said a Daoist wizard with no 'troops' is unlikely to be considered as a true master. Indeed there is a considerable period of time in his or her training that an apprentice wizard will be cultivating and forming relationships with Celestial Troops. This idea is similar to the use of familiar spirits in western magic. You cannot call what you haven't developed a reciprocal relationship with.

The final class of spirit dealt with in Luban are ghosts, the dead. In Chinese belief the human soul has two aspects. The Hun and the Po.

The Hun is the higher and immortal part of a human being

and is essentially inaccessible to most wizards.

Wizards will employ the lower part the Po, which is in essence a part that is left behind on earth after death for a lot longer. The Po however often consists of the lowest and meanest parts of human nature and on top of that, in most cases they only possess a rudimentary intelligence. However through a certain method of cultivation Po can be developed to become powerful beings in their own right. That in a nutshell is the basis of Chinese ghost magic.

Note To Reader: Some talismans included in this volume do not have corresponding text, 34 and 35 specifically, but we included them for the sake of completeness. However, in the text there are spells which have the same name and function and they can act as alternative talismanic forms.

For example, the Spell of Mud Mountain (Talisman 35) can be found in Spell 172

The Luban Shu
(Upper and Lower) Book I

Preamble

This Book reaches the household.

People prosper and wealth arises.

Make a thousand calls and there are a thousand responses.

Ten thousand invocations and there are ten thousand spirits.

One does not call one's own spirit.

One family becomes ten families.

Ten families become ten thousand families.

In the four directions wealth flows towards the family.

1. Qi Xi Fa Shen Tan
Setting Up The Divine Altar

This is a preliminary self-initiation rite before one undertakes cultivation in the methods and spells of the Luban tradition. The idea is to connect with the ancestral Master Luban to empower and connect the disciple to the Luban lineage of wandering mages.

The auspicious ceremony requires five fruits (to represent the Five Elements of Chinese cosmology), joss sticks, candles and spirit money.

(Note: Spirit money is NOT hell money which is purely for the dead).

One should first read the Heaven and Earth Spell and then the Immortal Teacher Luban Divine Method Spell.

The Heaven And Earth Spell

Heaven and Earth flow naturally,
Filthy Qi is dispersed,
Within the Cave is the Mystery of the Void,
A dazzling light of the Highest Origin,
The impressive strength of the Gods flows
in the eight directions,
Enabling me to flow with the Dao,
The Lingbao Talisman commands,
Announcing to the Nine Heavens,
Heaven's Net responds,
The Cave of the High Profundity Strength,
Slaying demons and binding evil,
Tens of thousands of people,

Central Mountain God utters the spell,
Of the Original Beginning Jade Script,
Holding it and reading it all the way through,
Preventing sickness and prolonging life,
In accord with the Five Holy Mountains,
The eight seas hear it and know,
The Demon King is bound,
Guarding me,
Inauspicious filth disperses like smoke,
The Qi of the Dao is eternal.

2. Immortal Master Luban
Divine Method Spell

Heaven purity, Earth spirit,
Luban Xianshi displays his power,
I sincerely request the Immortal Master to be present here,
I sincerely request the Immortal Master
to descend to this altar room,
The Immortal Master shall personally
descend here to instruct me in the method of the Craft,
I shall formally be a disciple of the Master,
This day forth confer the teaching and the method,
At night I shall learn in dreams to receive the transmission
of methods by dream-teaching,
I shall keep the secrets,
The Immortals of the Three Realms and the Assembly of
the Immortals who shall also come together and confer
the methods and dharmas of concealing the body, the ten
thousand methods will bring ten thousand fruits,
Treading and becoming one with the Five Elements,
Yin and Yang footsteps, Left to steps to Yin and Yang,
Descend today Immortal Master and confer the Immortal
Methods of the Cloud-Wandering Immortal Realm,
I request the Assembly of the Immortals!
I honour Luban Xian Shi who passes the method,
I honour Taishang Laojun.
Ji Ji Ru Lu Ling!

Now the auspicious hand (left hand) grasps three sticks of
incense, bow nine times and then stand up and perform the
Five Elements Step Technique.

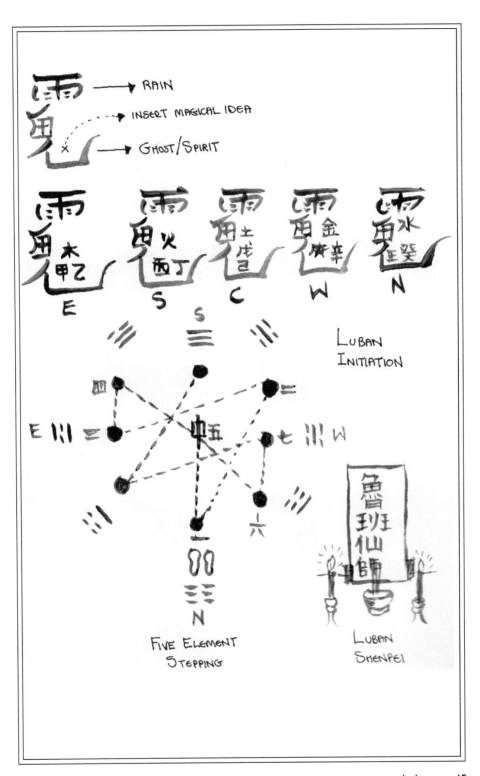

RAIN

INSERT MAGICAL IDEA

GHOST/SPIRIT

E

S

C

W

N

LUBAN
INITIATION

FIVE ELEMENT
STEPPING

LUBAN
SHENPEI

At each of the quarters write the forbidden words (seals) with the incense sticks. Step with the left foot first.

3. Untitled
Concealing Violations
And Ridding Of Evils Spell

Before any hope of magic there must be a purification. In Daoist tradition we, living life, give rise to all kinds of violations against the natural order of the Dao, in the realms of Heaven, Earth and in the realm of Humanity. With the burden of karma there is no hope of performing any magic due to karmic debt.

This spell is designed to wipe the slate clean so to speak. It is also used as we can tell from context to get rid of those violations which have impeded the flow of wealth and fortune into a house. The Luban magician conceals his violations from heaven. The magician would also perform this on the behalf of a client.

The Rooster is a significant symbol in this spell. The rooster represents the heavens and the Sun. It has a crest or crown that is often used in the practice of Daoist magic. The Rooster is revered for its purifying Yang energy.

Study and cultivate this method every day for seven days. Practice in the early morning before other people awaken. Do not let others know. With candles and joss sticks, pure in heart, recite the spell three times. Begin from the first day of a lunar month and end on the seventh day of the Moon.

The Spell:

Fuyi! It is not the first arising,
like a purple chicken wearing a five-colour garment.
Where did this rooster come from?

Tangseng went to the Western Heaven to fetch it,
the honoured Jade Emperor went to and fro
to announce the good news,
the people used it to hide (their violations),
Nature passes away and returns to the Realm of Heaven,
the Earth Evil (Disha) returns to the Earth God,
Demons and evil spirits, the Rooster points at them,
the Year Evil, the Month evil, the Day Evil, the Hour Evil,
the Rooster transforms the front of the home,
it transforms the rear of the home, the left of the house
and the right of the house, O the Gods respect the image
of the rooster and violations retreat from his image.
Metal! Wood! Water! Fire! Earth!
Those violations against the Five Elements,
all violations are transformed!

4. Untitled
Raising Water Spell

The raising water spell is learned over three months, on the first and fifteenth days of each month, on the second and sixth days of the third month.

On the first day of the month is when you begin, burning candles and three incense sticks. The best hour is that of Hai (9pm-11pm).

Pour some water into a small cup and use the hand to draw the Chiling Character (Fig.1) and read the spell twice. After the spell, drink the water. This will improve health, purify your body, purge violations and evil thoughts. Burn some paper money as you recite the spell, the hand drawing the Chiling character. It also covers violations and can be used to chase away evil spirits or exorcise them. You must be pure of intention and sincere or it cannot work.

The Spell

Fuyi! I request the Water God to come.
First arrives Pu'an and so this place is highly auspicious,
Heaven is Pu'an, Heaven and Earth are like as to Pu'an,
Earth is Pu'an, Pu'an Da Shen penetrates Heaven,
daily in the centre of the palm it is used, I honour Pu'an,
at this hour, at this place, I open this working, Heaven Evil
returns to Heaven and Earth Evil returns to Earth,
Year Evil, Month Evil, Day Evil, Hour Evil and the Evil
of the Wooden Horse are escorted far away from here.
I honour Taishang Laojun!
Ji Ji Ru Lu Ling!
The hand now traces the Chiling above the water.

With one point Qian Kun is great, The Sun is bright,
Po Luo generates all phenomena on Earth,
The Five Buddhas are set at the centre, the Three Celestial
Doors are on the outer, the Eternal High Blue Sky above,
the Upper is protected by the Dragon and Tiger Supreme
Crowned Emperor, the ever flowing river waters are forced
to turn back, the four thoughts and ten thousand reasons,
Eastern Mountain Temple God, Southern Mountain
Temple Master, Western Mountain Temple God, Northern
Mountain Earth Master, I request you to attend to this
burner and receive the incense smoke, Hong Zhou who
attained the Dao, Luban Xian Shi listens!
I respectfully request the Two Family Door Ancestors to
come, I honour the Three Doctrines Gods and Buddhas,
Peace comes to the family house, longevity,
prosperity by Tudi!
Hougong Buddha Qing Daren,
Zhaocai Tongzi,
Jin Bao Lanjun ye,
Hao Yu Jiutian Dong Chu,
Si Ming Taiyi Zao Wang Fu Jun,
Hou Gong Yu Chi Furen,
Ban Chai Tongzi,
Yub Shui Lang Jun,
Making right humankind,
The Upper has Pangu Xian Shi,
The Centre has Pangu Xianshi,
The Lower has Pangu Xian Shi,
Mo Dou Xian Shi,

FIG (1)
CHI LING

FIG (2)
USING CHICKEN'S
BLOOD.

FIG (3)
NINE
DRAGONS
FU

FIG 4.
A
PROTECT
FOETUS

FIGURE 4
B.
PROTECT
FOETUS

I request you all to attend this incense burner,
Raising water, reporting violations, protecting from disaster
by the Liujia, building or digging a ditch in the earth.
All violations are hidden!

Write this character on yellow paper with the blood of a chicken, burn it and let the ashes fall into the water to make all matters '100 times auspicious'. (Fig 2)

Many Chinese spells use a bowl of water as a means of transmission and communication of spiritual, cleansing and occult energies. The term 'Raising Water' or Qi shui is commonly used. The aim of this water spell as the text relates is primarily purification or the removal of accidental violations that give rise to impurities, doubts or wrong thoughts in the microcosm.

Various deities and Immortals are called to empower the water. Important among these are P'uan, who is often invoked in the Luban and other Southern traditions of witchcraft.

Pu'an was a Buddhist sage of the Ch'an School (Better known by its Japanese flowering, Zen) famed for his magical powers, so naturally he was called in such rituals. He lived from (1115-1169) and was originally a native of Jiangxi. He is so associated with the magic of averting disasters that his name is often seen on Tai Sui Talismans.

Other deities include the Four Great Mountains of the Cardinal Directions, the Wealth God Zhaocai and the creator God Pangu. Hao Yu Jiutian Dong Chu translates as Ninth Heaven Eastern Cook.

5. Cultivation Taboos

Luban Evil Days.

In Spring avoid Zi.

In Summer avoid Mao.

In Autumn avoid Wu.

In Winter avoid You.

Cutting with the Axe is evil:

In Spring Chen.

In Summer Wei.

In Autumn You.

In Winter Zi.

Cutting stone is evil:

In Spring, avoid Zi and Hai.

In Summer avoid Yin and Mao.

In Autumn avoid Si and Wu.

In Winter, avoid Shen and You.

The Days of the Wooden Horse Evil.

1st Lunar Month avoid Shen.

2nd Lunar Month avoid Wei.

3rd Lunar Month avoid You.

4th Lunar Month avoid Shen.

5th Lunar Month avoid Xu.

6th Lunar Month avoid Zi.

7th Lunar Month avoid Yin.

8th Lunar Month avoid Chou.

9th Lunar Month avoid Mao.

10th Lunar Month avoid Yin.

11th Lunar Month avoid Chen.
12th Lunar Month avoid Wu.

The taboos speak for themselves but mainly refer to building, cutting trees and quarrying. The Wooden Horse Days are days in which you should not begin any building or magical work.

In the Chinese calendar the days are marked by the Heavenly Stems and Earthly Branches in combination. The above taboos are marked by the Earthly Branches.

For more information see my *Practical Chinese Magic* and Appendix 2 for the Earthly Branches.

6. Famu, Kai Shan Zhi Sha.
The Method Of Cutting Trees And Quarrying In The Mountains Eliminating Evils

Anoint the axe head with chicken's blood so that accidents are avoided when chopping trees. This spell is used when quarrying in the mountains or chopping trees to protect the workers so that they are safe and sound and in addition there comes good fortune.

With incense and candles say:
The disciple bows to and honours Kaishan Zushi
(Opening Mountain Ancestral Master) with incense,
candles and wine offered to all the Gods to avoid
Heavenly Evil (Tian Sha) and Earth Evil (Di Sha),
Year Evil (Nian sha), Month Evil (Yue Sha)
Day Evil (Ri Sha) and Hour Evil (Shi Sha),
One Hundred and Twenty Four Evil Gods
and demons return to their respective directions!

7. Untitled
Building A House, Knocking Down A House Or Walls. Avoiding The Family Evil Of Construction And Renovation

Purify your cutting tool with wine, burn incense, candles, bright golden joss paper is needed as well as a red thread anointed with chicken's blood. It is burned in the North and the spell said as follows:

The Spell:

The Magical Power is vast, the Virtue of the Sages is bright,
All the Gods are invited, the Disciple's altar declares,
the Tu Gong and Tu Mu (Earth Lord and Earth Mother),
the Earth is profound and Heaven is high,
the Master's house is to be built/repaired,
Ten thousand blessings come, Celestial evils pass back to Heaven and Earthly evils pass back to Earth and are interred,
The Year evil and the Month evil are vanquished.
All taboos are lifted (BAI WU JIN JI!),
the disciple chants this spell and all the Gods return,
Great Fortune and Prosperity!!

(The money is burned in the burner.)

For the good of the family home it is best to start on the 1st day of the month, or the 9th, 19th, or 29th, performing the rites in the evening at the Hour of Hai (9-11pm).

You should also have some yang gao cakes that are broad and total a half jin in weight. Set three pure oil lamps, lit, and placed in the wall. One should dig three niches into the wall to hold the lamps.

At the commencement of the Hai hour, making sure nobody sees you, face the three lamps, kneeling on the ground, hands together at shoulder level and read the above Dharani Spell three times and burn the money in the tub.

Master it by cultivating it for six months, for three days in each of those months for a total of eighteen days.

The tribute of cakes cannot be changed and should be kept pure after the ritual. Use gummed paper to seal the cakes so they do not go off too soon.

After cultivation they can be eaten but it is taboo to give to others.

8. Bao Fan
Reporting A Violation

Have 0.1 Dou weight of husked rice, and a wooden bench or stool in the house underneath the central beam of the house.

Grasp some rice and cast it in the bowl, drop a little blood from a cockscomb on the talisman. One drop on top, one drop in the middle and a drop on the bottom. Burn it and let the ash fall into the water and drink it. Then recite the Report a Violation Spell.

The Spell

Pu'an Zushi, Great of Magical Power, Year after year, month after month he is with the family. No matter if the people meet the Three Evils, the Divine Water falls to the ground and penetrates all, the Heaven evil rises, the Heaven evil retreats, the Year evil rises and the year evil retreats, the month evil rises and the month evil retreats, the day evil rises and the day evil retreats, the hour evil rises and the hour evil retreats.

Pu'an Buddha sits in the centre. Fearing that it will not meet the Sun, the Great Earth is clothed in soil, Red sunlight is in the centre, the faithful fear the violation of the tomb, the kitchen violation, the house violation at the front and rear, digging high and filling low violations, Eastern wood violation, Southern Fire violation, Western Metal violation, Northern Water violation and Central Earth violation,

Eastern Five Li, South Five Li, West Five Li, North Five Li, Centre Five Li, Five by Five, Twenty Five Li!!!

RETREAT! RETREAT! RETREAT!

The Great Wheel detains evil.

The Ancestral Water strikes the rice of one sheng, and covers the evil and evil person, carrying that evil away.

In the direction that the evil retreats, yet money and silver are still in the Master's house and come as wished, covering evil there are no disputes.

If there are disputes, the Divine Spell generates no spirit!

To work the spell of the Bao Fan Zhou, you must choose the 1st or 3rd days of the 5th month. Or always use odd numbered days according to the Lunar Calendar. That is the 1st, the 7th, 9th, 11th, 13th, 15th, 17th, 21st, 23rd, 25th, 27th and 29th.

You can check the Chinese Almanac for the Days of Heavenly Star Descends to the Earth (Tianxing Xiafan) and for Tianyi (Celestial Doctor) Days which are particularly favourable for this action. At the hour of midnight, light joss sticks and candles and burn paper money and read the following spell:

Purity Master (Qing Zushi), a thousand times thousand Masters, ten thousand times ten thousands of Masters, the disciple requests the spell!

Say it three times and then say seven times:

Tianhou Jiang Shen water is drunk and using it the spirit comes near!'

It is taboo for the master to enjoy his wife or share the bedroom. Wash the face, rinse the mouth as in the tradition. Best cultivate this in the 1st, 3rd and 5th lunar months.

9. Jiulong Hua Gu Shui
Nine Dragons Transform A Bone Water

If there is a fishbone or the like stuck in the throat this is how one can cure it.

The Spell

FUYI! Nine Dragon Immortal Master (Jiulong Xian Shi) comes and helps the needy and the distressed.

Nine Dragons transform the bone water, transmitted from the Master to the Disciple.

Ling Guan Ma Yu (Lit. Spirit Horse Official), changes the illness of the throat, the well of water disaster, the blue sea is vast, the disciple cultivates success, a thousand invocations and there are a thousand responses, ten thousand invocations and there are ten thousand spirits, I honour Taishang Laojun's command.

Drink the bone water, transform the bone water, a thousand times a thousand transformations arrive with the long stream of flowing water, the depths of the throat change with the flow of water.

The Eastern Ocean has great sea water, The Ancestral Master arrives, the Teaching Father arrives, A thousand times a thousand fishbones transform and descend.

Use the middle finger in the bowl to draw the talisman in the midst of the water. Drink. (Fig. 3) Cultivate this spell in the same way as Bao Fan previously. It can cure the calamity on the spot and even aid someone who is not present.

10. Chanfu Nan Chan Shi Chui Sheng Shui Chui Sheng Fu.
Difficulties In Birth, Blowing Birth Water, Blowing Birth Talisman

The Nine Dragon Spell can also be used to effect an easier delivery when there are difficulties in labour.

The Spell

One, Transforming Nine Dragons Water,

Two, Transforming Wang Mu's place birth-water,

Three, Transforming into Guanyin's Inner Vase Water,

Four, Transforming into Western Heaven Hua Tuo's Water!

When using it, hold the Chui Sheng Fu talisman and blow the spell into the water after saying one, two, etc in the spell.

The Chui Sheng Fu is the same as the Nine Dragon Talisman. (Fig .3)

11. Antai, Bao Tai Fu
Protect The Pregnancy,
Avoid Miscarriage Talisman

In pregnancy it can be easy to miscarriage. Eat this talisman by burning and drinking in water or wear it to protect the mother and child.

It is best written with chicken blood. To cultivate this method one must practise it over a period of 49 days.

Find the appropriate days in the almanack (Lishu) and especially look for Tian Yi Xing Xia Fan (Heavenly Medicine Descends to Earth) days.

Practice after reciting the spell, draw a talisman, burn it to ashes and drink it in water. (Fig. 4)

Avoid sleeping with your wife for the period of 49 days, paying attention to self purity.

If you do not, it will not work.

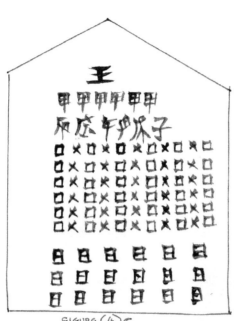

FIGURE (4)C.
PROTECT FOETUS

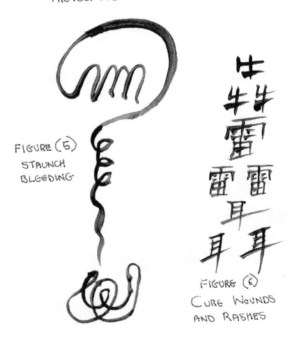

FIGURE (5)
STAUNCH
BLEEDING

FIGURE (6)
CURE WOUNDS
AND RASHES

12. Zhixue Zhou
Staunch Bleeding Spell

Write the talisman (fig 5) over the wound as you chant the spell. Stamp your foot on the ground and the bleeding stops.

The Spell

Fuyi! My hand grasps a great golden knife,
The bright red cinnabar road is obstructed,
The hand holds a little golden knife,
The lesser cinnabar road is obstructed,
Within, the blood cannot flow,
Without, the blood cannot run,
The man sees my sorrow,
The ghosts see my sorrow,
Ten people see my nine worried people,
Laojun sits at the cave entrance,
The blood dares not flow,
The Blood Official (Xue Gong) surnamed Qiu,
The Blood Mother (Xue Mu) surnamed Zhou,
Cannot flow, Cannot flow, Truly cannot flow!
The Ancestral Master reverses the stream.
Taishang Laojun.
Ji Ji Ru Lu Ling!

13. Zhi Du Chuang Yang Zi Zhou
Curing Poisoned Wounds
And Prickly Rashes

The stop bleeding spell and the curing of infected wounds and rashes are cultivated in the same way.

Practice over three days on the 1st, 3rd and 15th days of the lunar month, and on the 30th day. You can also consult the almanack for additional Tian She (Heaven Pardons) Days.

In total you need to cultivate this skill over a period of 7 days but will need a year to master it. Select an auspicious day. Observe the taboo to never let anyone see you practise it nor let anyone know.

Light incense and candles before the Family Gods and recite the spells with sincerity. If anyone sees you cultivate the practice is automatically invalid.

The Spell
The left (hand) strokes, and the right disperses,
The right strokes, the right disperses,
Copper pounds and it disperses,
Iron pounds and it disperses,
If you do not disperse,
I shall add five hundred fierce thunders to come
and disperse you,
I honour Taishang Laojun!
Ji Ji Ru Lu Ling!!.
As you say the spell, the hand is over the wound
or rash and draws the talisman. (fig 6)

14. Chui Yanjing Chui Huzi Zhou
Blowing Eyes
And Blowing Beard Spell

Practise 15 days in a month, from the first day of the Moon to the Fifteenth. Take care that nobody sees you and be sincere. Do it every evening at the Hour Of Hai (9pm-11pm) when it is quieter. You cannot be involved in sexual activity at this time.

Burn joss sticks and candles and say the spell seven times and burn money.

When blowing the eyes and blowing beards use the hand to draw the talisman. Hands are over the eyes as you read the command and draw the talisman. (Fig 7)

Blowing Beard is a Chinese idiom, meaning to do something with vigour, in this case blowing forcefully so the beard rise (Ed.)

The Spell

I request the Strong Wind Immortal (Da Feng Shi) to come, and Lesser Wind Immortal (Xiao Feng Xian Xian) to come, the wind is coming quickly, the wind will come, I request that so I shall not blow forever, the wind blows the eye, blowing the eye fire, blowing the water violation, blowing the wood violation, blowing the earth violation, blowing the metal violation, (at this point blow three times as you name each violation then carry on …)

Blowing the year evil, blowing the month evil, blowing the day evil, blowing the hour evil, blowing the man ghost calamity evil, blowing the 124 evil spirits (blow five times for each)

Blowing Zi, Chou, Yin, Mao, Chen, Si, Wu, Wei, Shen, You, Xu, Hai evils (blow seven times).

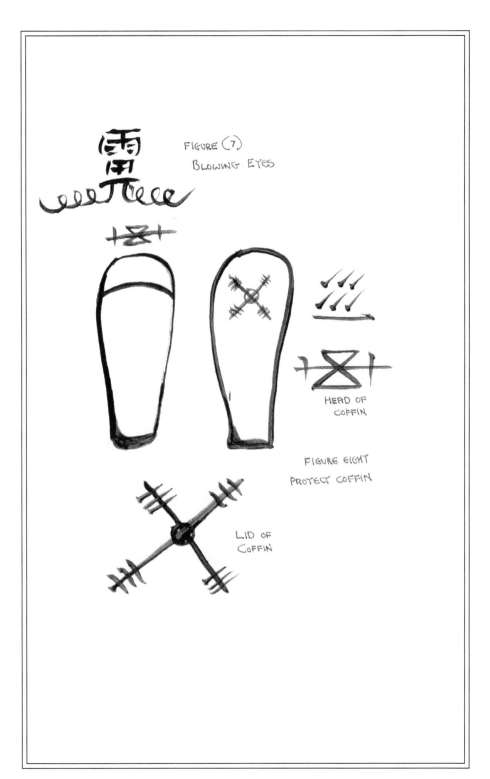

FIGURE (7.)
BLOWING EYES

HEAD OF
COFFIN

FIGURE EIGHT
PROTECT COFFIN

LID OF
COFFIN

15. Shou He Mu Yuan Gai Zhou Coffin Lid Spell

When a person dies and the coffin is shut it must be guarded against evil, violations or the sound of something moving or damage that can affect the life span of the living.

We use this spell and talisman to control and subdue such factors. For the two talismans use chicken's blood, but no need to stick on the chicken feathers. (Fig. 8)

The Spell

Fuyi! The Doa incense is sweet, the Lingbao worship is fragrant, the fragrant Dao goes to the Three Realms, throughout the Ten Directions. Reverently burning incense with a sincere heart I offer and request the Three Origins Three Great Officials, the Three Doctrine Masters Sakyamuni Buddha, Li Laojun and Kong Shangren, the Three Central Teachers who are Guanyin, Wenchang and Zushi, the Lower Three Masters who are Chuan Tzu, Tuzu and Yao Wang Zhenren, I request at this moment that you descend, I respectfully burn true incense and truly request, The Five Directions Earth Veins Dragon God (Dimai Long Shen, the Lord of the dragon veins or lines of Qi in the landscape according to the doctrine of Feng Shui), controller of this land, the place of the mansion of the earth, the Nine Complete Heavenly Emperor, the Purple Concubine Mansion of the Purple Flower Lady.

I respectfully burn incense with devotion and request the Dao Scholar who expounds the Dao of the Three Doctrines, Come and be here O Hong Zhou De Dao, Luban Ancestral Master comes to build the Spirit Tablet, the Master Zhang Lang builds skillfully with the axe, Tongzi Famu Langjun (Felling Tree Boy), the disciple bows his head in reverence, to the generations of great masters, I request you to come Ancestral Master, Teachers,Teacher Uncle,Teacher Younger Uncle, Senior Apprentice, Junior Masters and all Masters to shut and seal this coffin.

In the year ******* month*******day *******.

Request that the person whose name has passed on and is beneath the coffin lid, that Heaven opens the Yellow (ecliptic) Path, to great auspiciousness and fortune.

(Set up what is needed such as incense, flowers, joss money and wine for sprinkling) Then continue with the spell:

The Master's curved coffin lid,
One not defended by Heaven.
Two not defended by Earth.
So protect this loyal disciple,
Heaven has no envy, Earth has no envy,
The year has no evil, the month has no evil,
the day has no evil, the hour has no evil,
Jiang Taigong hereby lifts all taboos,
the round cover is shut, money is burned in the flames,
We request to receive security in this place,
supporting each other, vanquishing evil and safeguarding,
O Nanzhou Great Brightness today in this great country
of****and the province of **** in the city of *****of
renowned names we request the Gods.
The loyal worker has passed away and sleeps in this safe
and consecrated place, hands at the chest to honour
the Gods, the Upper (realms) give serenity.
(This last part is done 36 times)

Ji Ji Ru Lu Ling!

The Coffin Lid Spell is learned over a period of 49 days, beginning on the 1st day of a lunar month. In the third month it is accomplished. On the 4th month on the 27th day stop. The 1st day of the 5th month can be done, the 21st day of the 6th month is also good.

Set up the Luban Xian Shi Spirit Tablet and use red paper to write it and place it in the main room of the house. Sexual relations are forbidden or the power declines.

In the morning at the place of the Luban Spirit Tablet, place incense and candles and say the spells without anyone knowing or seeing you. Say it three times.

If not done secretly (Yingong) it is invalid.

It takes three purifications and a pure and calm mind to learn the arts of spirit.

16. Fozu Chuan Wan Bing Yi Wan Shui Zhou Buddha Transmitted The Ten Thousand (Cure) Illnesses By One Bowl Of Water

A bowl of water is set down, incense and candles above, whether it is for building or repairing, marriage or burying the dead, the sick person who is not in peace, all can be covered, protected and treated with this method.

The Spell

Fuyi! I dare not deal with this matter, having worries about this matter we hereby communicate with you the Gods,

Requesting the Gods, requesting our wish, request that you come O Xi Huang (Sun Emperor), Xuan Yuan Huang (the Lofty Ape Emperor), Shennong Huang, Tianshi Qipo, Tai Wu Leigong Shen Yi Bian Que, Yi Shen Zhang Zhong Jing, Taiyi Yu Shu He Liang Yi Hua Tuo Laozu, Yao Wang Seng Zun Ren and all the generations of the Three Dynasties Renowned Doctors, the disciple has come and money is presented with the request.

The Twenty-Eight Star Mansion Lords ... Jiao, Kang, Di, Fang, Xin, Wei, Ji, Dou, Niu, Nu, Xu, Wei, Shi, Bi, Kui, Lou, Wei, Mao, Bi, Zi, Shen, Jing, Gui, Liu, Xing, Zhang, Yi, Zhen!

The Five Eastern Roads are prosperous.

The Five Western Roads are prosperous.

The Five Southern Roads are prosperous.

The Five Northern Roads are prosperous.

The Five Central Roads are prosperous.

Five times five is twenty-five and they are all prosperous!

The disciple comes, wealth and money
are offered with our request,
Pu'an Zushi is great in magical power,
The Sun, the Moon and the Star Gods are in the centre
of the palm,
The fearless Nine Dragons rid of the Three Evils,
The talismans and heart together transform the emptiness,
One slaying the Eastern demons,
One hundred ghosts are extinguished without a trace,
Second, slaying the Southern demons,
Ghosts and evil spirits leave this altar,
Third, slaying the Western demons,
Ghosts and demons all must listen and depart,
Fourth, slaying the Northern demons,
Ghosts and demons flee and can never return,
Fifth, slaying the Central demons,
Forever they disintegrate without a trace.
The first request, the Eastern Direction JIA! YI! Wood!
The Eastern Five Li Dragon God returns to his station,
Second request, Southern Direction BING! DING! Fire!
Southern Five Li Dragon God returns to his station.
Third request, Western Direction, GENG! XIN! Metal!
Western Five Li Dragon God returns to his station.
Fourth request, Northern Direction, REN! GUI! Water!
Northern Five Li Dragon God returns to his station.
Fifth request, Central position, WU! JI! SOIL!
Central Five Li Dragon God returns to his station.
Eastern direction three evils,
Five times five is twenty five evils,
The Star Lord request answered,

A sound does not arise (ie purified),
The Nine Yin Oxen Immortal God (Yin Jiu Niu Xian Shen)
Makes a second shout and they do not rise,
The Nine Yin Oxen Immortal builds it (the talisman),
Qiu Xian Shi (Tomb Mound Master), Chen Fu Xian Shi,
Li de Zhang Xian Shi, ZaoFu Tongzi (Build Talisman Boy),
 Ci Fu Tong Lang (Command Talisman Official Boy),
Mu Shi Shenxiang, Du Jiao Meng Wang Da Liang,
Jiu Niu Po Tu Da Jiang Jun,
I request and honour Yang Gong Xian Shi, Bai He Shi,
Jiu Tian Xuan Nu Niang niang, Taishang Laojun.
Ji Ji Ru Lu Ling!

To learn this spell requires 49 days. Every day I chant it three times. In the second month you can cultivate it. Do it late at night when it is quiet.

Burn incense and candles. Palms together and on your knees bow. Hold in your hand the water bowl and the talisman and say the spell. Having read it three times, drink the water.

Learn it without lust in your heart and wash and bathe three times before sleep.

This method was transmitted secretly by the Buddha.

Talisman (Fig. 9)

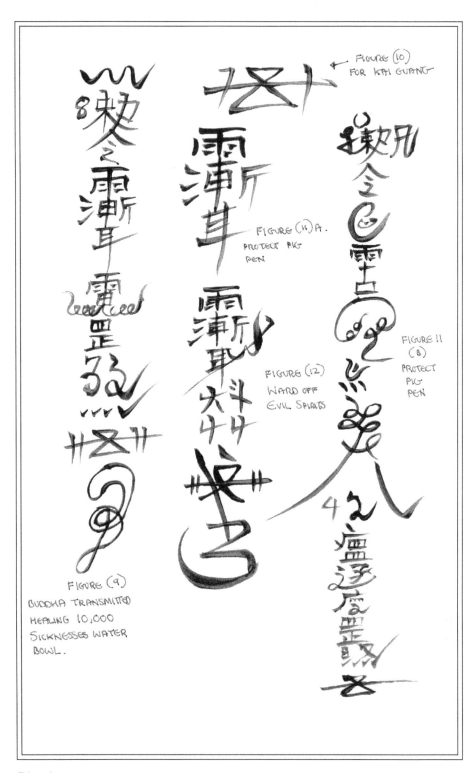

FIGURE (10)
FOR KAI GUANG

FIGURE (11) A.
PROTECT PIG
PEN

FIGURE (12)
WARD OFF
EVIL SPIRITS

FIGURE 11
(B)
PROTECT
PIG
PEN

FIGURE (9)
BUDDHA TRANSMITTED
HEALING 10,000
SICKNESSES WATER
BOWL.

17. Kai Guang
Of An Image

The Spell

Fuyi! An offering of paper money from the master,
Aligned in two rows,
Ten finger tips are straightened,
A drop of oil, shining and bright,
Vegetable seeds are cast outside on a barren hill,
But they shall blossom and bear fruit that people shall gather,
The farmer has skill in growing the fruits
and the craftsman have skills,
In Autumn, the people do not receive great power,
Thus the Disciple goes to consecrate,
Consecrate to initiate the light of the flame,
For a long time the light has not be illuminated,
Opening the light we ask the Sun
and the Moon light to open it,
The Sun and the Moon illuminates the four directions,
The light begins,
The rays of light shine upon the crown of the head,
Heaven and Earth, Qian and Kun illuminate
the Upper Heaven,
Opening the Dance of Light,
The nose is shining with light,
The nose smells the censer burner's eight treasure incense,
The light opens the light of the brow,
Light illuminates the brow,
The eight characters of the brow are in lines of two,
Open the light of the ears,

The light illuminates the ears,
The ears listen to the master of the family
and supports them,
Open the light of the eyes,
The light illuminates the eyes,
The left eye is Yin and the right eyes is Yang,
Open the light of the mouth,
Light illuminates the mouth,
The mouth has upper and lower 18 silver teeth,
Open the light of the throat,
The throat is an opening to the intestines,
Open the light of the hands.
The hands now shine with light,
The hands seize money and treasures
and bring them to the family home,
Open the light of the feet,
The feet shine with light,
The feet advance through the Nine Nations
and traverse the Four Directions,
Open the light of the knees,
The knees shine with light,
The two knees can enable travel upon the earth
and in harmony like twin mandarin ducks,
Open the light of the heart,
The heart shines with light,
The heart is bright and clear
and penetrates the Paradise of Heaven,
Open the light of the large intestine,
So it can serve the function of the large intestine,
The large intestine is two zhang in length,

Having the ability to function over every year,
over the twelve months,
and protects and keeps all safe,

Open the light of the Small Intestine,
In all the Twenty-Four Solar terms it functions,
Open all of the Five Organs and the Six Hollow Organs,
Therefore it channels metal, wood, water, fire and soil,
Open the 380 skeletal joints,
Open the 84000 hairs on the body!
Build and open it now!
The Spell of the Kai Guang acts,
I utter it with sincerity!

Luban Notes:
Recite it with your heart. There is no need to cultivate it. Use chicken blood to point the limbs and bodily parts as you name them.

Oral Teachings:
Kai guang is hugely important in Asian traditions such as Daoism and Buddhism but probably hearkens back to shamanic traditions.

A statue or image is considered 'dead' before Kai guang and without virtue. Worse still, the image may become inhabited by wandering spirits, lonely ghosts and even demons masquerading as Immortal or Gods. In this case the image becomes vampiric in nature feeding off the devotee rather than a benefit. Thus it is imperative that an image receives Kai guang before being seated in the home or an altar, or even worn in the form of a bracelet, necklace etc.

Kai means Open and Guang means light. That is, to fill a 'dead' image with the light of life and vitality.

There are various rituals associated with Kai guang but here we should focus on the Luban methodology.

The Luban itself merely gives a little advice, the sigil for consecration and the spell itself, but readers would have been aware of the ritual or taught the basics by a Luban Master.

Firstly you must consider the date, ie., select an auspicious date or Ze-Ri.

In the Maoshan tradition where the Luban ritual is sometimes used they are: In Spring and Autumn: In the periods of the Lunar Mansions of Xin, Wei, Bi or Zhang. (心,危 ,畢,張) In Summer and Winter the Mansions of Fang, Xu, Mao and Xing (房, 虛, 昴 星).

The fangshi should be equipped with the following:

Gushu (Ancient book. This is usually a page of scripture or a mantra written on paper. For example the Heart Sutra or the OM PADME HONG. It represents the wisdom of mind.)

RILI (Calendar. A page from an old almanack to represent the power of times and seasons.)

- Tong Qian (Copper coins to represent wealth and prosperity.)
- Bao Jing (A miniature mirror illuminates the good and exposes the evil for what it is.)
- Wu Gu (The Five Grains, i.e. rice, millet, soybeans, sesame and adzuki beans.
- A little gold and silver, pearls etc to fortify fortune.
  A cotton band made of five coloured threads of black,

yellow, white, red and azure to represent the five elements.
- Incense ash from a temple devoted to the deity in question (not always possible) and/or a talisman to allow the communication between Earth and Heaven).

Also needed are a brand new brush, cinnabar and or chicken's blood taken from the crown of a rooster, an incense burner, a Seven Star Sword or use of the sword jue, and a mirror.

The Altar is set up with the image to be consecrated covered with a red cloth, candles and incense and all the prepared tools.

Declare your intention, for example:

Today I ask you to consecrate this statue/picture etc,

I request the assistance of the Gods and Buddhas to consecrate this (...) deity with rays of light. Come! Assist your disciple to consecrate!

1. Wash and clean the statue
2. Insert the ancient book, calendar, coins, precious mirror, five grains, thread, gold and silver etc into the back, abdomen, base etc and then recover with the red cloth.
3. Holding up the sword or using the Sword Mudra say the Precious Sword Spell:
4. Carrying the Sword across the Land Under Heaven,
   Turn left and the Earth shakes,
   Turn right, the Sun, Moon and Stars,
   Heaven purifies, Earth is spirit,
   The hand grasps the precious sword and opens the bright light of (name of deity) and you shine with rays of light for over thousands of miles,
   An auspicious Day and hour!

This God's light opens and has a greatly auspicious visage,
A thousand do not have one exchange,
A year does not shun it, an hour does not block it
All taboos are lifted!
(so and so God) has great luck and prosperity.
I honour Taishang Laojun's command!
Ji Ji Ru Lu Ling!!!

5. Recite the spell as given in the Luban holding the pen and use cinnabar or rooster's blood to point each part as in the text.

6. Hold the precious mirror in your hand and reflect sunlight onto the deity:
   I hold in my hand the precious mirror
   to illuminate the Land Under Heaven,
   Illuminating, Heaven purifies,
   Illuminating Earth all living beings are blessed with longevity,
   Illuminating the people, they have long life,
   Illuminating (Say name of God) the three hun
   and seven po souls are illuminated to a higher state,
   You shall manifest great spiritual power,
   I thus illuminate your face and it is pure,
   I illuminate your body so the body is bright,
   Illuminating your entirety and the rays of light
   spread over a thousand miles!

The Luban also gives a seal, the standard Fu-dan or "gallbladder" as the consecration symbol. This should be written with cinnabar mixed in wine or cockscomb blood with the sword finger on the seat where the statue will be placed or on the base of the statue.

Talismans (Figs. 11a and 11b)

18. Untitled
The Stone Mason Sweeps The Pen

This is the Luban Method of cleansing and protecting an enclosure, stye or pen with domestic animals such as pigs.

The Twelve Branches Yearly Plague Kings

Zi Year Plague. ..	Zhou Da Wang
Chou Year Plague...	Yue Da Wang
Yin Year Plague…	Wei Da Wang
Mao Year Plague...	Zheng Da Wang
Chen Year Plague.. .	Chu Da Wang
Si Year Plague…	Wu Da Wang
Wu Year Plague…	Qin Da Wang
Wei Year Plague...	Song Da Wang
Shen Year Plague...	Qi Da Wang
You Year Plague…	Lu Da Wang
Xu Year Plague…	Zhao Da Wang
Hai Year Plague…	Liu Da Wang

The names of the Lords of the plagues are above and are placed on the door of the pen. For example in the years of Zi (the Rat) such as Wuzi, Bingzi, Gengzi and so on we shall request Zhou Da Wang to assist with the purifying of the enclosure in question.

To purify an enclosure, go to the gate of the enclosure, with wine, fruit, candles, joss paper for burning and a chicken. Also have a knife.

Firstly make a petition to the Enclosure Entrance Master

of the relevant year, i.e. the Plague King. Have in your hand a new broom and say the spell as follows once:

> Fuyi! The Disciple comes to this place
> called ………belonging to the family of………,
> One sweep to the East, Jia, Yi, Wood!
> A second sweep to the South, Bing, Ding, Fire!
> A third sweep to the West, Geng, Xin, Metal!
> A fourth sweep to the North, Ren, Gui, Water!
> A fifth sweep to the centre, Wu, Ji, Soil!
> Excrement and urine are swept away and dealt with,

(Hands hold the rooster (blood) and he writes the inner symbol with the point of the knife and continues the spell:)

> Plague water is not drunk, plague grass is not eaten, today the pigs grow a thousand jin, at night grows ten thousand jin on both sides, We congratulate the Master's family whose pigs become large porkers of three hundred jin!

Having drawn two talismans one is burned in a bowl of water and the water and ashes thrown into the pen. Another is pasted on the gate. The house owner or farmer should be the one to supply the materials for the offerings. After the Sweeping Ceremony the Master and the others can eat them. A taboo of the practice is that the sweeping cannot go through the railings but MUST go through the gate. After the Sweeping when all eat the fruit or meats the assembled people should not make loud noises.

19. Bi Xie Fu
Warding Off Evil Spirits Talisman

Use this talisman (Fig. 12) if you have to travel by night on lonely roads and to expel ghosts or demons you may encounter on such a journey.

The right hand middle finger should point to the Heavens and the right foot stamps on the ground when employing it.

20. Untitled
Sweeping The Pig-Pen Seasonal Epidemic Talisman And Warding Off Evil Talisman Appendix

Regardless of the month, the days of Tian Yi Shen (Heavenly Medicine/Doctor God days as found in any Chinese almanack) are the best.

In the early morning at the hour of Mao (5-7am), first wash your face and rinse out your mouth. No one can see you. Light incense and candles and request the thousands of Masters and millions of Gods to assist you, read the spell of the talisman three times.

If doing this for a client, do not dispute about money when sweeping or the spell will fail.

21. Untitled
Repairing A House, Raising The Stone, Cutting And Sending Ink Spell

This is a form of magic employed in building or repairing a house, and essentially is the placing of a talisman (Fig. 13) beneath the new structure.

Various Gods associated with protecting destiny, forgiving violations against the Dao of Heaven, the Masters of Daoism, Confucianism and Buddhism, and home protectors such as Door Guardians, Family Gods and Local Earth Spirit Gods are invoked. Then beginning with Dongfang Qing Di Tu Fu Shenjun, we have Eastern Azure Earth God, Southern Red, Western White, Northern Black and Central Yellow Gods).

This spell should be learned and cultivated on the first four days of a given Lunar Month and on the 15th day of a month.

Read the spell and have three oil lamps upon the shrine of the Earth God Tudi, along with incense and candles.

At the hour of Zi (11pm-1am) say it once in secret and burn paper money. Be sincere.

The Spell

Fu yi! The divine incense is in the burner, the people request you to descend from far away, a great pillar of true incense rises, with my whole heart I ask the Heaven, Earth and Water Officials, Great Earth, the Upper Origin High Official, the Bestowing Fortune Heavenly Official, the Middle Origin Second Official, the Official who Pardons Violations Earth Official, Purifying Great Earth, Universally as one, we request you all to come quickly and support us and descend here, to this realm, fearing the lonely soul, the distant ones come to this place and remain in this place.

The disciple (acting) for the people places the meritorious deed of the Ink, and thus we ask the distant ones to descend, the Three Heavenly Doors are without, honouring the Earth God (Tudi).

In the cold forest we meet, one place of both old and young lonely souls, come!

We request the arrival of the Family Gate Ancestors and the Family Ancestor Gods, the Upper Three Teachers Buddha, Li Laojun and Kong Shengren, and the Three Doctrines Masters Guanyin, Seven -Storeys and Wenchang Master, and the Lower Three Doctrines Masters, Chuan Zu Tu Zhu, Han Chao Hong Zhou Ling De Dao, Luban Xian Shi, Cai Lun Zhi Jiangren,

We request that you come, come to this place of the burner of incense,

With a whole heart we ask the Three Family Soil Official, the Nine Complete High Zhen Huang Da Di, the Concubine Palace Purple Flower Lady, Dongfang Qing di Tu Fu Shen Jun, Nanfang Chi Di Tu Fu Shen Jun, Xifang Bai Di Tu Fu Shen Jun, Beifang Hei Di Tu Fu Shenjun, Zhongyang Huang Di Tu Fu Shenjun, Tu Gong Tu Mu, Tu Zi Tu Sun!

The family .... (name) house in .... town/city,

I request Gaoshi Zu Wang to come and purify,

Zeng Shi Liu Shi to descend and purify,

Bi Shi Ye, Zhang Guo Fang Shi Hui, Yin Chuan Mingjiao Shi, He Chuan Yang Jiaoshi, Kuo Chuan Xin Jiaoshi, Bu Chuan Bu Jiao Chi, Di Ding Zi Jing, Yin Yang Hui Shang Qi Shi Qiao Jiang Xian Shi, Qian Qian Shizu Wan Wan ShiYe,

Requesting all the Gods and opening the incense pot with three offerings of incense.

One offering, two offerings, three offerings is perfection.
The rites cannot be measured, and today in
the Great Nation of…………..
in the province of……………
in the town of…………
with the family named………….we will build and repair.

Heaven has no envy, Earth has no envy, the people have no envy, the Year has no envy, the Month has no envy, the Day has no envy, the Disciple is here, to put ink below the stone and there are a hundred matters without taboo restrictions.

Great Fortune and Great Prosperity!!

22. Untitled
Crossbeams Evil Exorcism

Cross Beams and rafters are in feng shui considered extremely bad within a home when exposed. As well as being 'arrows' of poisonous sha qi they break up the general qi of a home and bring disharmony to a family as a whole and disharmony between man and wife. To counter this, both feng shui and practical magic have solutions such as placing certain objects in the beams or hanging red string charms thereto. The Luban offers this solution.

The Spell

Consult the Almanac for an auspicious day.

Obtain two almanacs and wrap them in gummed paper to form a package or bundle. Place it on the roofbeams close to the wall. In this way you will keep calamity away and serpents will not enter the house.

23. Untitled
Building The Stove

In old China the stove is of vital importance and is considered the heart of the house. Zuo zao means to repair or build a stove.

Old Chinese stoves were built of bricks and plastered over. Stoves should be odd numbers including numbers like 7 or 9 for the Big Dipper, 4 and 5 for the Five Lakes and Four Seas, and 1 and 2 for the 12 Earthly Stems.

Stove building has to use new soil obtained from a minimum depth of inches below ground, using well water and powdered pig's liver and wine.

The Spell

To prevent loss of oil and bring auspiciousness to the kitchen.

Find a cricket of the type that likes to warm itself at the stove, add it to water as well as the ashes of the talisman (Fig 14) shown. Mix it with the mud (cement) used to build the stove, light incense and candles.

24. Untitled
Mud, Wood And Stone
The Three Lines, Four Words
And Eight Sentences Spell

This spell marks the 'raising of the beam', that is fitting in place the main beam of the roof of the house. It is considered a vital and vulnerable moment in the construction of a house, hence this small ceremony.

Modern practitioners may well dispense with the sacrifice of the rooster and using cockscomb blood. One can instead use a carved image of a rooster and point the beam with cinnabar ink.

As can be seen the house owner will supply firecrackers, hong bao, silk banners in the five colours of white, black, azure, red and yellow and candy.

The Spell

Fu Yi! This rooster is not an extraordinary rooster, wearing a beautiful woollen garment, today it comes to the Master's house to be used in the crossbeams. This is a beautiful and auspicious day, the rooster is grasped firmly in my hand. We congratulate the master of the house on this auspicious day of prosperity.

Luban Xian Shi makes the roofbeam strong and so we welcome the Immortal Masters to come to this hall of prosperity.

Today the master's roofbeam is managed, silk banners and firecrackers will radiate joy, the rooster points to the head of the roofbeam.

Children and grandchildren await the rooster to point the

beam's centre and the descendants shall have great fortune and attract the salary of an official.

The rooster points to the end of the beam, and so the master's house will have six-stores of profits, at the front the beam is pointed and the home is full of gold, a point at the rear and fortune and happiness is boundless.

(The wizard seizes the rooster and ties it to the roofbeam with thick golden rope)

Fuyi! I am holding the golden rope to tie the strong roof beam, the weight is a thousand jin and the master's family shall have money and wealth!

(The folk hang the beam on the half wall and wait for the master to give a red packet to each (a red packet or hong bao is a small red envelope with a small gift of money), then they all pull the beam up into position.)

The Wooden beam is above the wall! The house is radiant with joy and the firecrackers are loud!

The master of the house rewards me (the master of the house offers a bag of candies and money) with candy and money.

We congratulate you at the hoisting of the beam, this house is forthwith prosperous and auspicious!

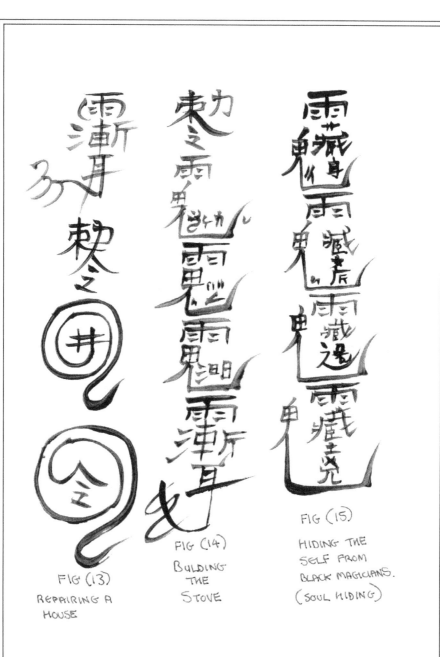

FIG (13)
REPAIRING A
HOUSE

FIG (14)
BUILDING
THE
STOVE

FIG (15)
HIDING THE
SELF FROM
BLACK MAGICIANS.
(SOUL HIDING)

25. Untitled
The Simple Method Of Raising A Beam

(This is an alternative method to 23)

On the beam the Luban wizard writes the characters for Official Salary so the descendants prosper. Below the beam are the characters of mud, wood and stone.

Then the family of the homeowner gather and together hoist up the beam, crying out to the homeowner for a gift of candy. The homeowner obliges and gives each participant some candy and a red envelope with money. The wizard ties a golden rope to the centre of the beam.

The Spell

Fuyi! This day is auspicious,
and the people are fortunate and prosperous!
Luban shows the bright cut trees.
The pine and cypress are youthful
and thus the roof beam is strong.
All four sides of the beam radiate scintillating beams
of light!

26. Untitled
Stepping On And Casting The Beam

This is a small spell when the first beam is laid across the main beam

The Spell

The Upper Heaven is a singing joyful swallow,
Cha! Cha!
The master's house places a beam upon a beam.
The Ten thousand high tower
is good for the running horse.
The pearly roof beam is laid on the upper shelf.
Today I speak four words and eight.
I congratulate the master's family!
They shall have wealth and rank,
wealth and fortune come to the people!

27. Untitled
The Carpenter's Sentence
Of The Main Door

The Spell

Heaven is high, the Earth is deep,

and they meet on this profound occasion,

The hand holds the axe to build the auspicious door,

The master's house shall be full of wealth and prosperity,

Precious gold will roll through the door,

Today the auspicious day has come to speak the Sentence of the Wealth Door,

One hundred matters are satisfied and there is great peace,

When this door is opened the evil spirits cannot enter,

In the night wicked people cannot come!!

28. Untitled Stonemason's Repair The House Spell

The Spell

Repairing the masonry of this house is the
Stonemason Ancestor Official,
The auspicious day has come to act upon
these tranquil foundations,
Jade stone lays the foundation and gold shall cover it,
Repairing the splendid house and the broad room,
Descendants have golden names,
They shall neither be the middling official
or the middling military officer!

29. Sheng Hun Zhou
Affecting The Soul Spell

(This is one of the first methods of 'punishing' mentioned in the Luban.)

You will have the hair of a man or woman that is one foot long. Arrange it on the earth as shown in the picture. Have the name and birthdate of the victim written on paper with chicken's blood.

Drive a knife with some force into the centre pinning the name-paper into the earth into the centre of the ring of earth.

Utter the spell:

Heaven is Pu'An Heaven,
Earth is Pu'An Earth,
Thousands of troops,
Thousands of Celestial Generals!
I request Taishang Laojun!
Ji Ji Ru Lu Ling!

With the knife in the centre, leave it fixed in the earth for half an hour and the victim will show signs of seizure, vomiting, intranquility and nervousness.

Solution: To take off this spell, hand in the Sword Seal, stamp on the earth three times with the right foot and cry 'Zou, Zou, Zou!!' (Go Go Go!) and take out the knife and the victim will recover.

30. Xian Hou Tian Bagua Fa
The Pre And Post Heaven Bagua Method

The pattern of the Pre-Heaven Bagua, in the centre is the Taiji Diagram that acts as the central master.

Below is the Post-Heaven Bagua in the middle of which is Taiji because Heaven is valued above all else.

Paint it to make a Celestial Plate (Tian Pan) and place it in the beams of a house. Pre-Heaven upwards and it will guard from evil. Paint it and position the Celestial Plate correctly, there can be no error.

31. Cang Shen Fa
Concealing Life Method

A popular series of spells in Chinese magic are the Cang Shen or Conceal Life Spells.

These spells are intended to make you invisible to malevolent spirits or rival sorcerers, as well as used by warriors engaged in warfare who want to remain unseen by the cruel hand of fate. This kind of magical spell has an ancient history and is even prominent in the famous work The Water Margin or Tales of the Marsh.

In the more powerful versions actual physical invisibility is implied but usually it aims at concealing the soul or by creating a kind of decoy diverting forces intended to reach the target at that instead.

In general Chinese magic this class of spell is a standard procedure in daily training and before important rituals.

The Spell
Hiding Body, Hiding Body, Truly Hiding Body,
Concealing me Zhenwu Dajiangjun
(Mysterious Warrior aka Black Turtle General of the North),
On the left the three hun souls
and on the right the seven Po souls,
Concealing those places I shall go,
Concealed in the wave-net at the bottom of the sea,
The canopy of Heaven covers the Earth,
The Earth covers Heaven,
If Heaven is exposed it is concealed by clouds
and mist so guarding the blue sky,
A thousand Evil Masters seek but cannot find,

Ten thousand Evil Masters seek but are blocked,

The Evil Masters seek but the Heavenly Thunderbolt transforms them to dust.

I sincerely request the Six Stars of the Southern Dipper and the Seven Stars of the Northern Dipper!

I honour Taishang Laojun!

Ji Ji Ru Lu Ling!!

Talisman Fig. 15 or 16

32. Cang Shen San Tian Nian Qu Hun Zhou Hiding The Soul For Three Days Spell

The Spell

Transforming body, Transforming body,
Truly transforming the body.
Transforming to a warrior, a warrior of great rank,
The first transformation to Buddha,
The second transformation to Li Laojun,
The third transformation to the Master Chuan Zhen Qu,
The fourth transformation of the four limbs
in warrior's armour,
The fifth transformation, the five lakes and waves rise up,
The sixth transformation, the Six Liujia Bingzi,
The seventh transformation the armies of the river
and earth mansion,
The eighth transformation Dong Yong exerts his body,
The ninth transformation,
the Equal with the Ninth Heaven Mysterious Girl,
The tenth transformation,
the Ten Great Fragrant Gods request the transformation
of the disciple's three immortal hun souls
and seven mortal po souls to converge.
I request the six stars of the Southern Dipper
and the seven stars of the Northern Dipper!
I honour Taishang Laojun.
Ji Ji Ru Lu Ling

Talisman Fig. 17

33. Jin Dao Li Jian Fa
Golden Knife Sharp Scissors Method

The Spell

I sincerely request the Profound Celestial Jade Emperor,
The Spirit-Cloud King's Palace sends out light.
Quickly, Quickly!
I request! Quickly Quickly Spirit!
I request the Golden Cloud Jade Snow King,
The Mother speedily comes,
To lend us the Golden Scissors,
The scissors descend upon a hempen rope,
The scissors cut the hempen rope,
The scissors cut the hempen rope and it falls broken,
Without mercy the evil sorcerer is sent the method,
Heavenly Thunder and Celestial Thunderbolts
crush your body,
I sincerely ask the six stars of the Southern Dipper
and the seven stars of the Northern Dipper.
I honour Taishang Laojun!
Ji Ji Ru Lu Ling!

Talisman Fig. 18

Solution to
The Golden Knife And Scissors Cutting Method

The Spell

The Three Treasures Cave,
within it are two wonderful and mysterious golden dragons
turned on their heads,

Copper heads and iron tails break.
The Jade Stone Golden Child binds it with ropes,
If they do not die, climb the mountain of stone
and break it,
I sincerely request the six stars of the Southern Dipper
and the seven stars of the Northern Dipper.
I honour Taishang Laojun.
Ji Ji Ru Lu Ling!

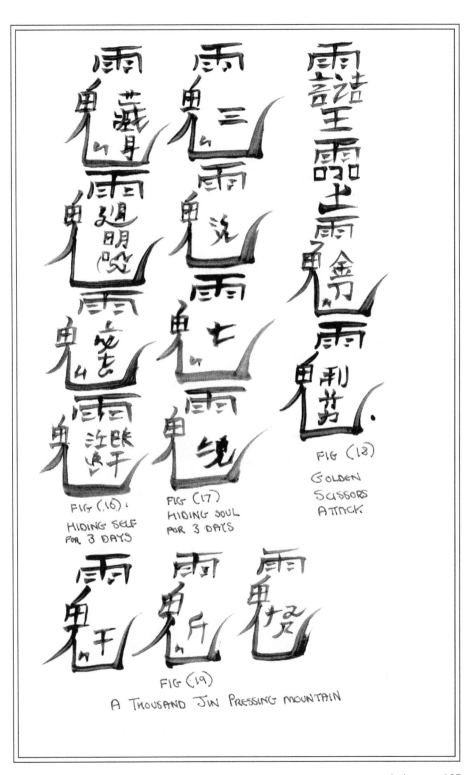

FIG (18)
GOLDEN
SCISSORS
ATTACK

FIG (16).
HIDING SELF
FOR 3 DAYS

FIG (17)
HIDING SOUL
FOR 3 DAYS

FIG (19)
A THOUSAND JIN PRESSING MOUNTAIN

34. Qian Jin Tuo Shan Zha Fa
A Thousand Jin Pressing Mountain Method

This is one of those famous methods of Chinese magic well known among Chinese magicians. Pressing is a means by which the target is constantly under pressure by unseen occult forces.

The Spell

I reverently request the Profound Heavenly Jade Emperor,
Great Heaven is not in accord with Earth,
Great Earth is not in accord with Heaven,
And I am not equal to Mount Taishan,
First request, a thousand jin comes to press,
Second request, ten thousand jin come to press,
One person presses ten people,
ten people press one hundred people,
one hundred people press a thousand people,
a thousand people press ten thousand people.
Cannot rise up!
I sincerely request the six Southern Dipper stars
and the seven stars of the Northern Dipper.
I honour Taishang Laojun !
Ji Ji Ru Lu Ling!

Talisman Fig. 19

Solution To The Thousand Jin Spell

I ask Laojun. Ji Ji Ru Lu Ling!
You still cannot rise, the Golden Restraint is now lifted,
If you still cannot rise the Silver Hook is lifted,
Still cannot rise the Nine Oxen lift you up,
The Nine Yin Oxen and the Nine Yang Oxen
control you and hook the mountain peak,
Listen! On the third day of the first sunset,
My Master will call you and allow you to rise up!
Ji Ji Ru Lu Ling!

Talisman Fig. 20

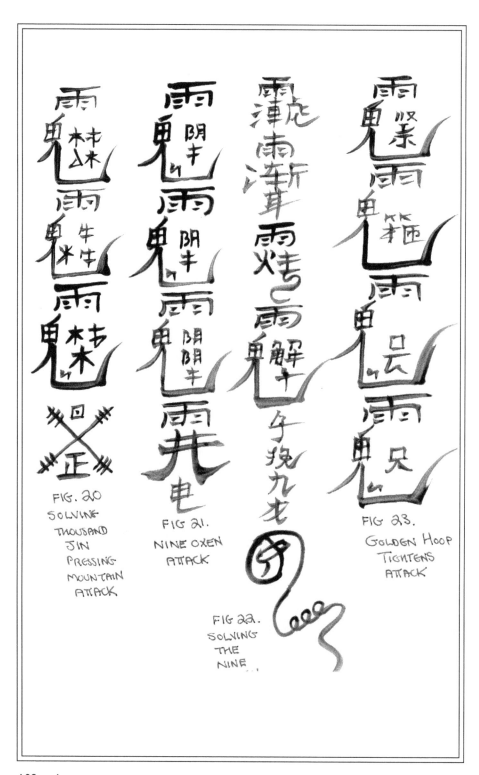

FIG. 20
SOLVING
THOUSAND
JIN
PRESSING
MOUNTAIN
ATTACK

FIG 21.
NINE OXEN
ATTACK

FIG 22.
SOLVING
THE
NINE ...

FIG 23.
GOLDEN HOOP
TIGHTENS
ATTACK

35. Jiu Niu Zao Fa
Making The Nine Oxen Method

The Spell

Heaven is endless and Earth is vast,
The disciple makes the Nine Oxen,
One is made and Heaven and Earth tremble,
The second is made and Gods and ghosts are startled,
The third is made and the mountains crumble
and stone splits,
The fourth is made and the evil sorcerer's head
and eyes become confused and dim,
Do not tarry, a thousand jin shall press,
Nine Oxen are together made,
Divided into two lines,
I sincerely request the six stars of the Southern Dipper
and the seven stars of the Northern Dipper.
I honour Taishang Laojun.
Ji Ji Ru Lu Ling!

Talisman Fig 21

Dismissing The Nine Oxen Method

I sincerely request Laojun,
I request Laojun,
Borrowing the Vast Western Heaven Official
Fan Heaven Seal NAMO A MI to dispel the body,
Unbind the body,
Quickly descend,
I request the Divine Teacher,
the Seventy-Two Men of Virtue who passed on the Way,
The disciple calls a thousand
and there are a thousand replies,
Ten thousand invocations and there are ten thousand spirits,
Dismiss and call back the Nine Oxen
to give relief to the body of the enemy,
I request the six stars of the Southern Dipper
and the seven stars of the Big Dipper.
I honour Taishang Laojun.
Ji Ji Ru Lu Ling!

Talisman Fig 22

36. Jing Gu Zhou Fa
The Golden Hoop Tightens Spell

This spell has an interesting history. Those familiar with the Chinese Classic *Journey to the West* will have heard of it. When Sun Wu Gong is ordered to accompany the priest Tangsheng to journey to Gandhara to fetch the Tripitaka Scriptures, the mischievous and pugnacious Monkey King has a golden hoop around his head that tightens when he is in danger of losing his reason or temper. Though Journey to the West was written in the 17th century, it was compiled from much earlier sources and folk legends. In fact the golden hoop may have originated as a device of Buddhist discipline encouraging constant awareness in the wearer.

The spell in fact calls upon Tang Sanzang, who was a real monk of the Tang Dynasty (602-664) who not only translated important scriptures, but personally journeyed to India and wrote a travelogue of the same.

The Spell

Tighten the hoop on the body,
Tighten the hoop on the body,
The Spell is upon their body,
Tighten the hoop on the evil master's forehead,
Quickly break the head,
and crush the eyes until there is unconsciousness,
Western Heaven calls Tang Sanzang,
The shores of the Southern China Sea request Guanyin,
The Spell of the Golden Hoop descends,
the spirit descends!!
Talisman Fig. 23

37. Tian Luo Di Wang Fa
Heaven Net Earth Trap Method

In this spell the evil master or sorcerer is entrapped and entangled by heavenly and earthly forces envisioned as a kind of net. In Chinese magic this is often actually made in the form of a hoop with a net with a spider web like arrangement of red threads. This heavenly and earthly net also functions to trap any spells or spirits the sorcerer may want to send. A similar idea appears in many cultures, of tangling thread patterns that trap spirits, nightmares and other evil forces. For example the sprite traps of English folk magic and the dreamcatchers of the native americans.

The Spell

Profound Heavenly Yu Huang Dadi Revered Jade One,
First stop, the Heavenly plague road,
Second stop, the Earth Plague door,
Third stop, man has the Way,
Fourth stop, Ghosts are robbed of entry,
Fifth stop, block the plague road,
Sixth stop, break the thief,
Seventh stop, break the evil master's road,
Eight stop, disaster and plague five temples gods,
Ninth stop, the evil shaman (or witch) path,
Tenth stop, My Master walks the Path,
The Master breaks it,
People can tread the path,
All evil masters and spirits cannot enter,
The Green faced and the Red faced
come to employ this method,

Stepping on the Heaven Net
and the Earth Trap there can be no mercy.
I sincerely request the six stars of the Southern Dipper
and the seven stars of the Northern Dipper.
I honour Taishang Laojun. Ji Ji Ru Lu Ling!!

Talisman Fig 24

FIG 24
HEAVEN NET
EARTH NET
TRAPPING
THE
SORCERER.

FIGURE 25
COPPER POLE
AND
IRON POLE
ATTACK

FIGURE 26
GOLDEN
SCISSORS
FLYING
KNIFE

FIGURE 27
FIVE THUNDERS
FLAMING OIL
POOLS ATTACK

38. Tong Nan Gan Tie Nan Gan
Copper Pole, Iron Pole

This is one of the many spells in Chinese magic that employ the character of Jing, the Well. The well character implies a deep abyss that sucks in evil forces and does not let them escape, a bit like the Phantom Zone in Superman. The Jing character is used as a kind of black hole that pulls in that which is unwanted into an unspecified endless abyss.

The Spell

At this place I draw the crossed lines of the Well character,
In this place where I draw it is a ten thousand deep abyss,
If there is an evil master or a demonic method,
Unaware it treads into the gaping well,
Treading on it, it is contained within and there is no mercy,
All evil spirits become as wind and dust,
I sincerely request the six stars of the Southern Dipper
and the seven stars of the Northern Dipper.
I honour Taishang Laojun! Ji Ji Ru Lu Ling!!

Talisman Fig. 25

39. Jin Jian Fei Dao Fa
Golden Scissors Flying Blades

Another famous Chinese magical technique is the golden scissors. The essence or spirit of the scissors is sent to attack the demon or black magician.

The Spell

Heaven Spirit, Earth Spirit,
Luban bestows upon me the Flying Knife
in order to deal with this matter,
If an evil master should come and attempt his evil method,
I grasp three golden knives that have no mercy,
The first cuts the serpent's head,
The second cuts the serpent's body,
The third skins it and dims its eyes,
The Western Heaven calls Tang san Zang,
The shores of the Southern Sea call out to Guanyin.
Ji Ji Ru Lu Ling!

Talisman Fig. 26

40. Wu Lei You Chi Hou Zhou
Five Thunder Fire Pools Of Oil Spell

Thunder magic is a particularly powerful form of magic that requires considerable time to cultivate and is beyond the scope of this volume.

In this spell the Luban master sends the essence of thunder fire to burn and consume evil energies, spirits, demons or even an evil master. The master would set out five small bowls filled with oil in the five thunder pattern on an altar or on the ground with the talismans shown burned in each bowl.

The Spell

This oil is not extraordinary oil,
Luban bestows on me
the Burning the Evil Master Method Oil,
The disciple wears on his head the fire cap
and wears the robes of fire,
Feet tread wearing the fire shoes.
In the east burning the evil master,
In the south burning the evil master,
In the west burning the evil master,
In the north burning the evil master,
In the centre burning the evil master,
He becomes as a pregnant lady,
All demons become dust.
I sincerely request the six stars of the Southern Dipper
and the seven stars of the Northern Dipper.
Ji Ji Ru Lu Ling!!

Talisman Fig. 27

41. Tie Weicheng Zhou
Spell Of the Iron Wall

This is a defence spell, perhaps to secure a ritual space or for defence in a magical war. A similar method was said to have been used by Master Hu, one of the founders of a branch of the Southern Maoshan Sect that today is most often represented by the True Heart Maoshan School. Master Hu became embroiled in a magical battle with the King of Thai Magic and used an iron wall technique such as this to neutralise the Thai master's otherwise powerful methods. The end result after various exchanges was that the Thai arjan (master) was killed.

The Spell:

Heaven is vast, Earth is vast,

Heaven Spirit, Earth Spirit,

The Disciple bows his head in respect,

Hong Zhou De Dao and Luguo Xian Shi,

Today we erect the Iron Wall,

Four sides and eight sides do not allow forms to be revealed,

A copper wall ten thousand zhang high,

The Evil Master cannot approach it,

Ten thousand methods cannot infringe upon my life,

One rope eight zhang long,

A cooper rope and an iron rope strengthen its core,

No matter if a golden sword or jade scissors,

The golden sword and jade scissors cannot cut it,

To this the disciple adds

the Descending Five Thunders, HONG!!

The evil master's evil methods become merely dust.

I request it by the six stars of the Southern Dipper

and the seven stars of the Northern Dipper!
I honour Taishang Laojun!
Ji Ji Ru Lu Ling!!

Talisman Fig 28

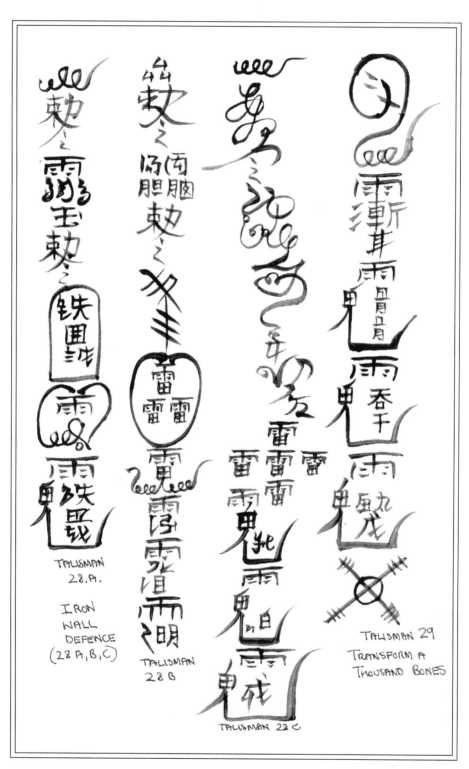

TALISMAN
28.A.

IRON
WALL
DEFENCE
(28 A, B, C)

TALISMAN
28 B

TALISMAN 28 C

TALISMAN 29
TRANSFORM A
THOUSAND BONES

42. Hua Gu Tun Qian
Transform A Thousand Swallowed Bones

As the name implies, this is a spell in the medical category for dealing with some object stuck in the throat. In some schools it was also used as a means of demonstrating shengong, magical-martial skills such as swallowing glass.

Don't Try It!

The Spell

Heaven Spirit, Earth Spirit,
I honour Longjun Zushi
(Dragon King of the Eastern Sea),
Medicine King, Caiyao Tongzi (Gathering Herbs Lad)
and Xun Yao Longjun (Seeking Herbs Official),
I ask that we meet in the East, South, West and North.
Sea Water Dragon King Holy Master,
Central Dragon Son and Dragon Grandson,
Five Directions Five Gods,
Zha Dragon God King,
Earth Veins Dragon God,
I sincerely ask you to quickly come,
Change a thousand bones that have been swallowed.
Ji Ji Ru Lu Ling!

The talisman would be pre drawn or drawn over the bowl of water and then drunk.

Talisman Fig. 29

43. Ding Gen Fa
Fix Root Method

One of the infamous spells of the Luban and Chinese magic generally is the Fix Root Method. As the name implies it is a spell whose aim is to cause a person to enter a curious trance-like state and become unable to move. Some sources relate that there is a difference between Fix Root and Fix Body. Fix Root will for example cause a person to repeat the same action over and over again as told in the little story in the introduction of this work.

The Spell

One, two, three, four, five.
Metal, Wood, Water, Fire, Earth.
You come but I will not come.
If a person shall come they are unaware
of this circle drawn large.
If a stranger comes here and they advance here,
they cannot speak or cry, you shall be motionless
as if weighed down by Mount Taishang
and forever there is no trace of you.
We sincerely request the six stars of the Southern Dipper
and the seven stars of the Northern Dipper.
I honour Taishang Laojun.
Ji Ji Ru Lu Ling!

Talisman Fig. 30

44. Jie Tuo Fa Zhou
Undo And Remove Method

This spell is for dismissing or neutralising another person's spells.

The Spell
I request Huli Zushi (the Fox Master)
to come and dismiss and withdraw the spell,
First request, Heaven dismisses the Master,
Second request, Earth dismisses the Master,
Come and dismiss and withdraw the person's
seven po and three hun souls,
One cut and the Mountain Spirit
joins with the Water Demon,
The Witch Master's evil dares not try to influence,
If there is a Green Youth
or a Whiter Person come with their methods,
The hands easily detain them
and lock them at the bottom of the sea!
Ji Ji Ru Lu Ling.

Talisman Fig. 31

45. Bai Jie Xie Fa
Banishing A Hundred
Evil Sorceries Method

The Spell

On the shores of the Southern Sea is one animal fur,
Day and night youthful and never ageing,
The peach of Wangmu comes to dispel and remove,
First banishing by Huang Yi Duan Gong,
The second banishing,
the Southern Sea Ten Thousand Methods,
The third banishing, the Hundred Skills Method,
The fourth Banishing, Three Master Pass the Method,
The fifth banishing, the Method of the Ironsmith,
The sixth banishing, the Method of the Flower Arranger,
The seventh banishing, the Method of the Brick-Layer,
The eighth banishing, the Method of the Stonemason,
The ninth banishing, the Method of the Carpenter,
The tenth banishing the Method of the Tailor,
Heaven and Earth banish,
The Year and Month banish,
The Day and Hour banish,
I request Huli Zushi and all the Masters of a hundred
and one ways to dispel and banish it!
I request by the six stars of the Southern Dipper
and the seven stars of the Northern Dipper!
I honour Taishang Laojun.
Ji Ji Ru Lu Ling.

Talisman Fig. 32

46. Kao Jiu Fa Zhou
Scorching Wine Method

One of the curious set of spells in the Luban seeks to wreak havoc in household chores in wine-making, cooking, making tofu and so forth. Place hand on the axe or upon a rock or stone. This spell is said to cause the wine to heat up and evaporate into nothing.

The Spell

I request Huli Xian Shi to come down from the mountain,
Follow the Golden Lock,
Today meeting a stranger and scorching wine,
Filling a cup with wine the lock closes the door,
The disciple grasps the command symbol on the axe.
It is not seen!
Ji Ji Ru Lu Ling!

Talisman Fig. 33

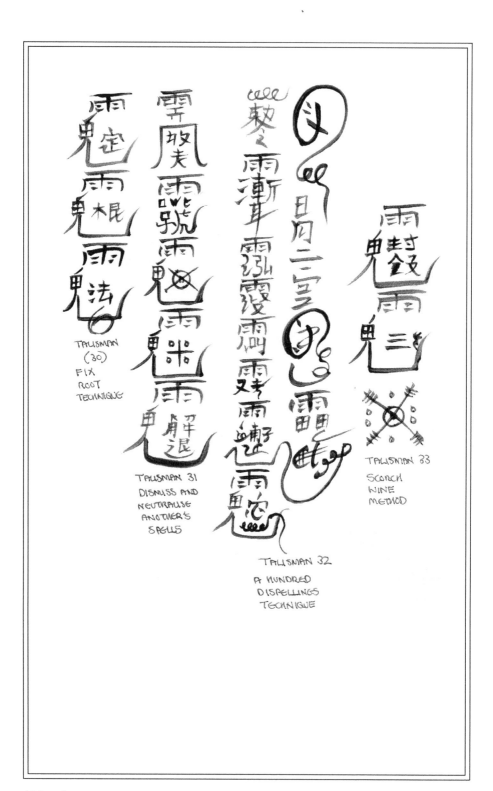

TALISMAN
(30)
FIX
ROOT
TECHNIQUE

TALISMAN 31
DISMISS AND
NEUTRALISE
ANOTHER'S
SPELLS

TALISMAN 32
A HUNDRED
DISPELLINGS
TECHNIQUE

TALISMAN 33
SCORCH
WINE
METHOD

47. Sha Zhu Fa Zhou
Killing Swine Method

The hand is upon a stone when using the spell.

The Spell

I with reverence call Sanshisan Gang Qi shi er Sha Zushi

(The thirty three strengths

and Seventy-Two Killings Master),

The disciple descends down the mountain,

The copper iron plate cangue,

A thousand killing knives cannot kill,

If there is an evil method

the Dao person comes to slaughter without end,

A thousand arrows pierce the heart and leave nothing.

I request the six stars of the Southern Dipper

and the seven stars of the Northern Dipper.

I honour Taishang Laojun.

Ji Ji Ru Lu Ling!

(Talisman Fig. 34)

48. Zhu Fan Zhu Rou Fa Zhou
Cooking Rice, Cooking Meat Method Spell

The Spell

Heaven is vast and Earth is vast,

The disciple holds the command symbol,

The rooster cannot crow,

The hen cannot cry out,

Meat in the pot leaps around,

Rice bubbles in the bowl,

Within a second the fire is extinguished and passes away,

It is cold and still,

Like shallow water,

Though you cry out it cannot be completed,

Meeting the unexpected,

The head is confused and the eyes are dim

and without form.

Ji Ji Ru Lu Ling.

(hands are on the door)

(Talisman Fig. 35)

49. Tui Doufu Fa Zhou
Pushing Tofu Method Spell

The Spell

One, two, three, four, five.
Metal, Wood, Water, Fire and Soil.
The blessings of the Gods.
The disciple's heart reads this spell.
Cooking beans, cooking beans, sifting.
The beans in the cauldron weep,
Born of the same root
and together they are decocted in excess,
Not clear, not clear, cannot be accomplished
and cannot work.
Seizing the thickness it changes to a basin of pure water,
A thousand spirits, ten thousand spirits!
Immediately the spirit approaches!
Ji Ji Ru Lu Ling!

(Talisman Fig. 36)

50. Jie Tui Zheng Ren Fa Zhou Dismiss And Banish The Entire Person Method

The Spell

Spirit Cloud precious
and wonderful in the midst of the profound,
Two golden dragons are upside down on their heads,
I request San Xiao Zushi (Three Clouds Master)
to quickly descend and come,
One banishing, Shijia Fo (Sakyamuni Buddha),
Second banishing, Li Laojun (Lao Tze),
Third banishing, My Master has passed the true words,
Fourth banishing, four limbs of the armoured troops,
Fifth banishing,
the waves of the Five Lakes rise and roll up,
Sixth banishing, Liu Jia and the Liu Bingzi,
(A class of spiritual or celestial warriors),
Seventh banishing, Mu Lian is in the Underworld,
Eight Banishing, Dong Yong Zi Mai Shen,
Ninth dispelling,
in ten thousand years shall not meet again

in a distant place,
Cast you out, cast out from this place
where you harm the good people.
I honour Taishang Laojun!
Ji Ji Ru Lu Ling!

(Talisman 37)

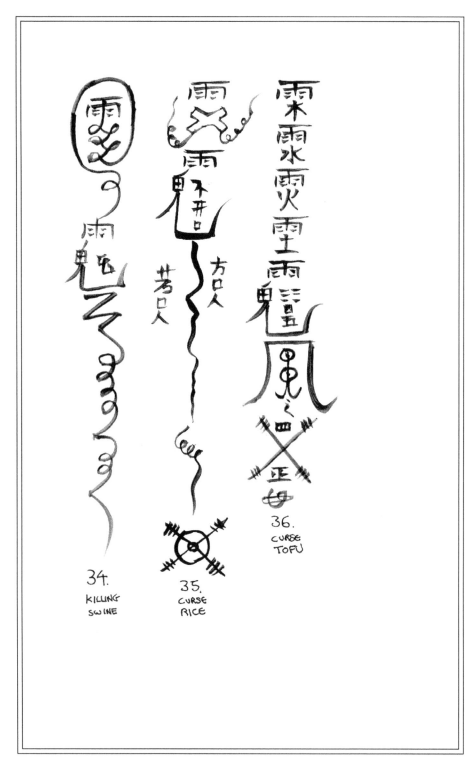

34.
KILLING
SWINE

35.
CURSE
RICE

36.
CURSE
TOFU

51. An Wei Cang Shen Fa
Tranquillity Place Hide Body Method

The Spell

Using long threads that are safe and pure,
The Sun rises in the East a little Yin,
The Master calls me to hide my body,
Three hun souls are hidden within a fresh cloud,
The seven po souls are hidden in the ninth heaven cloud,
The disciple hides within the Iron Ox's belly,
Hiding body, hiding body!
I sincerely request the six stars of the Southern Dipper
and the seven stars of the Northern Dipper.
I honour Taishang Laojun.
Ji Ji Ru Lu Ling !!

(Talisman Fig. 38)

52. Jin Guang Zhou
Golden Light Spell

This is a truncated version of the famous Golden Light Mantra, a basic of Daoist practice. For a full version see The Golden Light further in this book.

(Talisman Fig. 39)

29. GOLDEN LIGHT

37. DISPELLING MAGIC SET

38. HIDE SOUL

53. Untitled
Travelling On The Road Method

While travelling, the magician hides his soul from evil spirits, black magicians, undesirable people and the like.

The Spell
Laojun is in the midst of the cave dividing grass,
Though seemingly aged when he arrives
he appears not old,
People who come to fetch the grass have no use for it,
My Master fetches and brings the straw,
One hun soul is hidden in the Moon on the horizon,
Second hun soul is hidden
in the sound of the Buddha Thunder,
Alone the three hun souls are not yet hidden,
Eight shadows in the cave ask Laojun,
Alone the three souls become the three honoured Buddhas,
The seven Po souls become Zhenwu Shen,
Gods and Ghosts cannot hear them,
And the evil magical method becomes mere dust,
I ask the six stars of the Southern Dipper
and the seven stars of the Northern Dipper!
I honour Taishang Laojun!
Ji Ji Ru Lu Ling.

(Talisman Fig. 40)

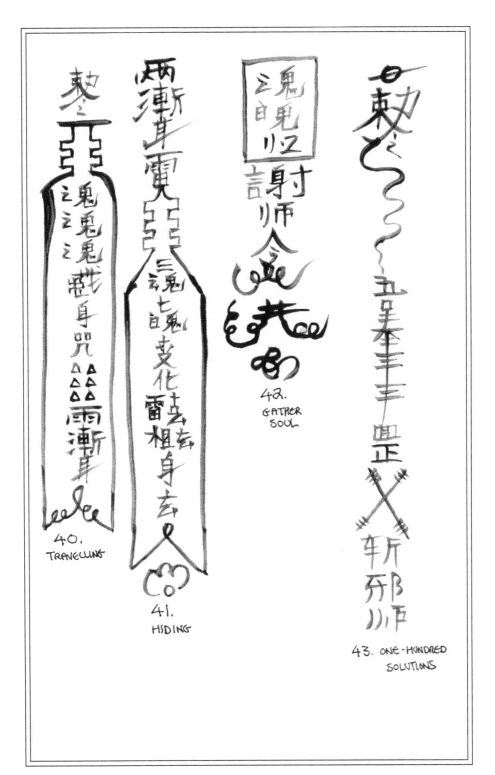

40.
TRAVELLING

41.
HIDING

42.
GATHER
SOUL

43. ONE-HUNDRED
SOLUTIONS

54. Wen Cangshen Zhou
Continual Hiding Spell

The Spell

Transform my body, change my body,
My Master assists me to change to Zhenwu Zushi,
Who has dishevelled hair
and is on the correct Temple Seat,
Terrifying those ghosts and demons
who are in the mortal world,
Great ghosts will see me and weep aloud,
Lesser ghosts will see me and their tears will fall,
Demons shall see me and I shall change them to dust,
The first transformation,
The second transformation,
I change into the Cloud of the Ninth Heaven,
Leigong and Lei Mu (the Thunder Mother) come quickly,
People see me and they shall have longevity.
Ghosts see me and they shall become dust.

(Talisman Fig. 41)

55. Xie Shi Shou Hun Zhou
Thanking The Master
And Retrieving Soul Spell

This is a common spell in Chinese magic in general known commonly as Shou Hun, to retrieve the Soul. Soul loss was a common ritual was and still is a common ritual used when it was perceived that the soul or part of the soul was lost through either accident, contact with evil spirits or sorcery.

The Spell

The Blue Sky is profound,
The purple cloud opens,
Vermillion Plum Second Immortal delivers
the hun soul to come,
Three hun souls thus return to the root-body,
Seven Po souls return to protect the root-body.
The Green Emperor guards the hun soul,
The White Emperor attends upon the po soul,
The Red Emperor cultivates Qi,
The Black Emperor penetrates the blood,
The Yellow Emperor is the Master of the Centre,
Ten thousand spirits do not rise,
The living hun soul quickly comes,
The dead soul quickly goes,
I invite you to come and quickly return.
I ask this by the six stars of the Southern Dipper
and the seven stars of the Northern Dipper!
I honour Taishang Laojun.
Ji Ji Ru Lu Ling!
(Talisman Fig. 42)

56. Bai Jie Zhou
One Hundred Solutions Spell

The Spell

Above, on Kunlun Mountain there is a nest made of straw,
The seventy two aged ones do not look old,
I request the Master to fetch the Heaven and the Earth,
All the Evil Master's methods are hereby removed
and dismissed,
One, two, three, four and five,
Metal, Wood, Water, Fire and Earth,
My Master commands that the evil magic
becomes nothing but soil,
I request this by the six stars of the Southern Dipper
and the seven stars of the Northern Dipper.
I honour Taishang Laojun.
Ji Ji Ru Lu Ling!

(Talisman Fig. 43)

57. Zhi Xue Fa
Stopping Bleeding Method

The Spell

Morning water boils at the ninth hour,

Seeing the water is not flowing, spirit approaches,

The Blood Official named Zhou,

The Blood Mother named Liu,

Born in the Southern Cloud Vast Prosperity Lake,

You call: 'Do not flow' and it does not flow,

Yet if it still flows Laojun is over their head.

I request it by the six stars of the Southern Dipper

and the seven stars of the Northern Dipper.

I honour Taishang Laojun.

Ji Ji Ru Lu Ling.

(Talisman Fig. 44)

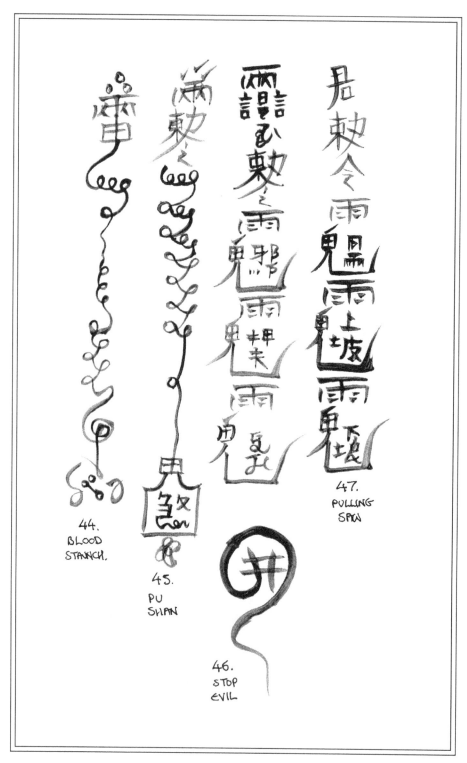

44.
BLOOD
STAUNCH.

45.
PU
SHAN

46.
STOP
EVIL

47.
PULLING
SPIN

58. Pushan Zhou
Pupu comes to the place on the cliff

The Spell

I today stand firm and you are lifted by a hundred people,
If people come they are startled by me,
I ask you that the Yang Life Destiny returns to Yin,
There is no fear of the evil masters,
My Master brings peace and brings down the iron pole,
The hand grasping it is brought to the ground
to command,
I today release to return the feelings
for the sake of Laojun's face!
I honour Taishang Laojun!
Ji Ji Ru Lu Ling!

(Talisman Fig. 45)

59. Che Ju Fa
Pulling The Saw Method

The Spell

Heaven is troubled, Earth is troubled,

Laojun bestows upon me the smooth and slippery fish,

And the Iron Egg Saw,

The saw pulls and astonishment arises,

You pull, I pull,

Cannot go up the hill or go down the hill,

All see you and laugh out loud hahaha,

All see you and laugh hahaha,

I sincerely request this by the six stars of the Southern Dipper and the seven stars of the Northern Dipper.

I honour Taishang Laojun,

Ji Ji Ru Lu Ling!

(Talisman Fig. 47)

60. Jie Che Ju Zhou
Dismiss the Pull Saw Spell

The Spell

I honour the command of Taishang Laojun,
Who descends the Mountain,
By command the demons
and spirits must turn back to the mountain,
The disciple's hand has seven blades of grass,
A hundred and one evil methods are all dismissed,
First request, Heaven undoes the Master,
Second request, the Year removes the Master,
Third request, the Teacher passes on (the power/method),
Quickly come, quickly come to dispel,
I ask it by the six stars of the Southern Dipper
and the seven stars of the Northern Dipper!
I honour Taishang Laojun,
Ji Ji Ru Ling!

(Talisman Fig. 48)

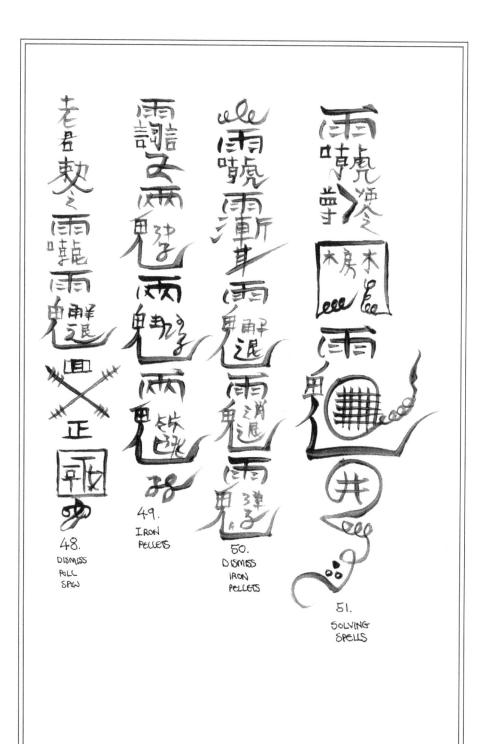

48.
DISMISS
POLL
SPELL

49.
IRON
PELLETS

50.
DISMISS
IRON
PELLETS

51.
SOLVING
SPELLS

61. Tie Danzi Zhou
Spell Of The Iron Pellets

The Spell

Smelting this spell in the midst of the censer of Laojun,

Three thousand three hundred and thirty iron pellets,

Iron sand,

The disciple descends the mountain

and carries them upwards,

Unexpectedly meeting one who turns the millstone,

Meeting one pulling a box,

The disciple releases a few iron pellets or iron sand,

Wooden box and millstone,

How can it be pushed or pulled?

The iron pellets and iron sand.

The box and millstone jump and rise upwards,

Left pushes and right jumps,

Right pushes and left jumps,

I sincerely request it by the six stars of the Southern Dipper

and the seven stars of the Northern Dipper!

I honour Taishang Laojun,

Ji Ji Ru Lu Ling!

(Talisman Fig. 49)

62. Jie Tie Danzi Zhou
Dismissing the Iron Pellets Spell

The Spell

Upper Heaven red clouds rise,

Luban Xianshi calls me to descend the mountain to end

the Iron Pellets, the Iron Sand, the Golden Pellets,

the Silver Pellets,

The disciple descends the mountain holding the decree,

Quickly! Yes!

One command and the box is fine

and the millstone is fine,

Left pushes, left is calm,

Right pushes, right is calm,

I sincerely request it by Taishang Laojun,

Ji Ji Ru Lu Ling!

(Talisman Fig. 50)

63. Ji Jie Fa
The Method of Solving Spells

The Spell

Hong Zhou De Dao,
Luban Xianshi transmits the true words,
In front are fifteen miles, behind are fifteen miles,
On the left are fifteen miles
and on the right are fifteen miles,
In the centre are fifteen miles,
The disciple uses his hand to point,
Azure Dragon and White Tiger descend the mountain
and come to fend off the rising,
No matter if it is wood and soil combine to rise up,
The Sun rises and initiates the work to succeed
in countering anything that arises.
I request it by the six stars of the Southern Dipper
and the Seven Stars of the Northern Dipper.
I honour Taishang Laojun,
Ji Ji Ru Lu Ling.

(Talisman Fig. 51)

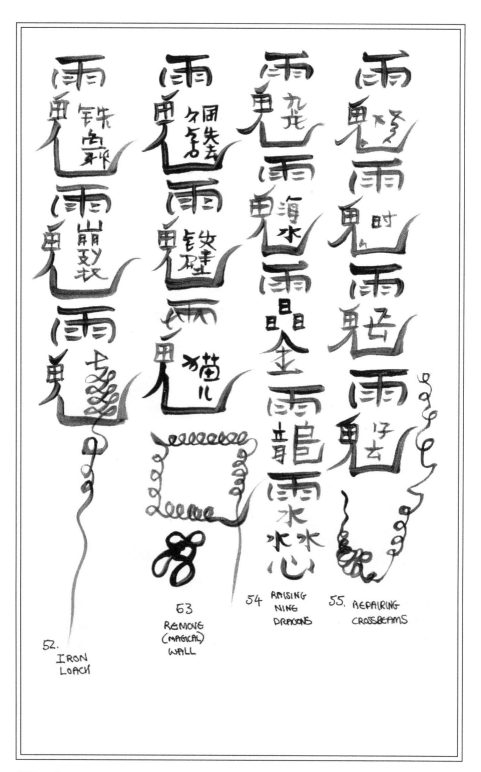

52. IRON LOACH

53. REMOVE (MAGICAL) WALL

54. RAISING NING DRAGONS

55. REPAIRING CROSSBEAMS

64. Tie Yu Qin Zhou
Iron Loach Spell

This unusual spell seems to use either a piece of iron shaped like the loach, a species of fish found in freshwater or perhaps the spirit of a sacrificed loach to smash through the defences of an opponent.

The Spell

Heaven is troubled, Earth is troubled,

Laojun bestows upon me the Iron Loach,

It dashes forth breaking Heaven,

It dashes forth breaking Earth,

Breaking both sides of the earthen wall,

I ask the Six Stars of the Southern Dipper,

I ask the Seven Stars of the Northern Dipper,

I honour Taishang Laojun,

Ji Ji Ru Lu Ling!

(Talisman Fig. 52)

65. Ban Qiang Fa
Removing The Wall Method

This also seems to be a method both to counter a rival sorcerer who launches a magical defence smashing technique such as the previous Iron Loach Spell. The idea is to construct a magical wall of defence.

The Spell

The sun rises in the East and comes to illuminate the west,
Below is safe with iron bricks,
A thousand loaches cannot hear (the command),
Ten thousand iron oxes build
and block the sides of the wall,
Rising up, there is an iron fence that defends the iron wall,
I fear not the evil master who comes with magical powers
to fight me,
If he releases the Iron Loach,
I release the Divine Cat to eat it!
I ask the Six Stars of the Southern Dipper,
I ask the Seven Stars of the Northern Dipper,
I honour Taishang Laojun.
Ji Ji Ru Lu Ling!

(Talisman Fig. 53)

66. Qi Jiu Long Shui Zhou
The Spell Of The Nine Dragons Water

Another spell of the Nine Dragon's Water, however, the method here is clearly more dynamic and is focused on attack of an evil master and/or exorcism.

The Spell

I honour the Eastern, Southern,
Western and Northern Sea Dragon Kings
and Sagely Masters.
The Central Dragon Son and the Dragon Grandson,
Quickly assist and bless this the method of seawater,
I ask you to raise up the flood of seawater,
The house beam is one chi high,
Sea water floods to the height of one zhang,
The flood waters reach up to the Upper Heavens,
In the flood waters gather the True Dragon Gods,
Meeting together in that place and flooding without mercy,
I ask the Six stars of the Southern Dipper,
I ask the Seven Stars of the Northern Dipper.
Ji Ji Ru Lu Ling!

(Talisman Fig. 54)

67. Untitled
Repairing The Building
Or Crossbeams Evil Countering Method

In this method when a repair of a house is made there is a belief that the ensuing chaos of reconstruction and repair disturbs the tranquillity of the house and can cause evil forces to take advantage of the upheaval to enter. This spell allays the evil and invites wealth and prosperity into the home.

The Spell

The master's house is being repaired
on this auspicious day,
And the Upper Heaven Purple Star is present,
The blessings of the Salary Wealth God (Lu Cai Shen)
shall come here,
Heaven descends and silver water shall flow here
to this house,
The left stream advances the noble sons of this house,
The right stream is of yellow gold.
I today order the people to prosper,
On this auspicious day,
The people shall prosper with wealth issuing everywhere
as from a spring!

(Talisman Fig. 55)

56. SEAL A
HUNDRED
MOUTHS

57. SLIPPERY
OIL
MOUNTAIN

68. Feng Bai Kou
Sealing A Hundred Mouths

This spell as the name suggests is aimed at sealing the mouths of gossips and back-biters.

The Spell

The Upper Heavenly Lei Gong roars,
The Lower Earthly Leigong covers a hundred mouths,
Upper Heavenly red mouth,
Year and Month red mouth,
Day and hour red mouth,
Within the yard and without the yard,
Closing all the hundred mouths,
Quarrelling red mouths,
Covered and detained in the
ten thousand zhang deep lake,
Heavenly Official of the Underworld helps,
The Officials of the Four Season Thrones detain them
within the very borders of the wilderness,
Into the deep pit of ten thousand zhang,
The white tiger drives them away to the Southern River,
By the Temple of the Golden Buddha,
A thousand years they shall not meet,
A thousand years there can be no chance of an encounter.
I sincerely request this by the Six Stars of the Southern
Dipper and the Seven Stars of the Northern Dipper.
I honour Taishang Laojun.
Ji Ji Ru Lu Ling!

(Talisman Fig. 56)

69. Inner Secret Of Setting Up The Altar Table Of The Craft

This is a method of setting up the altar of the magical craft in the home of yourself or a disciple. (See the spell in which the Ceremony of the roof beam was given. When a house is built, or moved into or when a house is blessed by placement of an altar the house beams are blessed)

The Spell

This is the Altar of the Great Disciple,
Grasping the great chicken to perform the ceremony,
The ceremony of the roof beam and the placement
of the upper beam are complete.
The flowers are golden and calamity avoided,
Great fortune and prosperity!
The highest fortune and prosperity.
The happy and holy occasion,
There is a making of wealth,
Jiang Taigong is here!
Bai Wu Jin Ji!

(Bai Wu Jin Ji is a magical formula meaning there are no taboos, all is allowed, that is freedom)

Upon the altar are gifts of wine in five bowls in the five directions.

Five coloured cloths, one foot long and two inches wide.

(These are long talismanic cloths on which are inscribed the talismans shown. The five colours are Azure for the East, Red for the South, White for the West, Black for the North and Yellow for the centre. These are sacred to the Dragon

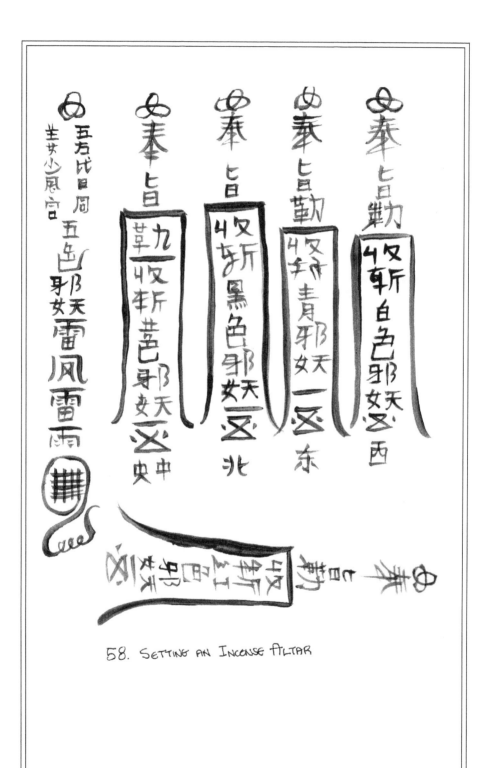

58. Setting an Incense Altar

Kings who rule the Five Elements of this altar. The cloths are draped so they hang off the edge of the altar.)

Offer three libations of wine in each of the five directions, light incense (five sticks) to the Azure, Red, White, Black and Yellow Dragon Emperors.

Request your wish and ring the bell.

At the end, thank the Dragons and ask them to leave the altar room to return to their homes.

(Talisman Fig. 58)

70. Qi Shui Antai Yizong
Chapter On Consecrating (Lit:Raising) Water To Protect The Unborn Child

The Spell

The sun rises and Yin and Yang illuminate the five
directions and so comes the Consecrating Water Official,
First rising, In the East Jia Yi and Wood,
Second rising, In the South Bing Ding and Fire.
Third rising, in the West Geng Xin and Metal,
Fourth rising, in the North, Ren Gui and Water,
Fifth rising, in the centre Wu Ji and Soil,
The Virtuous Star Lord descends to this mortal realm,
First sprinkling to the East,
the Embryo God (Taishen) is firm and strong.
Second spinkling to the Southern Taishen,
Third sprinkling to the Northern Taishen fixes in place.
Fourth sprinkling to the Western Taishen fixes in place
strongly.
Fifth sprinkling to the Central Tai Shen fixes with strength.
All is to satisfaction and disperses to the four directions.

(Draw the sign in the bowl with three joss sticks or sword
finger)

First sprinkling, Heaven opens,
Second sprinkling, Earth splits,
Third sprinkling, the people have longevity,
Fourth sprinkling, Ghosts are extinguished,
Fifth sprinkling, The six stars of the Southern Dipper
and the Seven Stars of the Northern Dipper
are attacking stars.

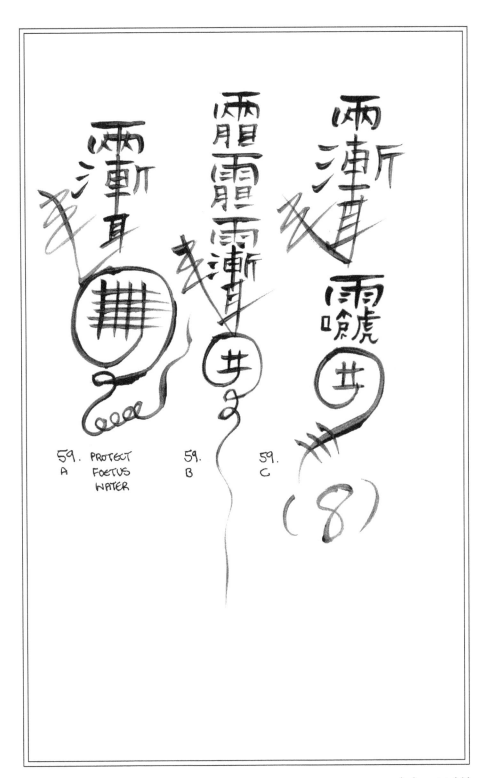

59.
A   PROTECT
     FOETUS
     WATER

59.
B

59.
C

I honour Taishang Laojun,
Ji Ji Ru Lu Ling!
Jiang Taigong is here and all spirits return.
Heaven and Earth have no enmity!

(Talismans Figs. 59a/b/c)

Pu'an Master has great magical power,
The Land Under Heaven is in your palm,
I have the East, South, West and North,
Pu'an is here forever and leaves no trace of filth,
Eastern Taishen,
Southern Taishen,
Western Taishen,
Northern Taishen,
Central Taishen,
Five miles covered by Taishen in the five directions,
Taishen give rise to a ten thousand zhang space
(of protection),
None can occupy the Earth,
None can occupy the directions,
I sincerely request the Six Stars of the Southern Dipper
and the Seven Stars of the Big Dipper.
I honour Taishang Laojun,
Ji Ji Ru Lu Ling!

The Master Pu'an brings forth Master Ling Ji and all the Masters
come here to consecrate this water and afterwards a hundred
taboos are gone.

Put a long red thread some 20 inches long into the centre
of the bowl. Patient drinks. Can carry the thread in a pouch.

The Luban Shu
Book II

Lesser Wood Metal Classic

Part 1.
Shen Dao : The Way Of The Spirits

71. Untitled
Contacting The Fox Spirits
As Teachers And Familiars

To cultivate this art one must find a quiet room. It is better if it were in the mountains or in the countryside far from the noise of chickens and dogs.

With a sincere heart you can cultivate this art whereby you meet the black and white fox folk who will transform into human form, usually within three to seven days or months depending.

You should choose the time of the Fox Moon, at the hour of Zi and set up an altar with a bright lamp, incense, a tablet (paiwei), maize wine (shaojiu), chicken breasts, eggs, cooked white rice, salt and a dish of fruits.

With a sincere heart make offerings at the altar. Also have a new mat on which to sit, stand or kneel.

Before the rites one should bathe, abstaining from meat and wine. Write three Dai Fu, or Substitute Talismans and wear them on your body. Press another beneath your tongue.

On the date of the invocation burn the talisman of Tudi, the Earth God and read the Tudi Zhou, or Earth God Spell seven times.

Have three Zhu Xian Fu (All Immortal Fu) and with sincerity recite the Ju Hu Zhou or Catch Fox Spell seven times.

Burn seven Tudi Zhou and again read the Tudi Spell seven times. At this moment a number of foxes may throw stones and soil at you in an attempt to scare you.

Keep your mind fixed on cultivating the method and utter

the San Ju Zhou (Three Sentences Spell) once and burn the Chiling Fu or the Talisman of Command.

Soon the foxes will transform into a human shape, perhaps old, perhaps young, both male and female. The older foxes become friends and the younger foxes like brothers and sisters, but you must be cautioned against forming a spousal relationship with them.

Explain to the assembled foxes that you apologise for troubling them, that there is a place of peace here for them and above all that there should be mutual respect. Say this kind of Oath:

> I am xxxxx, Shangdi has sent me to you as a friend in Dao, I wish you no harm, I ask that you may go East, West, North or South to procure and bring certain items, whether they are a thousand miles away or as near as eight hundred miles, the Book of Heaven spirit writing, magical fungi (zhi), herbs, cinnabar, medicines, treasured objects, money and other things that may be near or far for you.
>
> Do not cause trouble, work with me, assist me and aid me in the Arts of Dao and there will be the fruit of good merit of Shangdi, work for the merit of Shangdi and there will be longevity for the both of us, do not abandon me. I present this by the Upper Command Decree.
>
> Even if you uphold this Oath of the Clouds, if there is disloyalty, Thunder strikes the head and the Eagle claws out the eyes. We shall be sworn brothers/sisters. If illness shall come we shall assist each other, if there are trials and tribulations we shall rescue each other. There shall be no ingratitude.
>
> The Oath is complete!

Read the 79. Song Xian Zhou (Immortals Depart Spell) burning one Immortals Depart Talisman and then burn the paiwei or spirit tablet. Also burn the talismans you are wearing.

In the days to come you will receive money and goods, accept them.

You will not need to do this ritual every time. Once the Oath has been made.

In the quiet room set up a bed and an altar with food and drink and call the Brother or Sister Immortal.

Use cinnabar to write three Zhu Xian Fu (Chase Immortals Fu) and two Qing Xian Fu (Request Immortals Fu). Burn one and wear one.

The Spell

Heaven and Earth contain many extraordinary beings,
Each capable of an extraordinary destiny,
If you do not meet a master to teach you,
Even if a person's spirit cannot equal that of the Immortals,
Brother Immortal, Sister Immortal,
In the Mountain of the Immortals (Dongfu)
in the Ancient Temple,
the Ancient Mountain Dragon Tower,
We respectfully call the Great Fox Immortals,
Brother Fox-Twin Immortal,
Who has already attained the Dao,
And you Great Fox Immortal Maiden,
Fox Twin Immortal Girl,
Who has also achieved the Dao O Immortal Maiden,
Hear my summons to call you,
Come as quick as fire and show yourselves,
Fly unto here and descend to this place,

Do not merely manifest unclearly as in a dream,
Comply, do not disobey the Way of the Dao,
Do not violate the Law of Heaven,
By the Shang Qing (Upper Purity),
I command it by Dong Yu Dadi!
Ji Ji Ru Lu Ling chi ling!

Burn this talisman (Qing Xian Fu) if they do not come.
Afterwards burn the Zhui Xian Fu if they still do not come.
Again if they fail to appear burn the Cui Xian Fu.
Finally, if they still do not descend,
burn both the Chi Ling Fu and the Ju Shen Fu.

The Chi Ling Fu has the following spell,
known as the Three Points Spell to be read as it is burned:
The first point and Heaven purifies,
The second point and the Earth strikes,
The third point and ghosts and gods over a distance
of a thousand miles are startled.

Now read the names of the twenty eight mansions spell:
Wheel water attracting, Fiery winged serpent, Open
Moon Deer star sun horse willow soil river-deer ghost
metal sheep well water open ginseng water ape mouth
fire monkey concluding moon crow hair sun chicken
stomach soil man lou metal dog kui wood wolf bi shui
shu fire pig wei brains emptiness sun rat girl soil bat ox
metal ox half Dou Wood separate Ji water dog Wei
tranquil Xin Moon Fox Fang Sun Exemption family
soil Kang metal dragon horn wood flood dragon.
I invoke it by the Great Precious Witch Soil!
Ji Ji Ru Lu Ling!

72. Untitled
Calling Tudi Spell

Burn the Tudi Fu and read this spell:

O the Tudi God of this place your spirit rises,
Extending up to Heaven
and to the depths of the Underworld,
Alone I request that you not leave without merit
and rendering great service today,
By the name of the Script of the Upper Purity!
Ji Ji Ru Lu Ling!

73. Untitled
The Spell Of The Gong Cao

Recite this spell of the Gong Cao Gods (the Gods of the Year, Month, Day and Hour) and burn a Gong Cao Fu.

The Spell:

Three Realms Gong Cao,
Four Values Messengers,
I today command you to quickly come
and enter this wonderful altar,
Do not be tardy and disobey,
By the Court of Heaven!
Ji Ji Ru Lu Ling!

74. Ju Hu Zhou
The Spell Of Catching The Fox

If they still do not come to you burn a Qing Xian Fu and read this spell, then still failing to come burn the Zhui Xian Fu, then if again they do not descend, the Cui Xian Fu and Chi ling Fu.

The Spell

The first capturing, quickly simmer, quickly simmer,
quickly, quickly simmer (ji jian, ji jian, ji ji jian),
Come near even if you are eight hundred miles away,
even if you are a thousand miles distant,
I request you to quickly descend,
I cry out to you to come!
LING HONG HONG HONG OM ZHI LING!
I request it by Xinzhou Dragon Tiger Mountain Patriarch
Zhang Dao Ling's name.
Ji Ji Ru Lu Ling!

The second capturing, quickly come, quickly come,
quickly, quickly arrive!
Come even if you are eight hundred miles away,
come even if you are a thousand miles away.
I request that you quickly come.
I cry out to you to come!
You need not quickly retreat,
I sincerely ask by the name of the Xinzhou
Dragon Tiger Mountain Patriarch Zhang Dao Ling!
Ji Ji Ru Lu Ling!
OM LI NA HUN LI KA MI PO CI.

75. Er Ju Zhou
Spell of the Two Sentences

The Eastern Sea has great foreknowledge,
Grinding below is the unyielding sword
to become a sharp sword,
The bow is tight and the sword is unsheathed,
You quickly come and love me,
I have the favour of accomplished merit!
OM LI HONG
OM LI HONG
OM LI HONG
I request it in the name of the Xinzhou Dragon
Tiger Mountain Patriarch Zhang Dao Ling!
Ji Ji Ru Ling!

76. San Ju Zhou,
The Spell of the Third Sentence

In the beginning the Chaos of Hundun was divided,
A vast great void of fate (Taixu),
I request the spirit (jingling) to descend,
Arrive and speak.
Ji Ji Ru Lu Ling!
OM LING HONG
OM LING HONG
OM LING HONG
HONG HONG OM
OM LING HONG
NIU!

If the fox does not immediately transform into a human shape, say the Bianhua Ren Xing Zhou, 'Transform into Human Shape Spell'

77. Bianhua Ren Xing Zhou, Transform into Human Shape Spell

I today ask you to come to this altar,
Changed into a human form
and on good terms we shall become friends,
The Jade Emperor's Precious Name commanding decree,
Quickly transform!
I request it in the name of Xinzhou
Dragon-Tiger Mountain Patriarch Zhang Dao Ling!
Ji Ji Ru Lu Ling!

When you have formed an alliance with the Fox Immortal, burn the Song Xian Fu and say the Song Xian Zhou to the Fox until she goes.

78. The Song Xian Zhou or Dismiss Immortal Spell

Said three times:
Heaven Spirit, Earth Spirit,
Cut the bamboo, break the enchantment,
Disperse the evil spirits and demons,
Quietly leave the midst of this house,
I sincerely request it in the name of the
Xinzhou Dragon Tiger Mountain Patriarch
Zhang Dao Ling!
Ji Ji Ru Lu Ling!

If they do not leave, burn this Fu
and say the Song Xian Zhou seven times.

In the beginning the Chaos divided,
The primaeval vital principles Great Void,
Commands the spirit to arrive and follow the
Way of the Harmony of the Dao,
And yet the Fox did not come and resolved to hide.
I ask by the name of the Xinzhou Dragon Tiger
Mountain Patriarch Zhang Dao Ling!
Ji Ji Ru Lu Ling!
Om Li Hong,
Om Li Hong Hong Hong Om Li Hong. Niu!

This talisman is held up to ask the Fox Immortal to come.
You should wear three protective talismans or Hu Shen Fu
(Protect Body Talisman). It will keep you safe. Along with the

above spell. Use the Dou Moyu Di Jue or Dark Jade Emperor Dipper Hand Seal to hold it.

You may summon Tudi Shen to assist.

(Talismans Fig. 60-68)

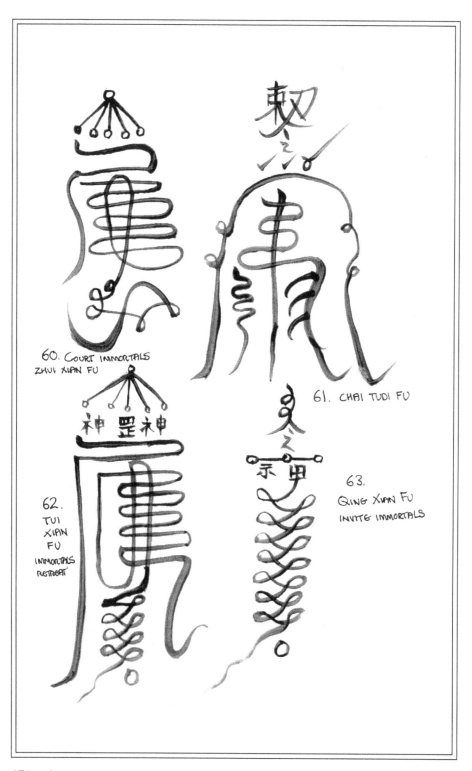

60. COURT IMMORTALS
ZHUI XIAN FU

61. CHAI TUDI FU

62.
TUI
XIAN
FU

IMMORTALS
RETREAT

63.
QING XIAN FU
INVITE IMMORTALS

66.
TRANSFORM
SHAPE
FU

64.
CHI-LING
COMMAND

65. CUI XIAN
HASTEN IMMORTALS

67.
SONG XIAN
FU
IMMORTALS
RETURN
TO
ORIGIN.

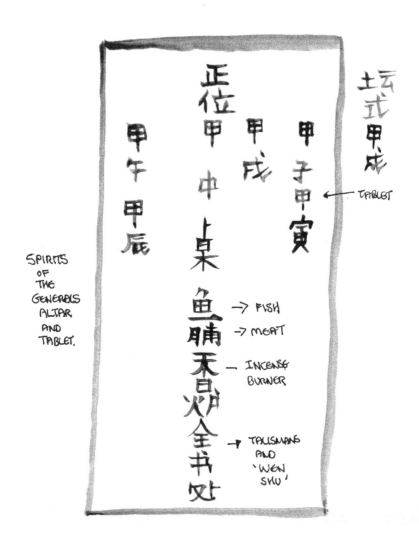

坛式甲戌

TABLET

正位甲中上桌
甲午甲辰
甲子甲寅
甲戌

SPIRITS
OF
THE
GENERALS
ALTAR
AND
TABLET.

→ FISH
→ MEAT
— INCENSE BURNER
→ TALISMANS AND 'WEN SHU'

Section II

The Evocation Of The Liu Jia
Spirit Generals

Being A Method
Of The Shen Dao (Part I)
Or Way Of The Gods,

With The Magic Of Ghost Warriors, Calling Thunder
And Sending Rain Or Winds, Flying Sand Hurtling
Stones, Plucking The Star, Dividing Your Form To
Many And The Like.

79. The Dao of Man

The Dao of Man is not the Dao of Heaven. It is said that Shandi secretly determines the Way of Dao in the hearts of the sages. For this reason it is not always handed down, the Sage cannot be in error or hear without having celestial bones and cannot see without spirit. Many do not have this opportunity. The seeker must have an immortal fate or destiny.

On an auspicious day in a clean and purified room or in the countryside we can start the operation. You can never be seen by others nor heard or the procedure is invalid.

Neither can it be done in an unclean house for reading the names of the Gods one must be careful. Nor pass it on to those people who are in error and without Dao in their hearts.

Even if a man offers a hundred pieces of precious gold and many treasures do not teach him if he is in error or you will come to fear the coming of calamities sent by Heaven.

If you pass it on to a man in error, a man of greed, of cruelty, of a bombastic nature, or one who is merely curious you will have inauspicious consequences. Do not pass to those who are not of the Dao.

Carefully create and use the spells according to the formula without error. The secret is a secret.

The Dao scholar will need to procure the following items:

A clean and pure room and a clean table to serve as an altar.

A fox's heart.

Three chicken eggs.

One tael of cinnabar.

One red peony.

Two taels of Chinese Cinnamon (Cinnamon cassia).

Seven large spiders.

Seven fireflies.

Two clean brushes.

Purified ink.

Ten pieces of paper.

Constructing The Command Decree, The Section Of The Secret Law

In the first three days of the Seventh Lunar Month, take the spiders, fireflies, cinnabar and grind them to a powder.

Fetch the chicken eggs and break them and remove the contents.

Put the powdered ingredients in the egg shell using layers of vellum paper to keep them separate.

Let it brood and so in seven days so it starts to incubate.

On the 21st day it will be done.

Peel off the shell of the eggs and take out the medicine and put it in a bag. This bag you will hang up in your incense room within a ding pot. (Ding is a three legged pot or urn).

Keep it there till the 10th month.

On the third day of this month fetch the fox's heart.

Divide the fox's heart into three pieces and seal it in the chicken eggs and incubate them for 21 days.

Peel off the shells, grind the fox's heart to a powder.

You now combine the two powders.

In the 12th month during the first 8 days use deer horn glue (lu jiaojiao) combined with warm water and mix all the ingredients to make a single paste. Shape into a shape similar to a candle with one rounded end and 4 cun long.

Dry it in the Sun.

You now have a magical cinnabar ink stick.

With a little water and a pure brush you can draw the Yang Command and then the Yin Command.

On the 12th month and on the 30th day, in the night time, eschewing the Three Evils, utter the

100. Pure Mouth Spell (see below)

101. Pure Body Spell

82. Peaceful Earth God Spell

103. Assemble the Gods Spell.

Use this ink to also write two Ju Shen Fu (Assemble the Gods Talismans) and a wash the body talisman. The Liujia Shen are lined up in a row on the altar table above the incense burner. Burn a stick of peach wood incense.

80 Jing Xin Zhou
Purifying The Heart Spell

Thousands upon thousands of flying rays of light
of bright spirit penetrate,
The Dragon-Tiger God generates the Qi
of the Revered Origin that is in perpetual change,
Thus generating Spirit,
I request it by Lingbao Great Master!
Ji Ji Ru Lu Ling

81. An Tudi Zhou
Peace To The Earth God

In the direction of the fields and lands,
With a hundred True Generosities,
the Revered respond to the matter at hand
and so the brightness of the Celestial Stars guard me,
Defending Spirit and transmitting the Sacred Sound.
I request it by Lingbao Great Master!
Ji Ji Ru Lu Ling!

82. Ju Shen Zhou
Calling the Gods

Kun! Li! Dou! Han! Piao! Huo! Sheng!
Ying! Kui! Gang! Zhi! Ri! Hua! Di! Bo! Mie! Meng!
This spell is a sincerely chanted
and reaches up to a thousand stars,
Meteors appear and cannot leave here!
By the Lingbao Great Master.
Ji Ji Ru Ling!

The Names Of The Six Jia Gods
I sincerely request,
Jia Zi Shui Jiang (Water General), Li Wen Zhong.
Jia Shen Jin Jiang (Metal General), Li Shou Quan.
Jia Wu Huo Jiang (Fire General), Li Shou Zuo.
Jia Chen Feng Jiang (Wind General), Li Shou Jin.
Jia Yin Mu Jiang, (Wood General), Li Shou Dao.
Jia Xu Tu Jiang, (Soil General), Li Shou Jing.
I command it by the name of the great Lingbao Master!
Ji Ji Ru Lu Ling!

83. Wenshu
Sparse Text

In this year, month, day and hour I present the True Disciple named XXXX born in the geng year of XXXXX and month of XX day of XXXX and in the hour of XX

Heaven and Earth True Qi of the Sun and Moon, Original Essence, the Four Emperors and Five Masters who have passed on the Way of the Dao and of Transformation and who have given true information (lit:wind) to realise that Samsara is a sea that opens to the bottomless Primaeval Essence (Hongmeng), thus teaching us how to cultivate with diligence to reach the Dao.

Today the profound script is presented to the Assembly of the Sages, and your honoured servant listens for a response, examining the mirror and summoning thunder, sending rain, plucking the star to the bucket, flying sand and stones, the heavenly divine protection, moving mountains and lifting houses, dividing appearance, sending the ghost warrior, the art of the wooden bird and the stone beast, visiting the treasury to fetch and find treasures, magical hiding, riding the crane to ascend to the clouds, instant travel in the night by boat, escaping by shrinking distance, concealing, commanding, multiplying and others of the 116 Immortal Skills that shall be bestowed in virtue of an alliance.

The sincere sparse script of the Upper Government Mountain Country, defends the passage of this person.

Presenting the Disciple XXXX .

In working the Skill we must recite it upon a Lunar New

Year's Day at midnight. Have ready the spells and three Ju Shen Fu talismans, the Yu Ti Fu.

Utter the Ju Shen Zhou having the biao wen (Taoist tube which holds the sparse script. This will be burnt and the letter passed to the spirits).

On the Altar should be the Liujia Spirit Tablet. (The spirit tablet will have the names of the Six Jia upon it as shown in the diagram overleaf). There should be a censer with one incense stick of peach in the centre, three dishes with dried fish meat.

The magician should hold one Ju Shen Talisman and then burn the biao wen. The Ju Shen Fu is worn on the head in a red headband, upon the left hand side.

Afterwards, prepare a large tub of warm water. Burn the Yu Ti Talisman so its ashes fall into the midst of the water.

Dip your left hand into the water and make three circles around your neck, then wash the eyes and both ears.

Undress and sit in the water and wash.

Take the basin indoors and empty it.

The left hand forms the Chen Wen hand seal, the right hand picks up the Talismans of Evocation (Zhang Ling).

Read the Ju Shen Zhou continually, countless times with impassioned feeling.

When the golden light covers you, the Ling Yin protects your body, keep reading.

This must be done daily until the xxxx day when finally the Jia Generals come. On that day the Spirit Tablet will move to the exactly correct location.

The Ju Shen Fu should not be lost but kept on the head on the left side.

On burning the Yuti talisman, it is the left hand in the

Chen Wen Hand Seal that is used to anoint the eyes and ears.

Cultivate without interruption every day. Focus your mind continually for six to seven days.

Then, one morning or evening you will hear, suddenly, a distinct voice coming from the altar saying 'Jiu' (Rescue).

You should be at first cautious and test what has entered the altar. Ask questions and discover who or what it is.

Having purified pens, write and record what you learn about the Great Immortal Art

Change the talisman every Jia day until the 27th day has passed.

When the Gods are familiar with the altar and their stations.

On the third or seventh day the god will show his true features, the colour of his clothes, armour and so on.

One reason people fail in knowing the true forms of spirits and contradict each other is that they fail to focus on asking and so getting true answers.

In five to seven days the spirits will come to partake of the food at the appointed place. You should change the dried fish for fresh foodstuffs, and every ten days change the talisman. (Probably referring to the Ju Shen Fu worn on the head), and keep the Spirit Tablet on the altar for the 60 day ritual cycle. (*60 days refers to the complete sexegenary cycle of stems and branches thus symbolising completion).

Firstly take hold of the Ling Zhang Talisman, in this case the Yin Zhang to write the character of fire, huo, 火, and say the name of the Jia General you are working with.

Suddenly if the operation is correct, the charcoal in the censer seems to brighten and the talisman is on fire.

Replace it with a new talisman.

In the location of the Spirit Tablet offer up fresh foods and hold the Chen Wen Hand Seal, and see if the talisman begins to shake or vibrate when you draw the 火 character. If it emits fire it has magic (shu ling). The Spirit Tablet on the altar appears to burn.

Hold the Ling Zhang and say the name of the Jia General and with the Yin Zhang draw the character of wind, feng, 風. If there follows a strong blast of wind raising dust into the air and ashes on the altar are blown away, it is accomplished.

Practising The Method

Beginning on the 8th day of the 10th Month (by the traditional Chinese Nongli calendar), fast, bathe and change clothes to fresh ones. Avoid the Three Evil Deeds so the rites of Liu Jia are a success. Abstain from meat and wine and all ill-smelling foods.

Wear the Ling Zhang on your head, but remove it when urinating, defecating or sleeping.

In nine years time you will not need the ling zhang, for your hands will have received the skill.

This is the secret of the Celestial Man and the magical secret of the Lingbao Great Method Teacher.

The lower ranking master may hear of it but cannot see it.

It will be necessary to swear an oath under the stars before opening the Book for fear of the Wrath of Heaven.

Shen Dao
Part 2
The Way Of The Gods

After nine years of practice and cultivation, fetch snow that has not touched the ground, 30 jin in amount and on the first day of the lunar month. To do this use a new pot made clean, the mouth of it open to the sky.

(No doubt this refers to the practice of gathering 'rootless water', water that has not touched the ground).

Use a fire of charcoal to boil the 30 jin of water. The master then holds the Yang Zhang in his left hand. Let him shake or flap the talisman from below to above twelve times.

When the pot of water seems to emit a bright light like lightning and a black mist spreads over it, take the pot off the fire. Wait for General XXXX to speak from within. At this point the master may feel an unconsciousness of the world, a sweating of the body until he wakes up. There is success.

Do this for one to two years and not only will you have merit, but your right hand can be used to call the General.

84. Calling Thunder And Sending Rain

Save the distressed and needy people by asking for rain.

Fetch five peach stones and line them up on the Altar, use the Yin Seal to write the character of thunder (LEI) in the air:

Call the name of the General and then shake the Yang Zhang many times until you hear a thunderclap. The sound of thunder will resound in correspondence to the number of times you wrote the character of Thunder with the Yin Zhang Fu.

By means of the Yang Zhang you can stop the storm.

If you wish to call the Dragons to send rain use two pieces of yellow paper, on each written the character of Dragon (Long):

龍

Cast these papers into the air and by means of the Yin Zhang Talisman invoke them to come, and by the Yang Zhang talisman to once again depart. Call out the name of the Jia General and of the Can Long (Grey Dragon, but also anciently azure), the dragon will fly up swiftly in a dense mist and rain will condense and fall.

Using the word water, (shui) will have a different effect. There will be rain and one part wind.

85. Zhai Xing Huan Dou Fa
Plucking The Star
And Transferring It
To A Bucket

If you wish to pluck a star and transfer it to a vessel such as a bucket to emit light, firstly, obtain a new bucket and inside place the 'Thunder Sounding in Five Directions Star'. (That is the pentagram in western nomenclature, drawn with cinnabar on yellow paper).

Then fetch a bamboo pole that is two feet long, and fix the pole into the centre of the bucket. Use five colour threads around the pole. On top of the bowl place a bowl.

Call the Jia General and use the Yin Zhang. Immediately stars seem to descend. Use the Yang Zhang, shaking it over the bucket and the brightness of the stars is gone.

Another way, for the Sun and Moon.

Fetch a Yin Mirror and stick or paint upon it the character of the Sun and Moon (Ri and Yue):

日月

Place the mirror in the bucket.

Crying out the name of the Jia General and using the Yin Zhang towards the Sun, inhale a breath and then blow on the mirror. Quickly turn up the mirror so it's reflecting surface faces down, there is a sudden darkness as if there is night.

Use the Yang Zhang and turn the mirror reflecting surface up to resolve the spell of darkness.

86. Feisha Zoushi
Flying Sand
And Hurtling Stones

This method can be used against demons or aggressors up to 2000 miles.

Quickly fetch up earth in your hand and call the name of the General, move the Yin Zhang in a circle and then throw the soil in the air, the General will see to it that a black mist of sand beats against the opponents eyes.

For hurtling stones, pick up a stone and call the General and wave the Yin Zhang as before and ten thousand stones come into being.

To stop it use the Yang Zhang, shake it and exhale once and the sand or stones will at once drop.

87. Tian Shen Hu Wei
The Divine Celestial Bodyguard

It is the wind that sends the Divine Celestial Heavenly General but only if you know his name. Using ink, write that name and then paste the name of the General on a door or window and call the name of the General. Inhale the solar Qi and by means of the Yin Zhang say the name of the person you wish to be guarded at night.

To stop, use the Yang Zhang by shaking it.

88. Yishi Gui Shen
A Serving Ghost Or Spirit

A person wishes to be successful in a new town or city or indeed, in one which he dwells. Let him obtain a picture of the Town God (Chenghuang) or Local EarthSpirit (Tudi). Use ink to write the name of the General and paste it on the heart of the image.

Use the Yin Zhang, shake it, and a wonderful 'person' will come and speak and answer you and serve you.

It is best if they are called at night.

To send the spirit away, remove the General's name and dismiss with the Yang Zhang.

If you want a Ghost Soldier to aid you, call the General and shake the Yin Zhang and he will come. Again dismiss in the usual way.

89. Yi Shan Ba Zai
Moving Mountain
And Raising Houses

A person who wants to shift or alter a mountain should have a blank sheet of paper and with black ink write the name of so and so mountain and ten li, one hundred li, one hundred li stop. Place it on a wooden stick and insert it into the mountain. Quickly call the name of the Jia General while holding the Yin Zhang, shake it and the mountain will appear to move,

The same action applies to a house.

90. Untitled
Changing Body

You wish that your own bodily form is divided and you disappear leaving a transformed object behind.

Fetch from the forest a bamboo branch that is exactly the same height as yourself and with six knots. With ink write your name and birthdate on a sheet of paper and insert it into the bamboo pole.

In an emergency, call the name of the General while holding the Yin Zhang and cast the bamboo pole down on the ground. Do not return to the Ancestors or you will die!

Your bodily form will appear to become a bamboo pole.

To change back, use the Yin Zhang to call the Jia General.

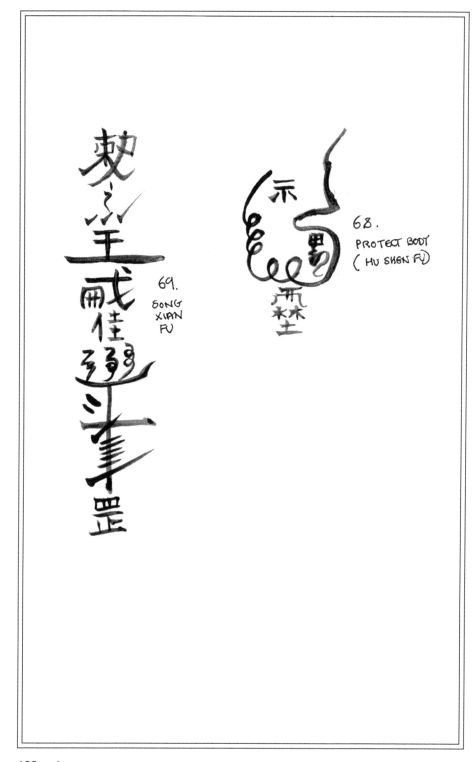

69.
SONG
XIAN
FU

68.
PROTECT BODY
(HU SHEN FU)

91. Untitled
Wooden Birds
And Stone Animals

Take two bird feathers and a rock, a fire-brick is ideal and make a large pile of stones.

To make poultry use chicken feathers, goose feathers, duck feathers and so on.

To make an animal use a pile of wood.

On top have a paper on which you have written 'chu', livestock:

畜

Call the General and use Yin Zhang, and a pig, sheep or horse will come.

Resolve it with Yang Zhang.

92. Tan Ku Qu Bao
Finding A Treasure Store

Desiring gold money first dig a hole without anyone seeing you, and with a bamboo pole and a net, sieve or winnowing fan cover the upper, middle and lower parts of the hole.

Call the Jia General with the Yin Zhang and cover. Call the General by means of the Yin Zhang, shaking the talisman. The money you desire should be written on silk and laid on top.

Countless other methods will be revealed by the Generals themselves.

(Talismans Figs. 70-72)

93. Jie Cao Dang Shang
Using Grass To Ward Off Injury

Preliminary Chant:

'Heaven's Profundity is Mysterious and Infinite,

The Soul and Heart is connected to all things,

In the East is rain and in the West is wind,

Stepping the Big Dipper step by step!'

Choose an auspicious day when rain comes from the East and wind comes from the west. Facing the Celestial Palace (ie the Big Dipper) do obeisance.

Quickly go up a barren hill when no one is around and pile up stones to form an altar. You will now prepare the ground to form the Big Dipper Altar which is to be at minimum six metres wide.

Each star will be represented by a hole which is dug at a depth of about 2 cun (roughly 3 inches) and in each hole you shall place an oil lamp.

This will be at the time the Dipper Stars come to the North East. The wick of each lamp must be thick so it stays alight.

When each lamp is bright, step on each star and say:

The Spell

'O Heaven quickly, Earth quickly!

Wind and Rain are in harmony with the Eastern Stars.

In the West the Moon is bright,

The spirit of the heart points to spirit,

Seeking the way to the Gate of Heaven!

I request the sweet dew of grass, of green grass!'

Tread the Dipper seven times and recite the spell at each

lamp seven times. Bow one hundred times at each lamp. Do not stop.

At each lamp pick some blades of grass and take them home. Place the grass you have picked in the shade to dry. When it is dry, grind it to a powder and place it in a bottle.

On a New Moon facing North do one hundred obeisances, then South to the Southern Court (Southern Dipper) and do one hundred obeisances. Repeat again on the Full Moon. The Grass is ready to use.

Mix with oil. Use the oil by applying it before battle. You cannot be hurt.

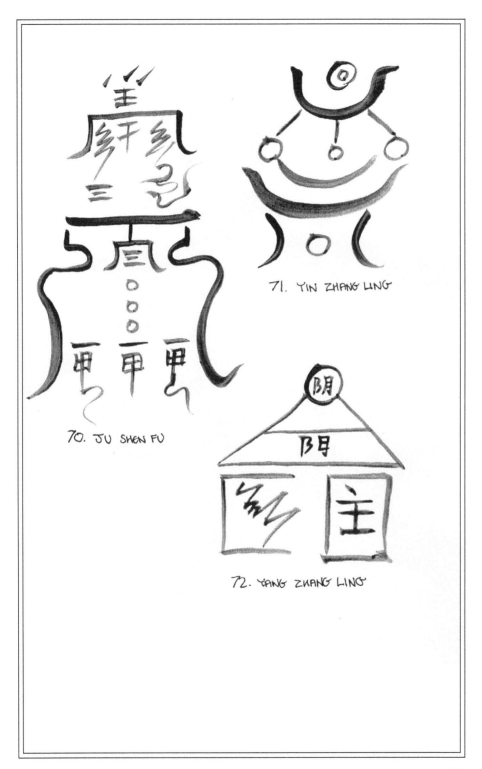

70. JU SHEN FU

71. YIN ZHANG LING

72. YANG ZHANG LING

94. Shiwu Jin Zei Dao Fa
Thief Detaining Method

On the first or fifteenth day of the lunar month, letting no one see you, read the spell seven times. Read it before Tu Shen (Earth God) or Shan Shen (Mountain God).

The right hand should be in the sword seal and the left foot forward in the ding step, with right behind.

At the front door place seven paper dolls, burn them as you read the spell seven times, blowing towards a wall or tree on which you have used a nail or needle to draw the talisman.

'Heaven assists, Earth assists,
Someone comes to seize an item,
If it is stolen, the Earth God and the Mountain God
will fix them with a cangue!
I honour Taishang Laojun!
Ji Ji Ru Lu Ling!

(Talisman Fig. 73)

73. Detaining a Thief

95. Qi Tian Bu Yun Xiantian Fa
Praying To Heaven To Seize
The Cloud Pre-Heaven Method

This spell or rather series of spells will need little introduction. It is pure weather magic with a number of rather interesting features. This talisman should be written twice on separate pieces of black paper. The secondary writing is written with cinnabar on a white cloth that is 1 foot and 5 inches long.

The Spell
Black Man, Black Horse, Black Qilin (unicorn),
the Black tiled house, Beat the drums and gong, noise
and darkness as the blackness passes through the Land

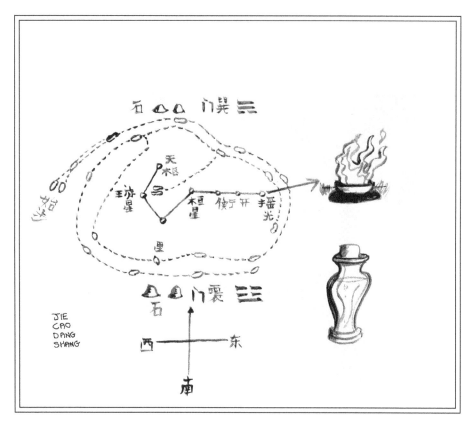

Under Heaven and there is no exit by which it can leave.
The Black Heavenly Teacher does not obey the Dao,
beneath in the Dark Underworld the Ten Kings open!

(This mysterious spell seems to be invoking the Yin power of water (water is both Yin and its elemental colour is black. The call to the Underworld is interesting. It specifically calls out to the Ten Kings who rule various Halls in the Chinese Underworld. Next follows an invocation to powers identified as yellow in colour, which is undoubtedly Earth.)

In the centre five yellow clouds arise,
five clouds one after the other and cover the sky.
A thousand spirit troops and ten thousand generals
carry my body, both military generals and scholars.
The descending spirit has weight in the five directions,
the clouds in the heavens open, the heavens open,
I come out!
I request it by Hunyuan Lao Zu's command!

The next spell in the 'weather' series seems to invoke wind and thunder specifically. To use this talisman, draw five of them using cinnabar ink. Use a white chicken and a white duck as an offering, turning towards the Five Directions, burn them to ashes in a bowl of water and drink. Alternatively you can paint the talismans on five pieces of peach or willow wood.

The magician has an altar with cooked offerings of chicken and duck and the five talismans laid out on the altar pointing to each of the five directions.one would have all the use implements of the Art such as incense, candles and so on.

The Spell

Fang Di Feng (God of the Wind) comes, Fang Di Feng comes! In the midst a violent blast of wind rises to the five directions. A fierce gale gathers upon the earth and opens the Upper and blows to Heaven.

The Earth, Sun and Moon become dim, it blows beneath the Five Sacred Mountains, Mount Tai collapses, even the Ten Halls and Palaces of the Gods make obeisance, it blows across the Yellow River and it is dried up, the mouths of the Three Rivers are broken, the land is plundered by the fierce wind, people are blown backwards, ancient trees are toppled, The Chang Jiang River's waters flow backwards, the Troops of the Eight Counties stations are halted!

I honour Hunyuan Lao Zu's command!

This talisman is for Thunder. (The Luban does not state the fact but they are used in the same manner as those for the Wind Spell above judging by the accompanying Five Elements and Directions diagram.)

The Spell

My spirit is not an extraordinary spirit, for it is not I but the Five Thunder Ancestor body that grasps the flaming light that is both high and deep, treading on the Wheel of Fire and making the rumbling sound.

Thunder arrives in the midst and the Yellow Emperor comes.

All the Five Thunders come!

HONG! HONG!

Startling the Kingdom of Heaven and the skies darken over the Earth, the seas darken and break, all the hundreds of Gods and Ghosts bow down.

The farmers and workers follow their hearts as lightning illuminates three thousand miles, the Eighteen Thunders transform my body!
I honour Wu Lei Wu Zu's command!

In this method draw the Thunder Characters on your palm and you shall resemble the Thunder God in all Ten Directions.

96. The Thirty Six Thunder Names

Na Erlang Xin Tian Jun
Hu Shi Zhe Zhen Tian Jun
Pang Liu Xie
Wei Niao
Guan Zhao
Kang Tian
Cui Liu
Tao Gao
Deng Gua
Weng Wang Yuanshi
Zhao Jiangjun
Wen Taibao
Song Zhao
Si Bao Yang
Wang Shi Chen Jiangjun
Gong Cao Tudi
Mu Yuanshi
Huo Yuan

The following spell is for rain. Go to your altar and use a bowl of pure and clean water from your location. Let this water be Heaven's Water (ie, rainwater that has never touched the earth). Using the right Thunder Hand Seal look up to Heaven and say:

Heaven Spirit. Earth Spirit, the Rain falls from the Palace of Heaven, Heaven and Earth descend.
The Five Dragons of Water arrive together,
The Five Waters arrive together,

Nine spit water and rescue the good people,
Fengbo (the Wind God) and Yushi (the Rain God)
come together.
Leigong's lightning descends,
Together the Wind and the Rain rises in purifying waves,
The Chang Jiang River is bottomless,
The Dragons of Rain descend,
Rain falls within the winds,
Lightning in the winds purifies the white Moon.
I honour Li Zhen Xian!

To stop the rain, burn the Seal of Hunyuan.
(Talismans Figs. 74-79)

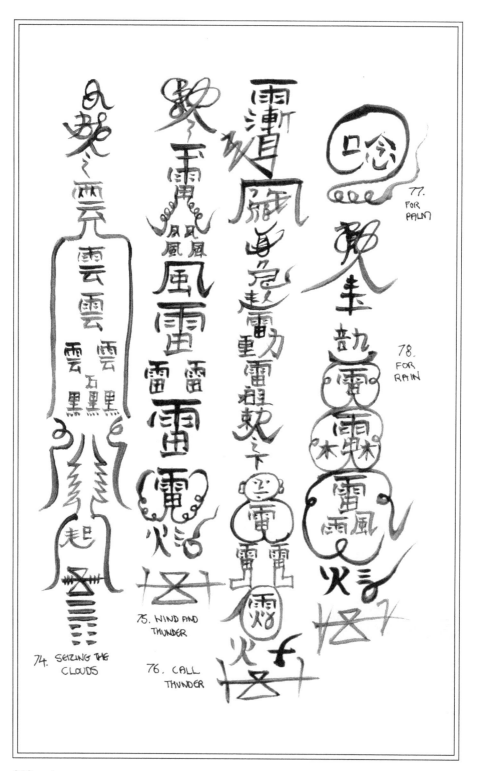

74. SEIZING THE CLOUDS

75. WIND AND THUNDER

76. CALL THUNDER

77. FOR PALM

78. FOR RAIN

97. Untitled
The Method Of The Five Seas

This talisman and its method are excellent and has been used for 10,000 years to send water to purify the land. One must use five bowls of water, the water having been gotten from a cave and cover it so dust does not settle on it. The five bowls are laid out on the altar in the five directions at midday. Using ash to draw the bagua trigrams on the floor before the altar. The magician steps onto the Kan symbol and his left hand holds the Five Seas Hand Seal.

The Spell

Rays of light descend from the Heavenly Palace
to the body,
Nine turtles spit water and the waves
of the Four Seas purify,
The waves of Taishan remove impurities
from the honoured house,
The element of Wood passes through,
Secretly all the unhealthy xie (qi) are carried
by the Heavenly Troops to the bottom of the sea.
O my Master is above in the blue sky,
And bubbling forth from the East, South, West and North
and centre are the Five Lakes and Four Seas waters,
Large waves arise to heaven,
and lesser waves sweep the earth,
Subduing the wicked with water!
I honour Hunyuan Zhen Xian,
Ji Ji Ru Lu Ling!

Read seven times and the powers of the sea and water shall come. (Talisman Fig. 80)

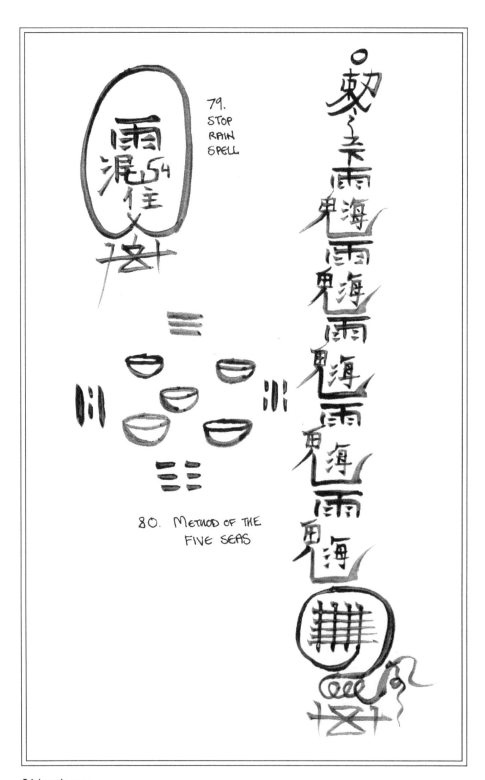

79.
STOP
RAIN
SPELL

80. METHOD OF THE
FIVE SEAS

98. Tong Shui Fa
Opening The Water Method

This is the first of a series of spells that are dedicated to using the five elements and other natural phenomena to hide the magician. It is a form of invisibility or escape used by magicians and warriors.

Such methods were integral to the magic of the divination system known as Qimen Dun Jia. Today Qimen is largely known as a 'divination' system with very few practitioners schooled in its magical elements. In ancient times magicians often worked with nobles and generals on the field of war and were expected not just to divine strategies but also offer magical solutions. These following spells represent part of that tradition.

This following talisman should be used before battle or when fleeing so you can escape by water, by ditches, rivers, lakes and seas. You will burn the talisman in the water.

The Spell

I do not punish myself,
I do not have an extraordinary body,
I am like Five-Kinds-Of-Body,
Wearing on my head a heavenly crown of diamonds,
I wear armour on my body and a helmet on my head,
Manifesting my power, following the King of the Sea
are his Troops and Generals,
Seeing water I penetrate its depths,
My three immortal souls (hun)
and seven mortal souls (po) are on the seabed,
Waves of water turn around and around me
guarding my body,

Try and see me!
One person comes and the water descendant
cannot be harmed by knives, nor cudgels,
nor spears. There is no pain.
The winds arrive and it cannot move the waves of water,
I honour Hunyuan Laozu's command!!

(Talisman Fig. 81)

99. Tong Shan Jue
Opening the Mountain Formula*

One should not take this talisman lightly, as it is a high method and a great Daoist skill. Use this method in times of famine, upheaval, when a city is under siege, in war and when a life finds itself on a dangerous road, or when the family are in danger of losing their lives. Then this talisman can be burned to hide the body, using the Five Mountains Hand Seal.

The Spell

My body is not an extraordinary body,
I am the Land Under Heaven Five Mountains
made manifest,
The eastern body acts and changes
to the Eastern Yue Mountain,
The right hand side body becomes
the Southern Nan Yue Mountain,
The left foot becomes the Western Xi Yue Mountain,
The right foot becomes Northern Bei Yue Mountain,
The body becomes the Five Wu Yue Mountains,
The eyes become Wudang Mountain,
The body Emei Mountain,
Large and small become the Five Mountains,
Going down the mountain the body is protected,
Ten thousand mountains protect the body,
I am high in the clouds and strong,
You are at the foot of the hill,
People see me and I am the Immortal Mountain,
I see you come with ten thousand knives to cut

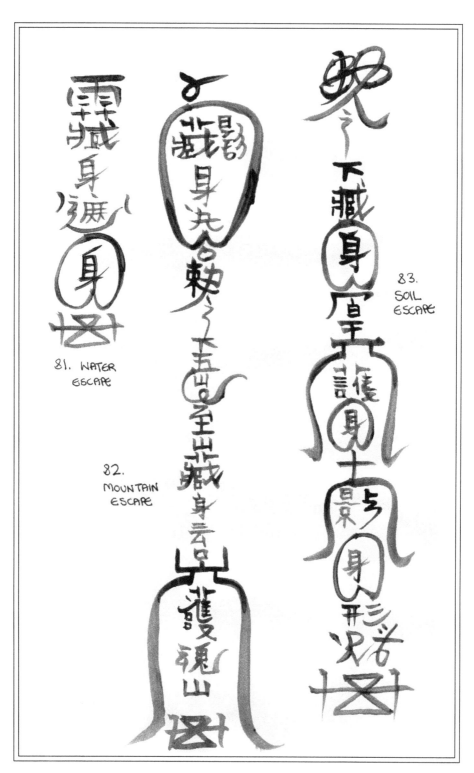

81. WATER
ESCAPE

82.
MOUNTAIN
ESCAPE

83.
SOIL
ESCAPE

and ten thousand swords but they are as soft as silk to me,
The mountain does not move. The mountain moves.
I honour Hunyuan Zushi's command!

(Talisman Fig. 82)

---

* An alternative handwritten manuscript renders it as Dun Shan
Jue, 'dun' meaning to escape, as in the Dun in QimenDunjia.

100. Tong Tu Jue
Open Soil Formula

This method is incomparable and a high method among Daoist skills. If there is evil on the road this talisman can be used to hide by the powers of the element of Soil. Choose a Liu Jia Day with Soil indications (i.e. stems and branches associated with soil, see my *Practical Chinese Magic*) and cultivate this at night.

Have incense arranged as customary and three of the talismans of Soil Penetration written in cinnabar ink. Go to the ancient tomb and fetch soil from the graves from the five directions. Place this soil upon the altar. One burns the talismans and mixes their ashes with a little water, soil and cinnabar and swallows a little. The right hand makes the Seal of Soil and the left the Hide Body Seal.

The Spell

One, Two, Three, Four, Five.
Metal, Wood, Water, Fire, Soil.
Ten thousand methods come together,
Guanyin comes to assist me,
I ask the Name and Harmonious Surname,
The Five Elements are my Mother,
The Ancestral Metal and Wood comes to hold the magus,
Five Earths are my body, My body are the Five Earths,
I today by ten thousand methods,
I shall enter the Earth three Zhang.
I am in the midst of the Seat of Earth,

Heaven and Earth come together to protect me.
I honour Hunyuan Xian Shi's command!

(Talisman Fig. 83)

101. Cang Shen Fa
Hide Body Method
(Hidden Stone Method)

This talisman uses whiter paper and cinnabar. You can practice this on the first day of a lunar month or one of the red-letter days according to the almanack.

Search for a yellow coloured stone and either find it in a mountain or river. One then places it in the centre of a river or on a mountain.

The talisman will be burned and its ashes in water drunk, read the spell and your spirit will be hidden in the stone.

The Spell

O hide my body,
change my body in its essence to be a stone.
My head is a large stone,
my body becomes the Stone General,
three hun souls hide in the belly of the stone,
my seven Po souls hide in the midst of the stone.
The white crane rises and a flying immortal crosses
the mountain. I am in the stone resting on the earth.
If someone knows where I am,
then I enter the goodly rock.
I have always been a stone within the cave,
people cannot come by the road
and ghosts cannot come by the hidden door.
Use Five Rocks Hand Seal.

(Talisman Fig. 84)

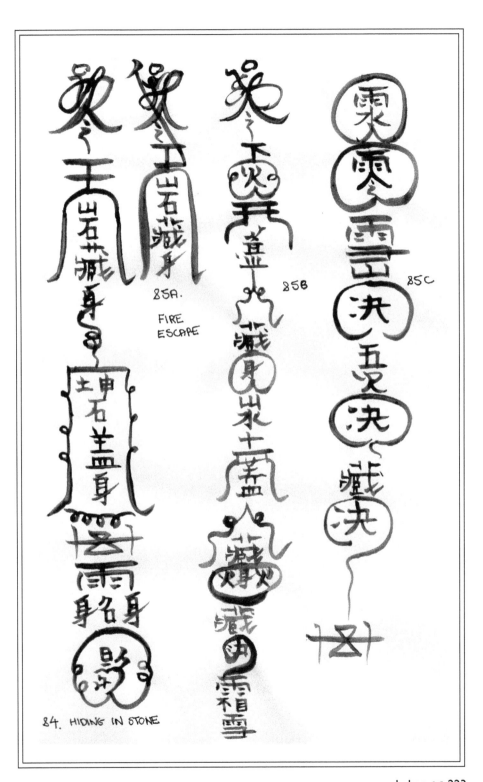

85A.
FIRE ESCAPE

85B

85C

84. HIDING IN STONE

102. Huo Dun Fa
Fire Escaping Method

Allows the magician to escape and be invisible by means of the element of fire.

The Spell

My spirit is not an extraordinary spirit.
I am the Southern Fire General, Houzai Jiangjun,
I am ten thousand zhang tall with green smoke rising,
My mouth spits forth blazing fire and blue smoke arises,
My spirit generates to a fiery shield for my body,
Meeting with fire that is one zhang high,
Five directions burning does not touch my body,
A person who tries to find me will see me
as a Fire Mountain,
A spirit who tries to see me will see me as a lantern,
An evil demon sees me and flees a thousand miles away,
An evil sorcerer sees me and his life passes away
and vanishes to nothingness,
I honour the command of Hunyuan Laozu!

This spell calls the Heaven and Earth Wind, Snow, Cloud, Lightning and Thunderstorms in the five directions. The left hand is in the Jade Seal and the right is in the Sword Seal. Breathe in three breaths of Qi to the dantian.

The Spell

Heaven is pure, Earth is spirit,
The Great Sage is sincere,
The Three Emperors assist me,
The Five Lords who have ten thousand methods

give me relief, sending their spirit that is purifying
and calming,
Purifying the heart so it is like Jia Geng.
On the left is the Big Dipper.
On the right the Seven Stars,
The Liu Ding protect my body,
I honour Feng Gao Ming, He Who Knows Fate,
Heaven bestows longevity
for as long as the universe endures.
I honour Taishang Laojun.
Ji Ji Ru Lu Jing!

(Talisman Fig. 85)

103. Teng Yun Jia Wu Fa
Rising Cloud and Driving Mist

Creates a magickal mist in which the wizard is concealed.

The Spell

My spirit is not an extraordinary spirit,
I am the White Crane Parent, Baihe Qinti,
My body is as tall as one zhang,
Riding the White Crane above the blue clouds,
Five coloured auspicious clouds come and hide me,
Clouds hide my form within their midst,
The Twenty Eight Lunar Mansions are on my left
and my right,
The lightning of Lei Gong follows me,
O clouds come, clouds come as a mist,
a mist gathers around my body,
The Sun and the Moon illuminate the clouds
and the mist and so my form appears scattered,
Today I will be in the clouds for a while,
I honour Hunyuan Laozu's command!

(Talisman Fig. 86)

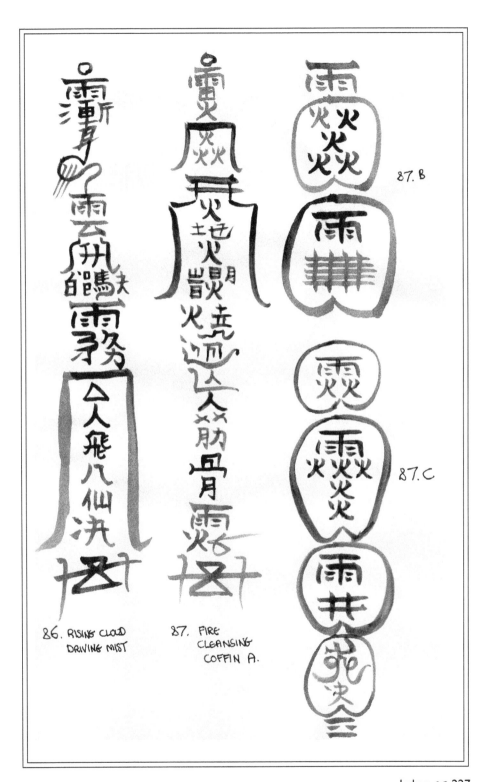

87. B

87. C

86. RISING CLOUD
DRIVING MIST

87. FIRE
CLEANSING
COFFIN A.

The Section Of Luban
Funeral Magic

In this section of the Luban are a number of spells related to coffins, the dead and the mourning procedure. Many folk traditions including that of the Luban have a number of methods aimed at the process of mourning for and burying the dead.

Protecting the coffin from evil spirits, purification protection of mourners and so on.

More unusual are spells to stop putrefaction of the corpse, an unpleasant problem in the days before the introduction of refrigeration and embalming.

Other spells have a punishing nature and seem quite unpleasant ... such as deliberately causing a corpse to liquify into a stinking soup that slops around in the bottom of the coffin, or making a coffin so heavy that no one is able to lift the casket and take it for proper burial. Not a pleasant curse by any means!

104. Bin Xian Huo Sang Fa
Mourning Rites Coffin Danger Fire Method

This method is utilised to rid of impurities or even evil spirits attracted to the yin energies present at a funeral as the coffin lies in wait.

The second set of spells use magical thunder fire to dry out a corpse to stop it from rotting and stinking before burial.

The talisman once written is placed on the chest of the deceased who lies in the coffin and the spell is read as another talisman of the same design is burned so its ashes fall into a bowl of water.

The Spell

With pure water, the Sun and Moon flowers open in the midst and store the power of the Northern Dipper, the San Tai descend within and remove evil filth, removing inauspiciousness, auspiciousness comes, true Qi comes and misfortune must leave, good fortune comes. The Divine Pool of Water becomes a lotus-throne, the demons detesting it leave.

By Earth leave!

By Heaven leave!

Pu'an removes all taboos.

I honour the command!

The person placed in the coffin has the talisman on his chest. For males it is on the left side and for females on the right side.

Use the Jade Knife hand seal.

Second spell to be read after water purification:

Heavenly Emperor, Earthly Emperor,

Jade Emperor orders me to mourn their passing,
There will be no foul smell, move and yet restrain,
the Five Thunders conceal it,
I request Heaven and Earth in the Year ......
Month..... Day...... and in this place..............,
Open the fire of the Five Thunders, quickly, quickly
come and send fire to come with great force, wearing
a cap of fire and a garments and armour of fire, a
pouch of fire hung from his belt, treading upon fire
and thunder, My Master quickly gives rise to the Five
Thunders and Five Fires which shall descend unto this
corpse and heat it so the thin and watery blood shall
never leak or flow like a stream, heat this corpse, the
five organs are transformed into jade-ash, the feet and
bones burn.

An offensive odour shall not arise, the fire is received
and enter's the person's belly, their five organs, liver
and gall, and the six soft organs of the cadaver of our
disciple named ...., passing through to the
Thirty-Three Heavens and like water leaving.
I request it by the command of Taishang Laojun True
Immortal's command!

Use this spell at the time of mourning, burn joss money
and recite it under your breath. Use the Mountain Plugs the
Sea Hand Seal and the Golden Lion Hand Seal.

Another to the same end:

The Spell

The heart aspires to return to life-destiny,
We request the pure Southern Fire Virtuous Star
to manifest its spiritual power,
General Copper Plate overpowers Iron Plate,
The Iron Plate overwhelms the Copper Plate,

Clashing with and knocking the Iron Hoop,
The Iron Nail and mirror are inverted,
The sharp iron nail is inverted,
The needle comes and changes the ingot to Eaglewood,
The root body diamond thunderbolt arises, quickly
and with power fire rises, and that fire strikes with force
to lift all taboos,
The crying mourners are struck
and have no defence from it,
The disease god comes and the demons leave
and request the Celestial Immortal True Person,
Earth Immortal True Person,
Tong Ling True Person of the Fire Ministry,
Golden Fire is seething and the Thunder Fire is scintillating,
Smoke and fire rise up,
The Fire rids of taboos,
I request the Five Thunder Patriarch's command,
Thunder strikes for three years without entering the water,
Within the river arises Celestial Troops,
My spirit is not an extraordinary spirit,
I am the Southern Powerful Fire Virtuous Star
(Nan Li Huo De Xing) come from the
Southern Bing-Ding Fire to kill the
Northern Water Virtuous Star,
I am come to Laojun's Palace,
Seeing beneath the ground the bones of the dead,
The throat is broken with three parts of Qi,
The body has a stench, O a sorry disaster,
Only the Patriarch God can open the great power
and sweep away the offensive smell so it can never arrive,

The first heating of the corpse,
The second heating of the corpse and it is dry,
The third heating of the corpse and the five organs
are preserved,
The fourth heating of the corpse
and the six organs are preserved,
Quickly the eyes open to see the Higher,
By this one altar cleansed by Heaven it is cleansed
as the Moon.
The entire body is transformed by heat.
If you disobey this command,
the Gods shall wipe you out,
The transformation changes the true person,
The honoured dead complies with the transformation,
Three arrays of the Purple Star disperse the rottenness
of the body,
Jiazi (Jiazi is a cycle of sixty in Chinese calendrical time)
becomes firewood of the Parasol Tree,
Ten thousand problems cannot rise up,
The Three Hun Souls become a single energy.
The Iron nail and the ingot cannot withdraw.
I honour Taishang Laojun!
Ji Ji Ru Lu Ling.

Use the Support of the Funeral Hand Seal and Locust Hand Seal.

In the first division of Heaven and Earth governing Qian and Kun, Sun, Moon and Thunder is ruled by Mars, Thunder Fire scorches the untamed ghosts, Earth Fire rises to scorch the criminals, Thunder Fire that is vast scorches the Land Under Heaven, intangible and eternal in its years, the Celestial Fire of the Thunder God arises, the Earth Fire of the Thunder God rises, the Year Fire of the Thunder God rises, The Month Fire of the Thunder God rises, the Day Fire of the Thunder God rises.

O the Fire of the Thunder God Master comes quickly, the Five Thunder Fire, with wondrous speed the Five Thunder Fire descends, My Master is within the midst of the fire, from within the auspicious person is fire, rising Thunder Fire scorches Jia, Yi, Bing, Ding, Wu, Ji, Geng, Xin, Ren and Gui.

For three years and five years there is no foul stench, having no tangible impression in Bing-Yin nor Ding-Mao, such is the stove and its fire power.

Secondly it rises up in Jia-Wu and Yi-Hai
as the Mountain Peak Fire.
Thirdly it rises in Wu-Zi and Ji-Chou
as the Thunderbolt Fire.
Fourthly it rises up in Jia-Chen
and Yi-Si as the Oil Lamp Fire.
Fifth, it rises up in Wu-Wu and Ji-Wei
as the Upper Celestial Fire.
I am the Master-Quickly-Rising Five Thunder Fire,
Transforming body to transform the corpse to be as dust.
I request the Celestial Immortal Zhenren,
Tong Ling Zhenren Fire Ministry,
Golden Fire is a seething fire as brilliant
as a candle flame that flies up swiftly,
The Jade Emperor commands that you scorch the body!
I honour Taishang Laojun!
Ji Ji Ru Lu Ling!
(Talisman Fig. 87)

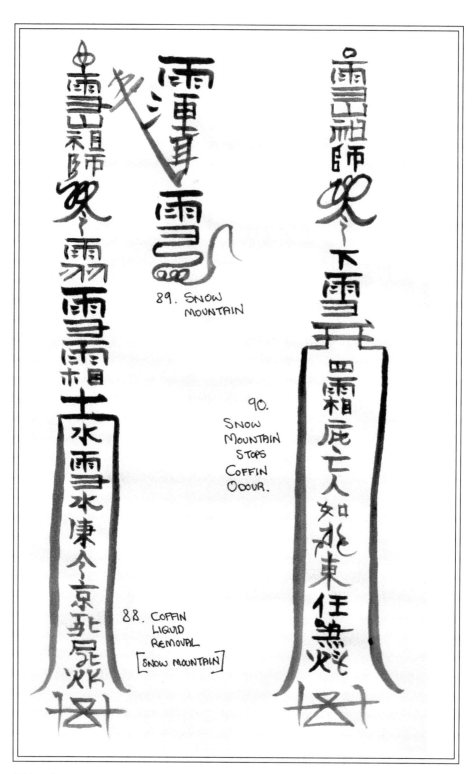

89. SNOW MOUNTAIN

90. SNOW MOUNTAIN STOPS COFFIN ODOUR.

88. COFFIN LIQUID REMOVAL [SNOW MOUNTAIN]

105. This talisman transforms and is a higher magic

Today the Origin of Ten Thousand Years, Years, Years, Immortal Fragrance seizes the upright person, dressing them and covering them.

Covering the upper part and not in opposition to the lower.

The thick liquid cannot manifest on any of the four sides and there can be no stench.

Go and act, Bian Fa Zhong Wang

(Transforming the Midst Method King)

This paper originated from the paper of Cai Lun, and this paper is on the heart of the man and written on the four sides of the coffin and pasted thereon. It forbids the liquid to run and the corpse water shall vanish, the blood Qi and blood water is concealed within. Nine sand waters and sweat in the inner and outer coffin are so transformed by the Diamond Thunderbolt.

This talisman seals for three to five years.

(Talisman Fig. 88)

106. Untitled
Coffin Water Funeral Method

This talisman will assist the corpse in the coffin not to release water, purifying the filth and is placed on the chest. Left for males and right for females. Left hand makes the Five Thunders Seal and the right makes the Snow Mountain Seal.

The Spell:

Heaven is splendorous, Earth is splendorous,
I call the Snow Mountain Great Dragon King to rise,
By the command of the Jade Emperor,
Snow Water descends from the Celestial Snow Mountain,
Floating tenderly comes powdery frosty snow,
Snow Mountain Tongzi also comes with frost
and snow though the mountain is unseen,
Coming to the body to transform it to a Snow Mountain,
Like an iron vessel with two feet as white as snow,
The body is like that vessel,
The head becomes snow and there can be no foul odour,
The corpse becomes wood and wind
and so water is not leaked,
The belly and internal organs become a calabash
of snow and no stench arises,
Five Inner Organs change to snow,
The Yang Water is pure and enters like a cool wind
into the four limbs.
The Six Soft Organs and Five Inner Organs become cold,
The warmth disappears in the body of xxxx and the Upper
Thirty-Three Heavens come with frost and snow,
Forever there is no stench,
By the Wheel of the Big Dipper Stars,

I honour the Snow Mountain Patriarch's command!

(To be read five to six times)

The Snow Mountain Spell
The heart aspires to return to the ceremony of life.
With reverence I request the Eastern Green Emperor,
The Southern Red Emperor,
The Western White Emperor,
The Northern Black Emperor,
The Central Yellow Emperor,
The Snow Mountain Lady bubbles forth
frost and snow ten thousand in height,
I request the Snow Mountain Dragon Tree King
to arise and cause frost and snow to descend
from the Heavenly Hall in the Geng Period (ie at night),
Through the Five Watches
(five two hour periods of the night watch)
till the golden rooster comes to herald the dawn,
Mountain trees loudly sway,
opening the doors and there are a thousand years of snow,
In the family home there is a frost of some 10,000 in weight,
The four walls of the house are surrounded
by the power of the Snow Mountain command,
Seeing the frost and snow, cannot see the house,
The coffin changes to a hall of frost and snow,
It covers the person within,
The person becomes the Snow Mountain Official,
It becomes frozen and is cold and icy
like an iron vessel during both the day and the night.
Freezing solid! Bang! Bang!
The Evil Master seeing the first strike of cold is afraid,

Demons seeing it pass into nothingness,
Covering the corpse there is no stench,
Beneath there is no leaking of liquid,
Insects are stopped by snow within the belly,
Foul odours cannot enter the precious box,
All four sides do not emit a stench,
It shall be stopped by Fa Zhong Wang.
I honour Taishang Laojun.
Ji Ji Ru Lu Ling!

(Talisman Fig. 89)

107. Water Stops The Offensive Odour Spell

The Spell

The first Control and the coffin is as a Snow Mountain,
The second control, and the coffin is as frost and snow,
The third control and the odour is bound
and smells like the ocean,
The fourth control, and insects pass up
to the Heavenly Hall,
The lower coffin with one bowl of pure water,
Washing and bathing the dead so it becomes
a precious box,
The four directions are forever without a stench,
Assist the body to change O Fa Zhong Wang.

Funeral Leakage Method

One must enter the funeral place without anyone knowing. Use two sewing needles, blow three times on them and use the Diamond Place hand seal. Place some ash into the coffin and secretly place the needles, one at the head and one at the feet.

The Spell

Using left and right Dao hand seals say:
Heaven is troubled, Earth is troubled,
I the Master lay down some iron,
The iron wall bores downwards,
Quickly repent in private and the evil flees
this person's five zang organs and six fu organs,
Within the coffin the corpse water flows downwards
and passes into the village of the dead
and covers the base,

High and low the stench is gone
and the true unpleasantness stops,
The Evil Master sees it
and removes himself a thousand miles away,
The Six Relatives and all family dependants bow their heads,
I honour the command of Taishang True
Immortal's command!

(Talisman Fig. 90)

91. STOP COFFIN LEAKING

92. A THOUSAND JIN METHOD

93. SOLVING THOUSAND JIN

94. TRANSFORM CORPSE

108. Stopping Funeral Leakage Method

The Spell

Heaven hurries, Earth hurries,
My master descends to the mortal world
to stop the funeral leakage,
The purple copper plate is placed on the bottom,
The iron plate is bound to the wall (of the coffin),
Stopping the Huang He River's three mouths,
Stopping the ten thousand mile Wu Shan river,
Covering all so there is no stench beneath,
Nor will there be any foetid thick liquid,
The Southern Direction Fire the so called
Bing-Ding Fire wards off the odour,
And mosquitoes and flies are swept away by the light!

(Talisman Fig. 91)

109. A Thousand Jin Method

This talisman is used when there is a funeral announced. One goes to the house and places the Heavy Weight Talisman at the site of or on the coffin. It cannot be lifted.

The Spell

The sun rises in the east, Black Yang Yang,
Illumination and we see the Master's house,
A corpse is in there and I request
that I can come to the funeral,
Left and right sides both rise,
Soft foot, Soft hand.
The coffin is a thousand jin stone,
This stone is ten thousand jin at this funeral,
Nine oxen pull it and cannot move it,
They push and are flustered,
Trying a rope it shall snap in two,
Trying two poles they pull apart,
If struck with stick or axe,
Their menace is sent beneath the stone.
I honour the command of Hunyuan Zushi.

(Talisman Figs. 92-93)

110. Transform Funeral Method

This talisman is used at a funeral and is drawn on an axe head but you cannot let anyone see you do it. (That is the mage puts the talisman paper on an axe head and draws it).

Put the talisman paper on the side of the coffin seam and quietly say

The Spell
Si Da Tian Wang (Four Guardian Kings of Heaven),
The sun sets behind the western hills,
Ten thousand rays of light illuminate this scene,
The family has a corpse in the coffin,
I ask you send that power so the coffin
cannot seal the dead body,
The cadaver becomes a slurry and a thick liquid.
I honour the command of Hunyuan True Immortal!

(Talisman Fig. 94)

The Solution To The Above
This talisman will be used in the East. Gather up twenty-one blades of cogon grass and twist them together. Use three of these at the funeral. Using the Sword Hand Seal read the spell to purify the filth.

The Spell
My spirit is not an extraordinary spirit,
I am Hunyuan Laozu, the True Great True-Person comes,
The Jade Emperor shall not avoid helping me in this matter,
Assist me in this mortal world to slay the evil spirits,
My hand grasping a Seven Star Sword
that vanquishes demons,

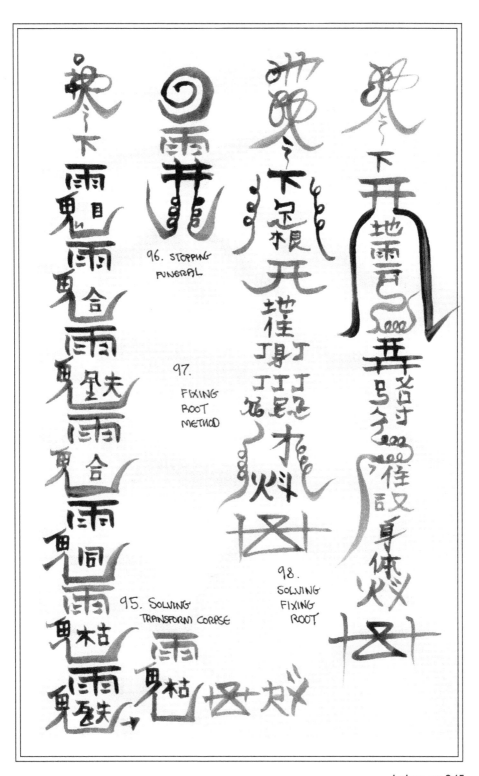

96. STOPPING FUNERAL

97. FIXING ROOT METHOD

95. SOLVING TRANSFORM CORPSE

98. SOLVING FIXING ROOT

Treading on the Wheel of Thunder that rumbles
with a deep resonance,
Having a thousand jin iron and steel chain,
Turning the coffin in four directions,
A green silk comes to seal the stench at once
and rises to the clouds,
The Eight Great Diamond Thunderbolts quickly come,
Gently raising it to the courtyard.

Use the Fend off the Funeral Magic Hand Seal towards an axe and blow once, cry 'Go' !!!

(Talisman Fig. 95)

Another Solution Against Evil Funeral Magic

This is to be used at the funeral. With seven straws and a root of Chinese Gromwell make a grass man and place it with the body with the talisman.

(Talisman Fig. 96)

Book III
Luban Magical Methods
$\left(\text{The Orphan Luban's Classic}\right)$
Part 1

111. Ding Gen Fa
Fixing The Root Method

This talisman will be placed at a crossroads centre point. Use the Copper and Iron Hand seal.

The Spell

Ding! Ding! (Nail! Nail!)
My teacher assists me to nail and fix this person,
Iron and Copper nail fixes them to stop,
Fixing them to stop their feet
and the sinews of their four limbs,
Fixing the two feet and their heels are weakened
so they cannot travel,
The head is swimming and they cannot see,
The three immortal souls
and seven mortal souls do not gerd the body,
Each day we summon justice.
I honour the command of Hunyuan Zhen Xian!

Use the Five Nails Hand Seal (nn)
and the Stop Body Hand Seal. (nn)
(Talisman Fig. 97)

Solution To Fixing Root Method

I respectfully ask the Liu Din Generals,
I ask all of the Dao to act,
Three souls gerd the body
and the seven souls return to the body!
(Talisman Fig. 98)

99. Scissors

100. Release Chains

101. Escape Cangue

102. Send Wooden Board

112. The Scissors Method

This talisman strikes the body and is written on a vertical long cotton cloth. It cannot be seen by others.

Use the Golden Scissors Hand Seal.

Read the spell once through and blow once.

Burn four Scissors Talismans.

(Talisman 99)

The Spell

Precious scissors sharp and cutting,

The scissors can never be broken,

Even when cutting ropes and branches of trees,

Meeting the silk official it cuts

and in two parts that which is cut falls,

The Divine Immortals cannot know it,

The filth that are ghosts cannot see it,

I am weary of you and you are held in a stupor.

I honour Taishang Laojun

Ji Ji Ru Lu Ling

113. Releasing Locks Or Chains

With this method a person who has broken the law and finds themselves in iron chains and the neck and body locked can free themselves.

No one can see the magician enact the spell. Have a wooden table and upon it burn the talisman shown near the town or burn in water near a tree.

The Spell

Heaven Spirit, Earth Spirit,
I am the Great True Person embodied,
The Great King Dao Method comes to turn the lock,
My Spirit can unlock and free this person,
The iron changes to a wooden box lock
and a thousand years old it becomes dust,
Both hands become as diamond vajras
and both escape secretly,
Transforming my body, in secret my body is transformed,
Yes my body is secretly changed,
By this wooden table, the copper lock locks the table,
The iron lock locks the table,
I point to the lock and command it to stop,
The table receives the iron lock.
My body rises free.
I honour Hunyuan Zhen Xian's command!

(Talisman Fig. 100)

Use the Escape Lock Hand Seal

114. Escaping The Cangue

The cangue is an ancient device which consisted of a heavy board that snapped around the neck of the prisoner and was locked.

The text goes on to say that this is a difficult magic to use, it cannot be seen by others.

The exponent uses the Wooden Peg Hand Seal, burns the talisman of cangue escape and then forms a Jade Seal with his left hand and a Transforming Hand Seal with his right. Finally he makes the Carrying a Thousand Jin Axe hand seal.

The Spell

My spirit and my body are not an extraordinary spirit,
I am Hunyuan Lao Zu Shen,
I am the Great Tru Dao Person,
I have violated the law of the land,
Come to turn the lock
and assist me to open the wooden cangue so I am free,
The wooden cangue is opened,
Freeing my body,
Transforming to become a wooden pillar,
I am wearing the cangue,
I free myself and become a wooden pillar
that is burning with fire,
The cangue stops holding the person,
Come and intervene in my hour of need
O Heavenly Palace,
I honour Hunyuan Zushi's command!

(Talisman Fig. 101)

115. Sending The Wooden Board Method

This is a form of occult attack used to entrap a rival or wicked person. This talisman and method is dreaded by the people who defy the law of the land.

To restrain them we use the Zhuban, the bamboo clappers to strike them on the spot.

The Spell

My spirit is not an extraordinary spirit,
It transforms into a heavenly stone,
It transforms into a stone of Earth,
I have a strength of body,
Earth and Heaven come to protect my head,
And to defend my body,
But the Bamboo Clappers strike like a stone,
The stone is above their head
and there come troubles and headaches,
A bundle of sticks strikes once and the clappers cry out!
My Master Rising Nine Clouds
(Shi Teng Zai Jiu Xiao Yun) acts!
I honour Hunyuan Taishang Laojun.
Ji Ji Ru Lu Ling!

(Talisman Fig. 102)

116. Wooden Rods Press The Legs Method

A similar magical attacking method except the evil person's legs are the target.

The Spell

My body is not an extraordinary spirit,
I am as a thousand year old tree root,
It appears that to mortals I have no use,
Luban descends to build a table with four feet,
And it shall be sent to torture the legs with aches
and pains.
My master is hidden in the nine clouds,
I honour Hun Yuan Zushi's command!

(Talisman Fig. 103)

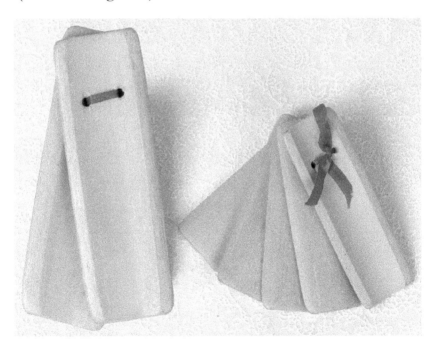

As the wizard chants the spell he will sound the clappers.

117. Escaping Prison Method

This talisman and method is used to aid those in prison. Perform this at night at the fifth watch before the rooster has crowed, at the hour of You and towards the West.

The Spell

My body is not an extraordinary body,
I am the Four Great Heavenly Kings embodied
and having the Six Jia and Six Ding Generals,
Eight thousand troops are on my left
and three thousand troops are on my right,
The Six Ding and Six Jia Generals descend
and those divine Gods come to assist me,
One step and there suddenly appears ten thousand doors,
People are fascinated by the ghost and are confused,
The walls break and the stones tumble above the clouds.
I honour Hun Yuan Lao Zhu's command!
Quickly make in succession the Eight Golden Thunderbolt,
Six Ding and Six Jia and White Crane Flying
Immortal hand seals.
The man can leave the prison.

Use the Jade Emperor hand seal and the Sword Seal.

(Talisman Fig. 104)

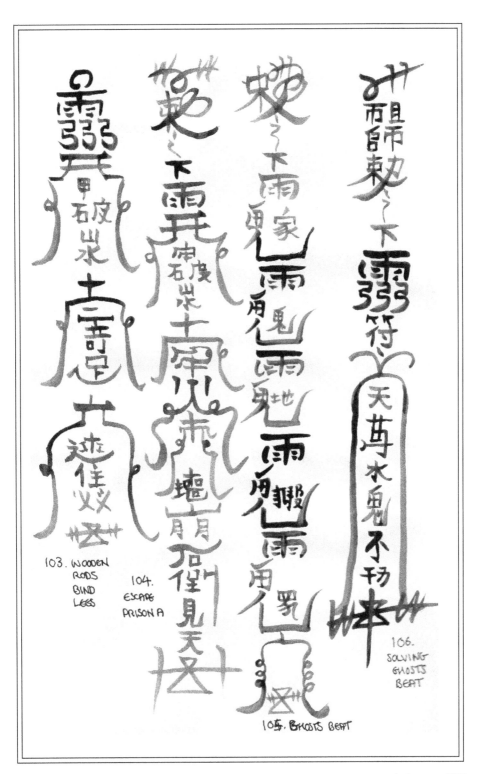

103. WOODEN RODS BIND LEGS

104. ESCAPE PRISON A

105. GHOSTS BEAT

106. SOLVING GHOSTS BEAT

118. Sending Ghosts Into A House

Another infamous spell of the Luban and other folk traditions of which many stories are told. It is a method of sending spirits or ghosts into a home that has offended the magician. Accounts of the practice have it that the home would be assailed with the sounds of phantom screaming, sobbing and knocking, spontaneous poltergeist phenomena and so on. There are a number of varieties of this punishing spell in most Chinese folk traditions.

This talisman is aimed at a family to plague the heart and mind of the enemy's household.

At a suitable time, in league with their door gods (Door Gods or Men Shen were set up to guard the home, a magician would first bribe or bypass them to send magic into a household).

One draws the spell on five white paper dolls and places them in the house or shrine area. (Failing this the sorcerer would find some way to place the five white paper dolls which represent ghosts near the house or in some hidden part of the house). Burn them (transforming the ghost dolls to a yin nature) while using the Five Ghosts Using Five Fires Hand Seal (or more simply according to Master Lang, use the Five Ghosts Hand Seal.)

The Spell

Heaven and Earth Ghost God causes ten thousand spirits to secure the door,

Striking the walls, crying out the name of the family,

Crying out names and toying with the people within,

Watching them,

Clean dishes become filthy,

Pots are burned, lamps are lit, doors are opened,
Though they look they cannot be seen,
Listened for they are not heard.
In compliance with destiny,
The wind and fire do not cease.
I honour Hun Yuan Zushi's command!

(Talisman Fig.105)

Solution

This talisman is drawn upon five human shapes on white paper, place them in the midst of a basin and then use a peach or willow broom to sweep the house.

The Spell

Ghosts and Gods, Heaven and Earth forms you,
I ask that this spirit leaves this place,
Bringing them into this basin and transforming them
into these ghost-spirit dolls,
Stricken with fear let the demons flee,
Inauspiciousness disperses, the Dao is in this place,
I command it so by Hunyuan Zushi!

The text then suggests reciting the Bao Guang Zhou, a simile for the Golden Light Spell known to all Daoists.

(Talisman Fig. 106)

119. The Thunder Altar Punishes The Ghost Method

This method is used to treat a sickness when an illness is grave and recovery seems unlikely. The essence of the spell is that a demon or ghost is the cause of the illness and it is disintegrated by thunder and light. Strong Yang dissipating Yin.

Have a doll resembling the likeness of the person or use five paper dolls to represent the sick person. They cannot be seen by anyone else.

Have the talisman written on the five paper dolls and have the patient eat one that has been burned to ashes and put in water.

The five paper figures and another talisman are burned at the front gate of the house. Use the ashes to make a circle.

Towards the East say the Bao Guang Zhou (Precious Light Spell) and place an earthen jar in the centre of the circle. Towards the east place a single candle.

The sick person remains in the bedroom but in the dark, his or her lights are not on.

The Master makes the Zhao Tian Jue or Illuminating Heaven Hand Seal with his left hand and the Hua Wu Lei or Light of the Five Thunders with his right hand.

The Spell

Ancestral Master Celestial God,
The Divine Head manifests spiritual power,
The Liu Ding and Liu Jia protects the body,
Celestial Troops and Terrestrial Generals do not tarry,
Stopping the Five Ways Ghosts
and Gods of Heaven and Earth from taking shape,

These Gods I know,
A thousand calls and there are a thousand responses,
Ten thousand calls and there are ten thousand spirits,
Men and women have form and are strong,
The Lord cannot be disobeyed and sends the thunderbolt,
Ghosts and demons are terror stricken,
Demonic forms disintegrate,
Golden Light quickly appears and the misty Qi
seethes and rises,
I honour the command of Hunyuan Zushi!

(Read the Treasure Light Spell)
This spell will cause the spirit to rise and vibrate and Gods and Ghosts will be seen which can be terrifying to those who are present.

(Talisman Fig. 107)

120. Yin Shen Fa
Invisibility Method

Hiding the body Hand Seal at the time of battle or other critical time, then people cannot see you but you can see people.

The Spell
The Samadhi Secret transforms my body,
Sakyamuni Buddha the honoured one comes,
Amitabha Buddha comes appearing in a golden body,
Following, concealing and causing my body
to become concealed,
Concealing from ten thousand people,
I see the forms of others but ten thousand people
cannot see me,
Rain and Wind come, Follow me Rain and Wind
and enact the method,
On the first manifestation the Divine Immortals
cannot see me,
On the second manifestation ghosts do not see me.
I honour Hunyuan Zushi's command.
Ji Ji Ru Lu Ling.

(Talisman Fig. 108)

121. Ji Shen Fa
Sending Life Method

A common method of Chinese magic is to transfer one's identity to an object that is difficult for an enemy, say a rival magician or a demon or spirit, to an object such as a stone or tree or even a blade of grass. Such is the following spell.

This talisman when two people are engaged in battle, draw it and use the Hide Body Hand Seal. Note that the talisman would be drawn in the palm of the left hand.

The Spell

Gazing into the distant forest,
Seeing a tree in the midst,
With its green base and ancient roots,
For most this tree has no use,
My Master comes
and sends my root-life principle to the tree,
My Master sends it to the tree,
A thousand swords
and ten thousand axes are received by its person.
I honour Hun Yuan Zushi!
Ji Ji Ru Lu Ling!

(Talisman Fig. 109)

122. Jiu Niu Jue
Nine Oxen Formula

There are a whole family of Nine Oxen Spells used for a whole number of purposes, but nearly all are summoning strength or weight and the power of gravity. For example to increase one's own physical strength or to makan object immovable.

The Spell

Yin Yang Nine Oxen come,
Calamity is sent to harm the people and it cannot be quelled,
Trampling they dry up the streams,
They eat the people's grain and rice,
Drinking water no longer flows,
A thousand jin of force breaks the iron clasp,
Seeking too disturb both the inner and outer coffins,
Corpse water flows,
Pulling open wood and stone built things,
The axe will not cut,
Ropes cannot pull the roots of the tree,
Buildings collapse and stones tumble,
I honour Taishang Iron Ox Master!
Ji Ji Ru Lu Ling!
(Talisman Fig.110)

Solution

Jin Tong (Golden Boy),
Tong Tong resides in the Celestial Palace,
Communing with Heaven and knowing the ten thousand methods since childhood,

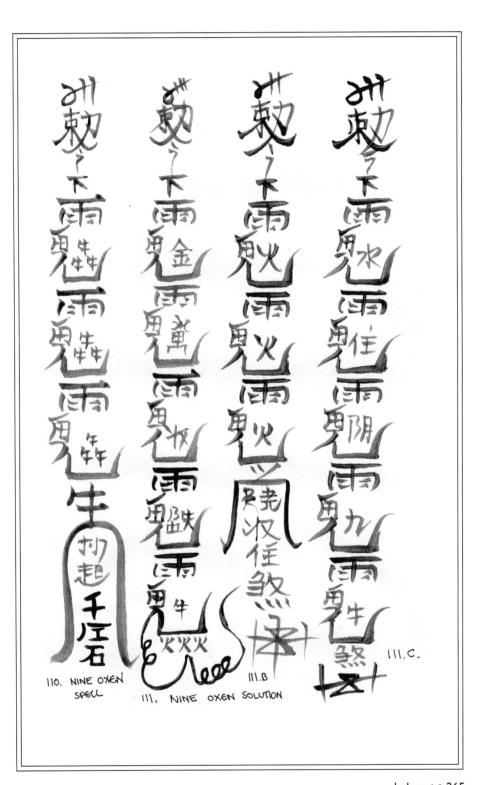

110. NINE OXEN SPELL

111. NINE OXEN SOLUTION

111.B

111.C.

My Master quickly descends from the Heavenly Palace,
Hands grasping the thousand jin axe and iron chain,
Piercing the nostrils of the oxen
and the thousand jin cannot move,
Ten thousand axes cannot act,
I harness the Nine Oxen,
The Nine Oxen are quickly driven back up
to the Heavenly Palace,
(Use the Thousand Jin Whip Hand Seal)

(Talisman Fig. 111)

123. Xian Tong Fa
The Immortal Youth Method

Another classic spell of Chinese magic and found in most folk traditions. This practice originated with willow figures used to communicate with the dead, a way of communing with the ancestors. This method seems to be what is known as the 'Ear Report Spirit', a kind of magical familiar that informs the magician of important information rather like a ghostly spy. Ear Report Spirits are again another common and well respected spell within the Chinese magic community.

It is best this operation is begun on the fifth lunar month or the ninth lunar month and towards the direction of the west.

(In Chinese esoteric thought, West is the direction of the dead and of the ancestors. Author's note)

Once begun, do not look back and others cannot see or it is ineffective. Search for a willow tree and carve the figure of a xian tong (Immortal Youth) two cun high (1 cun=3.33 cm).

Write, with cinnabar ink the talisman shown seven times.

Obtain adzuki beans, a stone, some insects, and mix with calamus, and forsythia suspensia (commonly called Golden Bell).

Place these materials in the abdomen of the wooden figure together with the ashes of the talisman. Place the Xiantong on your altar, offering fresh flowers and incense sticks.

The Spell

Xian Tong Tong stands in the midst of the clouds,
My Master summons you to quickly descend
from the Celestial Palace,
Having communion with Heaven and with the divinity of

Earth and able to inform us of calamities,
The Wen (Scholarly) and Wu (Martial) Officials petition
but do not demand wealth,
The spirit named Tong Wang Nu shall speak clearly,
Performing a great service to reveal the Upper Purity Script.
I honour Hun Yuan Lao Zu.
Ji Ji Ru Lu Ling.

(Talisman Fig. 112)

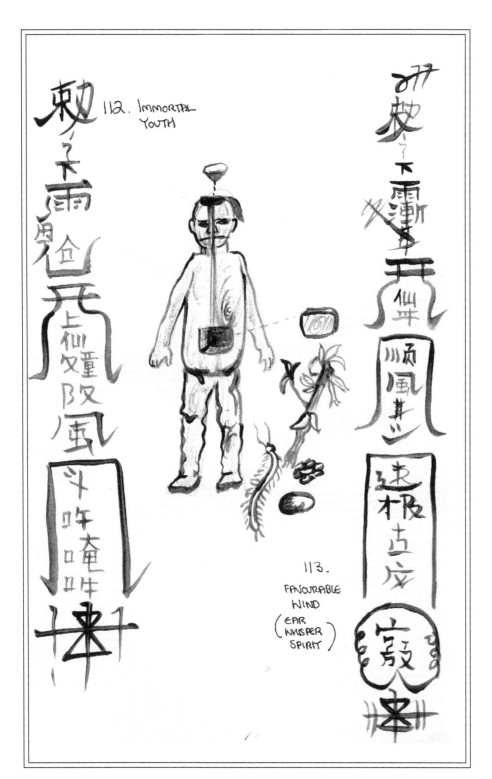

112. Immortal Youth

113. Favourable Wind (Ear Whisper Spirit)

124. Shunfeng Fu Fa
Favourable Wind Method

This is another 'Ear Report Spirit' method. Favourable Wind refers to whispered secrets. In this example however there is no wooden image used and the communion with the Ear Report spirit is done directly without a physical medium.

Have three liang of talc, three cicada shells, three of calamus root, three of forsythia suspensa and some jujube kernels. Powder them.

The talisman is concocted in water and drunk, one per day for a hundred days, once in the morning and once in the evening.

The Spell

I request Tian Shen Baoshen Shijie Bao (Heavenly Divine
Ear Reporting God Wandering Clouds
and Reporting) to truly come,
My master invites the Immortal Wind to come and whisper
in my ear the knowledge of disaster,
happiness or auspiciousness,
Report and respond.
Follow and protect my body.
I request it by Hun Yuan Zushi!
Ji Ji Ru Lu Ling!

(Talisman Fig. 113)

125. Bi Xing Wu Shen Fu
Closing Body Talisman

This spiritual talisman will help in times of great danger and allows one to hide quickly.

In times of danger when at the roadside stand within the grass and trees, holding the talisman and a handful of grass and tree leaves, inhale qi from the east and blow on the talisman and herbage. Repeat three times and say:

The Spell

Heaven opens, Earth opens,
Open the Grass and Trees Immortal comes,
My Master stands in the grass and trees,
The Sun, Moon and Stars protect my body,
The people have no need to fear the cold of the frost
or snow,
In Spring and Summer no need to fear the fire
nor hot weather,
The grass and trees do not know such things,
The Sun is bright in the blue sky.

(Talisman Fig. 114)

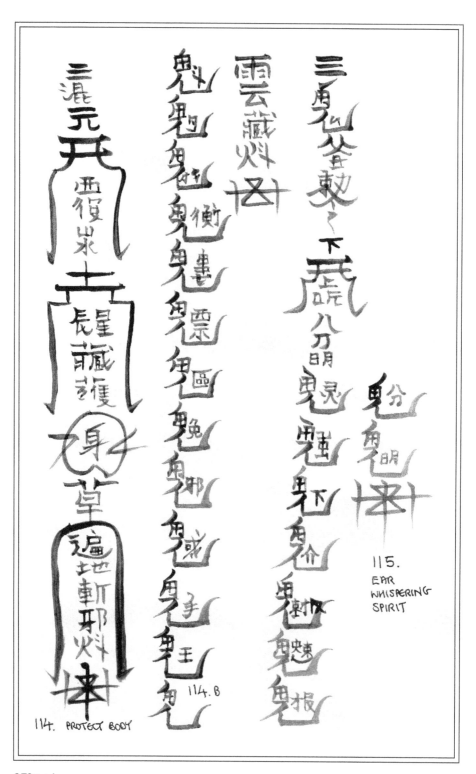

114. PROTECT BODY

114.B

115.
EAR
WHISPERING
SPIRIT

126. Another Method
For The Willow Boy

This spell when used with sincerity is marvellous. On the 9th month on the 9th day at the hour of Chen facing west.

Search for a willow tree and carve a human figure such as an immortal youth, but also carve the five internal organs.

Give it a drop of your own blood in a hole bored through the top of its head. Draw seven of the talismans in cinnabar.

Using the figure with five precious organs and cinnabar inked talismans and establishing it as a seat of a spirit, it becomes a means to communicate with Heaven.

It will communicate to those on Earth those things as matters of impending calamities, joys, life, death and good or ill fortune.

You can know if matters to be dealt with will be auspicious or inauspicious by a certain voice that will speak to you.

Never ask and never reply is the taboo.

If you listen you can avoid the inauspicious and hasten fortune.

Do not reveal it.

The Spell

Celestial Youths and Maidens
who reside in the Heavenly Palace,
Bright and intelligent musician cleverly uses
the celestial spirit and mind to communicate,
The tongue speaks,
The clever liver opens,
Eyes see to the very limits,
Yan Fu Immortal opens it,

The ears hear nine times and the lungs open,
The nose smells fragrances in the ten directions,
The mouth eats fine vegetables and meats,
Its life and destiny open the five internal organs,
The Eight apertures meet the Master
and he descends promptly from the Heavenly Palace,
Protect my body!
O intelligent spirit, speak!
Do not leave,
We offer fragrant flowers to your left and right,
Report good and evil, break ill fortune in all the ten directions,
O manifest and respond spirit,
Secretly defend my home from unclean ghosts who
can now not come within a thousand miles of this place,
I offer incense to you at this altar,
Come I declare,
By He Yun Feng (Cloud Wind He),
I honour Hunyuan Zushi!
Ji Ji Ru Lu Ling!

(Talisman Fig. 115)

127. A Spell Against Thieves

In this talisman method we deal with a thief who dares to enter a house. Using ash sifted, reading the Precious Light Spell, paint the image of the thief as shown.

Read the Thunder Ancestor Spell (Lei Zu Zhou) before the talisman.

Using a toothed iron rake, heat it until it is red hot. Seven talismans have been prepared, a scoop of rice is placed over the heart of the figure drawn in ash. On top of the rice place a small oil lamp.

This lamp should burn until it goes out even after the spell has finished.

Hold the hot rake over the heart, and then the belly. Recite the spell three times. In three days they may die. If they do not die then within six months. They will not die if they return what has been stolen.

The Spell

I sincerely request Thunder Ancestor Great Worthy
(Lei Zu Da Tianzun),
Whose hand grasps a copper mallet weighing
a thousand jin,
Leading Five Thunders Samadhi Fire and the stars
of the Big Dipper to descend to this mortal world,
Lightning illuminates three thousand miles,
At the family home of xxxx the thief has come,
A copper nail is held and an iron hammer,
We request you to slay this violator,
A copper nail enters the heart of the thief,
An iron nail enters his heart,
Three nails are fixed in his belly,

116A.

116B

PUNISH THIEF

Piercing his intestines and breaking his stomach,
Giving pain in his liver and heart,
The three hun souls and seven po souls pass away
and disintegrate,
Thirty seven days seeing and hearing me,
I honour the Ninth Heaven Responding Immortal Meng
Ji Pu Transforming Worthy!
(Jiu Tian Ying Xian Meng Ji Pu Hua Tianzun).
Ji Ji Ru Lu Ling.

(Talisman Fig. 116)

128. Bao Chan Tuoke Fa
The Precious Cicada
Slips Off Its Shell Method

This is the first of a class of spells known as *Beauty Takes Off her Clothes*. The aim is obvious, is to cause a woman or indeed a man to undress. It is said to cause a kind of temporary confusion or even insanity to cause the recipient of this witchcraft to suddenly start taking off their clothes.

Similar spells are to be found in the western grimoires, where in one, *The Grimorium Verum*, it is said to inspire pity rather than desire.

While the aim is erotic, there also seems to be a secondary intention of causing great embarrassment, perhaps to one who has offended our Chinese warlock.

This talisman cannot be seen by others. It is placed at the roadside and burned as you say the spell:

Man/Woman who is on the road take off your underwear,
Take off your clothes,
The upper and lower clothes are taken off so you are naked.
I honour Hunyuan Zhen Xian's command!

(Use the Golden Cicada Slips its shell hand seal)

(Talisman Fig. 117)

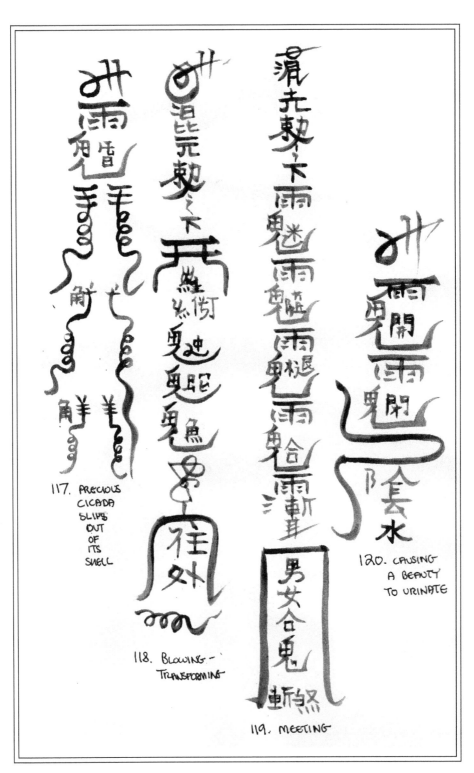

117. PRECIOUS CICADA SLIPS OUT OF ITS SHELL

118. BLOWING — TRANSFORMING

119. MEETING

120. CAUSING A BEAUTY TO URINATE

129. Chui Bian Fa
Blow And Transform Method

This talisman is used when you encounter people on a journey who have food and drink, fruits, pastries and so on. You are hungry and ask for some food but they refuse you.

Grasp some grass or tree leaves, soil, stones and blow three times upon them and say the spell:

Heaven hurries, Earth hurries,
My family calls the Transport Food Official (Yun Shi Lang),
Receiving my first breath it transforms into a mosquito,
A toad jumps to the side,
It becomes a cloud-bird flying in the midst,
It changes to a serpent in the grass and hides there within,
My Master has a hunger within,
Crying in hunger for ten thousand years of food.
I honour Hunyuan Zhen Xian's command!

(Talisman Fig. 118)

130. Fuhui Fa
Going to Meet Method

Mi hun is a Chinese term for specific kinds of magic to confuse or disorient the soul of the target in question.

This is a seduction spell.
This talisman is used when you see a young lady
that you desire. You think of her but cannot meet her.
Bring seven copies of the talisman with you.
If you wish to meet her, burn them in a cup and drink.
She will quickly come and both are gratified.

The Spell
Heaven and Earth, Qian and Kun,
Men and women meet to become one,
You desire me, I desire you,
Match with me when the bell rings,
A beautiful encounter is fulfilled,
You come to be with one,
Speak and respond to my feelings
I honour Jiu Tian Xuan Nu.
Ji Ji Ru Lu Ling!

(Use Mi hun Hand Seal and Yin and Yang Hand Seal)

(Talisman Fig. 119)

131. Meinu Jie Shen Yiniao Fa
The Beautiful Woman
Wants To Relieve Urine

This is an odd spell even by the Luban's terms. The idea is to make a woman suddenly want to go to the bathroom to relieve herself. The idea seems to be to reinforce spells of a love drawing type to encourage her (or him) to meet in a secret tryst.

This talisman is used in the case of a married woman who cannot for some reason follow the secret enchantment (eg, a love drawing spell). The woman is made to go to the toilet to relieve herself.

You pick up a pinch of soil and hold in the centre of your palm and blow on it twice, then draw the talisman with the soil and, using the Open and Close Hand Seal say the spell:

The union is accomplished,
A pill is wrapped and placed in the box,
Open the box and they want to urinate,
Closing the box and they stop,
For one day they cannot stop,
The woman, the girl,
Heaven and Earth,
Yin and Yang,
Father generates Mother and it is accomplished.
The six soft organs and five hard organs open,
The heart, the large intestines, the small intestines, the spleen,
the stomach, the gallbladder all cause the urinary bladder

to open and water to come.
Urinate, fiercely and quickly piss!
I honour Jiu Tian Xuan Nu,
Ji Ji Ru Lu Ling! Command it!

(Talisman Fig. 120)

132. Nan She Xian Xing Fa
Southern Serpent Form Manifests Method

The magician finds a sloughed snakeskin that is intact and takes it to his place of working.

Using seven talismans, burn them to ashes and put them in the snakeskin.

If you meet someone who is friendly and you wish to liven things up, take out the snakeskin and draw the taboo word, read the spell and you will seem to be a ghostly serpent when the spirit enters the snakeskin.

The Spell

Come change into the Snake-Man Admirable Spirit
and enter this girdle,
Be three yards long,
My master holds in his hand the Grass Dragon and snakes,
Seizing them in his hand and concealing them,
In the first transformation its body emerges
two yards and five,
A head appears and a yellow dragon tail,
Everyone sees it and their courage is shaken,
The Southern Serpent emits rays of light from its mouth.
I honour Hun Yuan Laozu's command!

(Talisman Fig. 121)

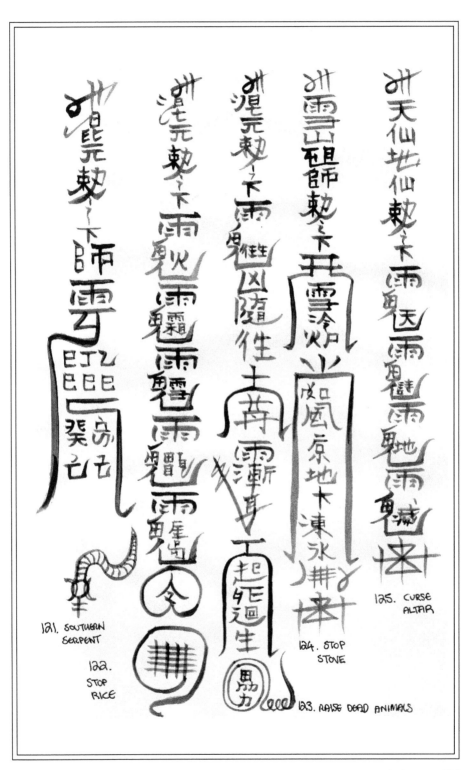

121. SOUTHERN
SERPENT

122.
STOP
RICE

123. RAISE DEAD ANIMALS

124. STOP
STOVE

125. CURSE
ALTAR

133. Zhu Fan Ruo Chi Fa
Cooking Rice Method

This is a popular spell in all editions of the Luban. It is an act of magical sabotage to cause a person's rice not to cook. See the story in the beginning of this volume for an example of how this passed into popular folk tales.

The Spell

The Sun rises in the East,
There is a Yin Light,
I see the family preparing a meal,
You today will cook rice,
I today lay down a stone of frost,
On meat, vegetables and on rice,
There comes snow and in the pot goes frost and snow,
Fires enter to cook but a thousand layers of iron,
The rice that has been cooked I dare not taste,
The frost and snow have kept the rice cold,
But my rice is fragrant and warm.
I honour Hun Lao Zu's command!
(Hand seal of Snow Mountain takes away fire)

(Talisman Fig. 122)

134. Zhu Sheng Pinglei
Pigs And Cattle Spell

This spell causes dead animals to be reanimated.

This talisman searches for the six domestic animals, sheep, oxen, horses, pigs, chickens and ducks. If their skin is peeled or bellies broken, use the talisman and the dead animal moves.

The Spell
All domestic animals are generated by Heaven and Earth,
Three Souls guard the body
and open fate to attain tranquillity,
Peel and remove the fur
and understand the Decree of Heaven,
With three sounds the three souls are everlasting,
Nor is the mortal soul lost or deviant.
I honour Hun Yuan Lao Zu's command!

(Use the Nine Oxen Hand seal

(Talisman Fig. 123)

135. Lu Huo Gong Jiang Fa
The Fire Stove
of the Craftsman Method

The aim of this method was to punish a Smith so that his fire doesn't reach the required temperature and thus make his work impossible.

This talisman is used against a place where copper, iron, silver or gold are hammered.

The spell should be read quietly:

The blacksmith's furnace is warded off
by the Kan Water Palace above,
Your charcoal fire is pressed by ten jin,
Your fire-stove is one yard high,
Snow and frost is ten thousand zhang deep,
The bellows are frost,
The flames are high and rise to dissipate,
Iron is like the cold wind.
I honour Hunyuan Laozu's command.

The wizard uses Snow Mountain, Cold Frost and Protect Body hand seals.

(Talisman Fig. 124)

136. Wang En Bei Yi Fa
A punishing spell causing difficulties and even insanity to the target

This talisman is for those who are unkind and disrespectful of their elders, and whose mothers have difficulties.

Go to their ancestral altar and put beneath this talisman of fierce and insanity influence.

Burn incense and say:

The Spell

A lesser pupil is learning to be a Master,
Disobedient to their parents
and even to their own flesh and blood,
Forgetting the Teachers and the Elders,
Deceiving the Gods and spirits,
Making rash decisions of disaster or joy,
Asking the Divine Immortals to subdue,
The Heavenly Thunderbolt comes to hide the dishonour.
I honour the command of Hunyuan Laozu!

(Talisman Fig. 125)

137. Zao Yao Shao Wa Fa
Tile/Brick Maker's Kiln Method

Similar to the Fire Stove of the Craftsman method except it is directed at the work of tile, brick and pottery makers. You wish to take away the fire of a tile maker. Go to the kiln with the talisman and quietly read:

The Spell

Rising Plum Kiln Master,

Your kiln is on Kan and above is Gen,

Today we are wedding off the heat,

The kiln is ice cold,

The fire is placed on Gen and the clay pot burns,

The earthen jar is yellowed,

Yellow breaks and festers,

Cannot be used by the good people.

I honour Hunyuan Zhen Xian's command!

The master uses the Snow Mountain Stops Kiln Hand Seal.

(Talisman Fig. 126)

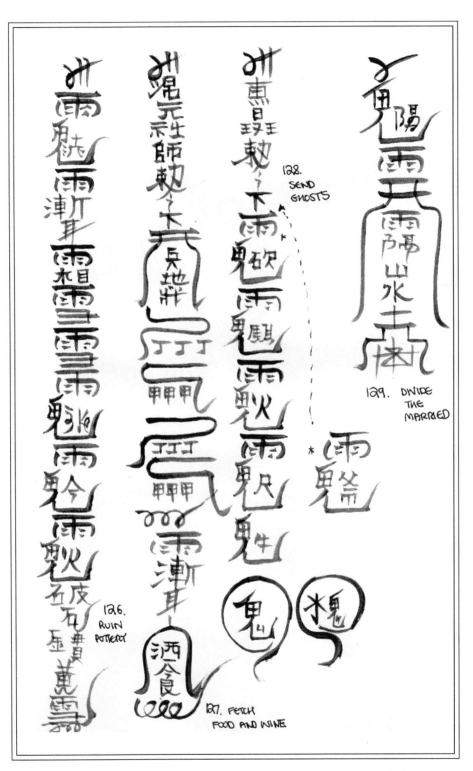

128. SEND GHOSTS

129. DIVIDE THE MARRIED

126. RUIN POTTERY

127. FETCH FOOD AND WINE

138. Qu Jiu Shi Fa
Fetching Wine And Food Method

With this spell at the market, a store or inn, three to five people see food and wine but they lack it.

Draw the talisman and say:

The Spell
I sincerely request the Liu Jia and Liu Ding Divine
Heavenly Troops and Earth Generals to protect my body,
(Name of store, inn etc) fetch wine from within,
fetch snacks from the (store name),
fetch flavoursome cakes, fetch a beautiful bottle filled
with wine, for the bowl is not filled.
I honour Hunyuan Zhen Xian's command.

Use the hand seal of Liu Jia and Liu Ding.

(Talisman Fig.127)

139. Mujiang Qi Zao Fa
Carpenter Builds the House Method

A carpenter has built a house for a man who is not worthy and there has been quarrelling.

The craftsman may use this method having ink, ruler and timber. Cut a hole in the wood and insert this talisman and say the spell. The owner's house will be full of ghosts and spirits day and night, there will be no tranquillity and no balance of Yin and Yang.

The Spell

I the craftsman (your name) arose to build this house,
Venus is on the ecliptic and brings intranquillity,
Master Luban places it on the beams
and the work is complete and the price is calamity,
The doors and walls resound as if struck,
There are loud whisperings,
The owner feels misfortune.
I honour the command of Luban Xian Shi !

(Talisman Fig.128)

140. Hunyin Jia Qu Fa
Breaking Marriage Method

A terrible and unhealthy marriage is broken by magic. Their names are written on the paper and buried at the crossroads.

The Spell
Manifesting the (name of family)
Yin and Yang Harmony of Man
and Wife Immortal comes,
Heaven and Earth takes away
the woman's adornments and dowry,
No food is provided,
Their beds are separated,
They do not sleep in the same bed.
I honour the command of Taishang Laojun.
Ji Ji Ru Lu Ling

(Yin and Yang Separation hand seal)

(Talisman Fig. 129)

141. Ji Ya Zi Zhi Fa
Chickens And Ducks Come Method

This method should not be done in the road but near a house that possesses chickens and ducks.

Draw it in a place where you want the chickens and ducks to come to you and say:

The Spell

(Family name of owners of the fowl).....

your chickens bellies are hungry and without rice to eat,

The Immortals gave me a thousand years worth of rice

and all come to me and beg for food to eat,

Enchanting and casting a spell over the chickens,

Enchanting so even the Immortals do not see,

The Gods do not know,

Seek me who am .....(name)

and are surnamed (........),

I honour Tian Shang Shen,

Chickens and ducks are moved

from the rebuked neighbours to my house.

I honour Hun Yuan Lao Zu!

Ji Ji Ru Lu Ling!

(Use Binding Hoop Hand Seal)

(Talisman Fig. 130)

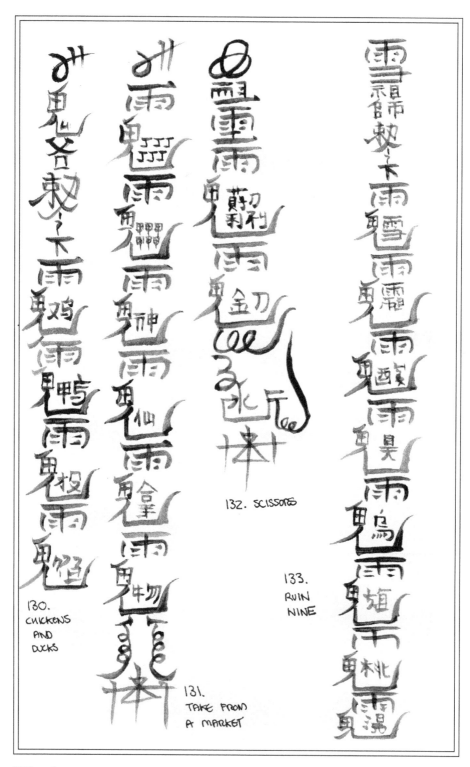

132. SCISSORS

133. RUIN NINE

130. CHICKENS AND DUCKS

131. TAKE FROM A MARKET

142. Yu Chang Na Wu Fa
Seizing Things From A Market

You are in the city market and see rare and curious things of all kinds.

The Spell

Immortal Lin is in the market,
at the market with precious items,
Chun Qiang and General Liu Yi holds out his hand to
touch the precious things in care of the trader,
It weighs not a thousand jin,
I reverently seize and take the spirit
and all creatures follow me,
The Liu Jia attends me and protects my body,
The Liu Jia Immortal protects life
and they are not aware of my approach.
I honour Hunyuan Zhen Xian!
Ji Ji Ru Lu Ling!

Liu Jia Hand Seal on the right and Heaven
and Earth Seal on the left.

(Talisman Fig. 131)

143. Jian Dao Fa
The Scissors method again

I will repeat that this is a magical combat method and is still in common use today. With this method one strikes the opponent quickly. Holding scissors in your hand blows once to release it.

When holding the scissors in your hand, say the spell and draw the talisman:

The Spell
Spirit Scissors are sharp,
In one word the scissors cut the rope
and cut the tree branch,
A hundred times I use it,
I break the matter in two and dispel it,
Immortals cannot see it,
Ghosts cannot perceive it,
Today I grasp it in my hand,
You will enter a mental stupor!
I honour Tai Shang Zhen Xian!
Ji Ji Ru Lu Ling!

(Talisman Fig. 132)

144. Zao Jiu Fu
This spell appears to ruin wine

Read the spell under your breath.

The Spell

The Sun rises in the East,
The Mysterious black Yang is within,
Holding yellow grass, carrying it swiftly,
The rice in the valley is ripe,
My Master quickly sends down frost,
Your wine becomes mealy thrice over,
I send down the Dark Plum three times at the Yin hour,
Yeast descends at the Mao hour,
At the Wu hour it is fragrant,
One vat is plum and another vat is peach broth,
Even if fed to swine they will not drink it,
Dogs will not taste it.
I honour Taishang Laojun Zu!
Ji Ji Ru Lu Ling!

Use Frost and Snow Hand Seal
and Stop Fire Hand Seal.

(Talisman Fig. 133)

145. Ao Tang Fa
Cooking Candy/Wine Method

(Similar to the above) This talisman transforms what is within a jar or a bowl, read it under your breath.

The Spell

The Sun rises in the East and is a point of red,
Cooking wine (or sugar) the mother works to no avail,
Polished rice is in the pot,
There is cold rice,
The steamer is cold and comes to an empty heart,
You descend into malt and it is nothing,
I bewitch the yeast,
From 3am to 5am, From 5am to 7am it smells foul,
It is as ice, as pus boiling in a pot.
The water boils like a vast expanse of water,
If fed to swine they will not eat it,
People cannot bear it,
Dogs cannot eat it.
I honour Hun Yuan Mu Jing Xian Shi!

(Talisman Fig. 137)

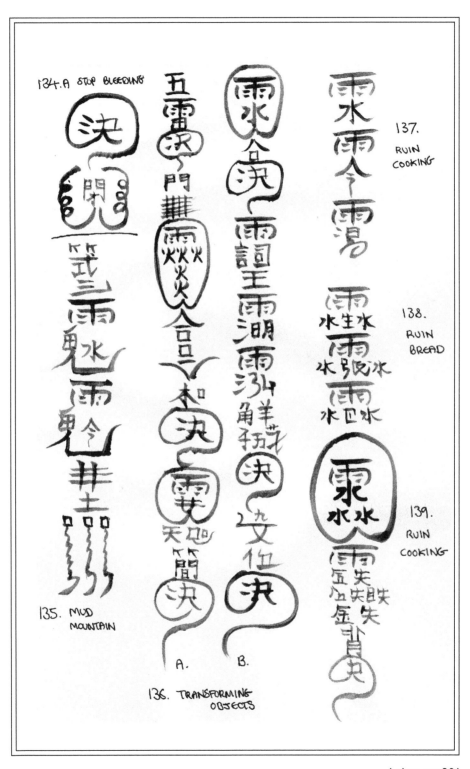

134. A STOP BLEEDING

135. MUD MOUNTAIN

136. TRANSFORMING OBJECTS

A.   B.

137. RUIN COOKING

138. RUIN BREAD

139. RUIN COOKING

146. Untitled
Cooking Bread Method

In your fingers hold the talisman and secretly place it in the house you want to enchant, then say:

The Spell

The Sun rises in the East,
There is Black Yang within,
Seeing the person cooking rice/flour,
Rice/flour is in the pot,
Cooked on the stove of firewood,
Fire burning and cold water clash,
Heat and steam are in the midst,
The rice/flour becomes as ice,
The firewood is as cold as iron,
I am the Skilled One who arrives,
And you give rise to foods that are inedible.
The Spirit Immortal Wood-Metal comes,
I honour Hun Yuan Mu Jing Xianshi
Ji Ji Ru Lu Ling!

(Talisman Fig. 138)

147. Chu Zong Zao Fa
Kitchen Chef Cooking Method

If you encounter a cook or chef who is an unworthy person you can deal with them with this.

The talisman is released near their food and burned while you utter:

The Spell

Going to the house and seeing the cook,
The red bowl of vegetables becomes snow and frost,
Frost and snow are sent forth,
Frost enters the bowl,
The red fire burns and becomes principally ashes,
Snow and frost on the iron clashes and becomes steam,
The food is hard and raw,
The meat is raw,
My meat is cooked.
Your food is sour and mine is fragrant,
Cold and sour cannot be eaten,
Quickly, quickly go by my request O Mu Jin!
I honour Hun Yuan Mu Jin Master.
Ji Ji Ru Lu Ling!

(Talisman Figs. 139 and 140)

148. Cun Bian Qiwu
The Method Of Transforming Things

An unusual method whose immediate purpose is not apparent until you reach the end of the spell. It is the magical disguising and empowerment of one's abode in cases of magical rivalry.

The Spell
Gazing up to the blue heavens,
The Ancestral Master causes the spirit to be present,
Opening the heart and transforming things,
Changing the house to a Golden Luan Bird Palace,
People change to Liujia Gods,
Oxen and horses become qilins and lions,
Chickens and ducks become Immortal beings,
Dogs and cats become large ravenous yellow tigers,
Men and women become Golden Lads and Jade Girls,
Others become Heavenly Troops and I am a General,
A heavenly pot becomes a steamer emitting dark clouds,
The kitchen stove becomes
the Heaven and Earth Net that covers all,
Bamboo turns into the Heavenly River (Milky Way),
Cotton becomes clouds and water becomes honey-dew,
Wine becomes the waters of the Yangtze River,
Wine cups become the Eastern Great Sea Royal Court,
A stream of three thousand eight hundred miles flows,
Fire becomes the Five Thunder Thunderbolt Fire,
Grains become the store of the Heavenly Stars,
Wine barrels become the Five Lakes and Four Seas,
The Mud-Palm protects all,

Strong Tongzi (Celestial boys)
become great armoured Gods,
A room becomes a golden dragon,
The bed straws become dragon skin,
The rug becomes a dragon mat,
Fire tongs become a great Jia God,
Firewood becomes the Liu Jia
and Liu Jia Divine Generals,
If there is an evil master he becomes
as soft as a married woman,
Like a pregnant woman,
The Five Thunders strike the midst of the well.
I sincerely ask the Six Stars of the Southern Dipper
and the Seven Stars of the Northern Dipper.
I honour Hun Yuan Laozu!
Ji Ji Ru Lu Ling

(Talisman Fig. 136)

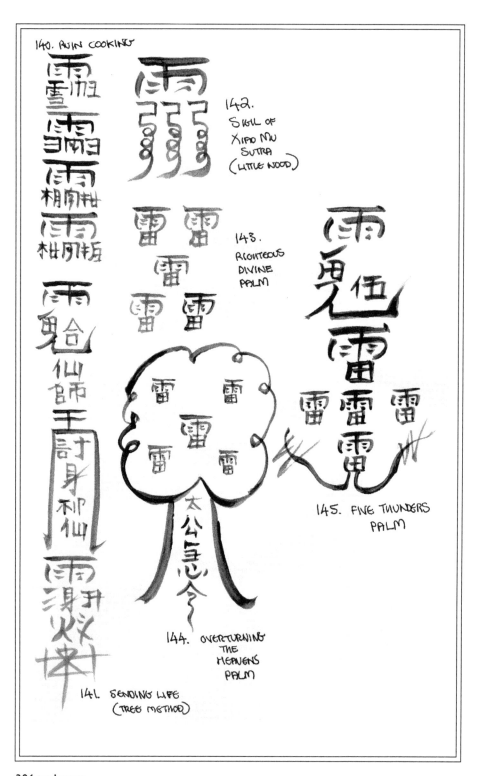

140. RUIN COOKING

142. SKILL OF XIAO MU SUTRA (LITTLE WOOD)

143. RIGHTEOUS DIVINE PALM

145. FIVE THUNDERS PALM

144. OVERTURNING THE HEAVENS PALM

141. SENDING LIFE (TREE METHOD)

The Orphan's Luban Classic
Part 2

149. Mu Jin Zhen Jing
The Wood And Metal True Sutra

O cultivate thyself to immortalhood and see the Great Sage Mu Jing.

It has the power to illuminate the heart so it shines brightly and you shall possess the Dao Virtue (Dao De). Read the Five Classics and approach the Gate of Dao and cultivate what you have learned.

The Method Skill or Dharma Skill complies with the Gods and Immortals and you will become a Master (Fashu).

Accomplish it and gather merit from good deeds.

Avoid deceiving the heart, avoid possessing an impure body and the confusion of the Five Impurities.

This text is endless and untiring.

On the 1st and 15th days abstain from meat and wine, show filial piety to your parents, do not neglect or disrespect the Teacher, endure cultivation and Heaven will support your life.

The Six Ding and Six Jia will be on your left and right. All the Gods will support you and the Ten Thousand Sages will protect you.

The family household becomes prosperous, the house bright, for using the skills of the spirit brings prosperity to the heart.

If you do not use the methods and talismans of this Sutra, the Ten Thousand Sages examine your life and you are not prosperous. Caution!

The name of this book is the Little Wood Sutra.

It was handed down by Hun Yuan to the mortal world

with the desire to enlighten the spirit, protect and deal with life's calamities and sufferings.

The Nine Nations will know how to defeat suffering!

The Immortal Hunyuan Zhenjun knows Heaven and Earth and was born on the first lunar month on the nineteenth day at the hour of Yin.

(Talisman Fig. 142)

150. Zheng Shen Zhang
Righteous Divine Palm

I respectfully honour the purity of the Celestial Five Hundred Fierce Thunders, the disciple asks that you drive away evil spirits and strike the Heavens to open the flowers, to strike the Earth to split open great trees, strike and tear up by the roots, the Disciple shall strike evil and evil becomes ash.

I honour Taishang Laojun.

Ji Ji Ru Lu Ling!

The Spell

Xuan Yuan commands the decree to cause
the Thunder Troops to descend,
Come and support me, come to me!
HONG HONG!
Swiftly soar upwards,
The demons of the five elements and you monstrous spirits,
The people shall have longevity,
If ghosts hear this they shall perish.
I have the Jade Command and sweep away evil!
Ji Ji Ru Lu Ling!

(Talisman Fig. 143)

151. Fan Tian Zhang
Overturning the Heavens Palm

Wu Wen Dasheng (Five Demons Great Sage),
Wu Wen Dasheng seizes you and presses you,
From behind the Yin Mountain,
She Cheng Cheng Da Sheng,
The great are driven back as are the lesser,
If you do not retreat the disciple rises to appear
as five hundred fierce thunders,
That strike and the thunderbolt smashes you
into fragments!
I honour Taishang Laojun Assisting Heavenly Palace,
Ji Ji Ru Lu Ling!

All the Great Celestial Leigong Thunderbolts descend,
Lei Kong Tong Ling (Thunder Sky Commander)
is followed by a retinue of 8000 troops,
Heavenly Thunder, Earth cannot tolerate it,
If you disobey the Thunderbolt claps,
The three hun souls and the seven po souls
disintegrate into dust.
I honour Taishang Laojun,
Ji Ji Ru Lu Ling!

(Talisman Fig. 144-145)

152. Da Dao Zhou
The Great Knife Spell

The Spell

Di Yue Sheng,
Upper Celestial Spirit Wisdom Wind,
Seizing Ghosts and Gods with great weapons,
A hundred and ten thousand assist the Dao and Heaven,
Having a righteous heart the holy and virtuous Sages
will agree with me,
Knowing my heart and supporting my loyalty the Sages
shall transform (evil) into dust and sand,
Millions of troops come to aid the people,
For there is a sincerity between Master and Disciple,
Requesting the Sages to decapitate the heads of demons,
Blood shall run and drip,
Request the Sages to gather the hun and po souls,
The Holy Sages rise from Heaven and enter the Earth,
Request the Sages to quickly seize that which is evil,
To come personally and seize it,
We request the Sages to disperse calamities
in this mortal world,
Even the fires are extinguished,
Requesting the Sages that if disease is seen in the five organs,
Then there is a healthy qi in all the houses
and ten thousand illnesses are all appeased,
With all my heart I act upon the Daoist teachings
and methods of the Sages that they may prosper,
I act night and day,
Thus the Sages descend as I burn incense with diligence,

I rely upon the Sages,
The sharp knife shall cut,
The Sages support me but do not support those
whose heart is not sincere,
I work to create perfect merit on this day
of the First Moon.
Ji Ji Ru Lu Ling!

(Talisman Fig. 146)

153. Untitled
The heart of man is perilous,

The Spell

The heart of the Dao has energy
that can accomplish the spell,
If we do not retreat the spell is accomplished,
Reciting the Great Compassion Mantra of the Master
stirs the Gods and awakens them,
All evil spirits make obeisance,
He arises who is named Shou Shizi Hou Lohan
(Roaring Lion Lohan),
The Four Sages of the Four Wheels bow,
The Eight Celestial Kings of the Eight Wheels arise,
The Eight Thunderbolts
and the Eight Greater Thunderbolts that slay evil arise,
The Hand that Grasps the Great Wheel
and illuminates the ten directions descends,
Celestial demons surrender,
Earth demons are exposed,
Di Jia La Po He subdues the demons,
The Dao itself slays the demons,
I honour the Assembly of the Immortals and Sages.

Ji Ji Ru Lu Ling!

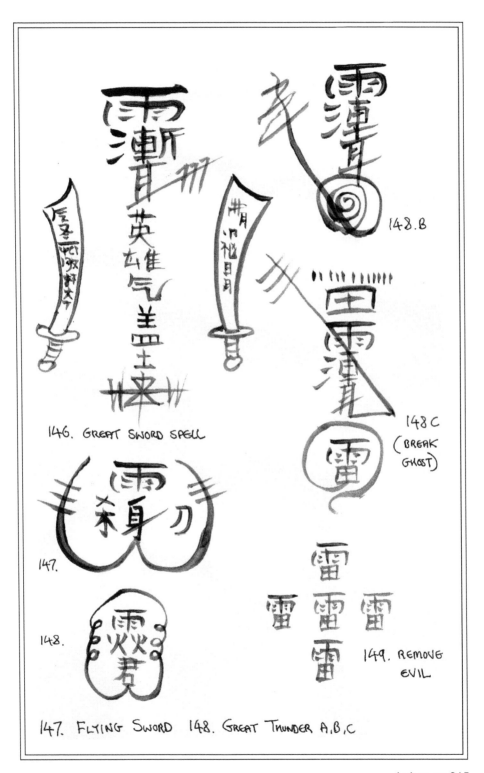

146. GREAT SWORD SPELL

148.B

148C
(BREAK
GHOST)

147.

148.

149. REMOVE
EVIL

147. FLYING SWORD   148. GREAT THUNDER A,B,C

154. Fei Dao Zhou
The Spell Of The Flying Sword

I reverently ask the Central Gods
and Spirits of the Flying Knife to go forth
and slay the non-righteous beings,
The Flying Knife has twenty-four energies (qi).
I honour Tongtian Jiaozhu
(The Master who Communes with Heaven),
Ji Ji Ru Lu Ling!

(Talisman Fig. 147)

155. Lei Hong Zhou
The Great Thunder Spell

I respectfully call the Celestial Great Leigong,
The Thunderbolt of Yin Lightning shakes the void,
Southern Bing Ding Fire burns the Heavens
and they are broken,
It burns the Earth and the earth cracks,
I honour Taishang Laojun and all the Gods
Ji Ji Ru Lu Ling!

(Talisman Fig. 148a)

The Ways of the Dao are rare,
The Southern Spring passes to the Northern River,
The Assembly (of Sages) help the characters,
Descending to this world the power of magic,
The High Ones come and a fierce wind blows,
The Low Ones come and enter the earth
and are concealed therein,
When they come I seize you and bury you in the well forever
and you cannot free yourself.
I honour Taishang Laojun.
Ji Ji Ru Lu Ling.

(Talisman Fig. 148b)

Open the Gates of Heaven
Close the Gates of Hell,
The Gates of Man are guarded,

Block the Ghost Road,
Pierce the Ghost heart,
Break the Ghost Belly,
People come and they control the Gate,
Ghosts come but they have no path,
I honour Taishang Laojun!
Ji Ji Ru Lu Ling!

(Talisman Fig. 148c)

156. Tui Sha
Removing Evil

The Spell

Heaven evil, Earth evil,

Year evil, Month evil,

Day evil. Hour evil,

One hundred and Twenty demons retreat,

If they refuse to retreat we shall use the Rising Five Hundred

Fierce Thunders to strike and repulse you!

I honour Taishang Laojun.

Ji Ji Ru Lu Ling.

(Talisman Fig. 149)

157. The Five Thunder Fire

The Spell

From the highest descends the Tianda Leigong
Thunderbolt through the void of space,
In the void are three million troops sparkling
and glistening and enacting with honour,
Above in the midst of the blue heavens,
Is the Heavenly Thunder,
The Earth acts without mercy,
Stubborn ghosts who refuse to obey,
The Celestial Thunderbolt disintegrates you into dust,
Xuan Yuan Gao Shangdi
(The High Emperor of Mysterious Origin),
Yuhuang Da Tianzun (Jade Emperor),
Command it.
As man is Yang and Woman is Yin,
Yin and Yang command it.

158. Untitled
The Jade Emperor
in the Year of Bing-Wu

The Spell

Upon the first Lunar Month upon the ninth day,
At the hour of Wu was born,
Xuan Yuan orders the decree that activates the
Thunder Troops to descend and to go to that place
with cudgels in their hands to strike the demons
until they are nothing but dust,
Ghosts and the demons of the Five Elements
shall perish that man has longevity,
I honour the Command of Striking Technique
that sweeps away evil!
(This talisman will cause diseases to be gone)

(Talisman Fig. 150)

159. Sanmei Zhen Huo
Samadhi True Fire

Taiji divides the high and profound spirit,
I request the Upper Script Heavenly Personage
(Shang Shu Tianren) to come
and aid in the cultivation of samadhi fire,
The True Dao God (Xiu Zheng Dao Shen) comes,
And the Immortal Spirit Who Writes Truth
(Zuo Zheng Xian Shen) comes,
Generating three times three thousand reality teachings
which know the tens of thousands of years,
Come to the altar and open this precious hall,
Pass on to the disciple the way of cultivating
the True Samadhi Fire of the Spirit of the Sun,
That in the disciple's body there arises a transformation
of fire,
Burning the mountain of snow and burning all to dust,
The disciple uses the rising five hundred fierce thunder
fires that can burn even the waters of the Yellow River
and make it flow backwards.
Five directions using the five hundred thunder fires
to burn the waters of the Yellow River
and cause it to flow backwards.
The disciple uses the Rising Southern Bing-Ding Fires
so even the Snow Mountain becomes but dust.
I honour Taishang Laojun.
Ji Ji Ru Lu Ling!

(Talisman Fig. 151)

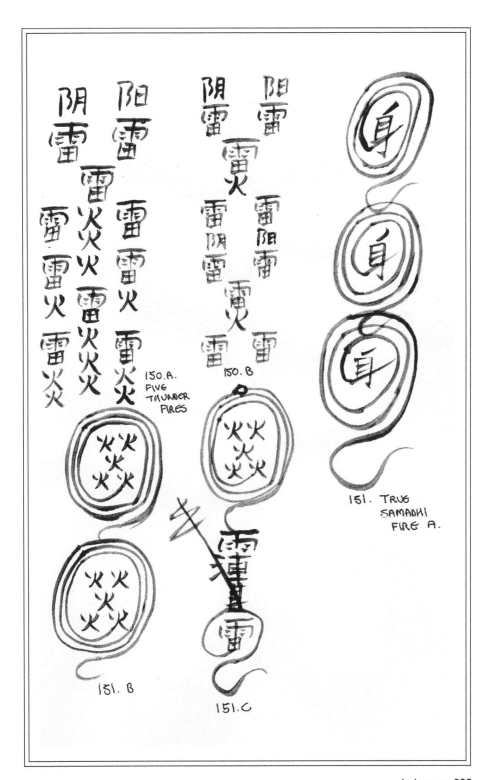

150.A.
FIVE
THUNDER
FIRES

150.B

151. TRUE
SAMADHI
FIRE A.

151. B

151.C

160. Jiulong Shui
Nine Dragons Water Spells

The Spell

On the great road, upon the side is the mouth of a well,
In the well are nine long dragons,
Transforming into nine Dragon Gods Water.
As the wind strokes the waters they change,
Nine turtle gods transform the water,
The spirits Bamboo Bone, Gold, Silver, Copper
and Iron Officials are in eighteen places!
I honour Taishang Laojun

Ji Ji Ru Lu Ling!

(Talisman Fig. 152)

This bowl becomes the Great Eastern Sea
The throat becomes a well ten thousand deep,
Nine Dragons return to the cave,
The Buddha Pu'an, the Azure Dragon,
the White Tiger come to the mountain of water.
Nine Dragons, Nine Phoenixes,
Nine Sage Masters of the Three Doctrines,
Sages of the Buddha Gate rise up to instruct,
The Sages of the Dao Gate rise up to teach,
The Medicine King rises up to teach,
Sun Gong Zhen Ren and Herb Gathering Child Immortal,
Cultivating Immortal Pill Immortal
(Lian Dian Xianshi) come,

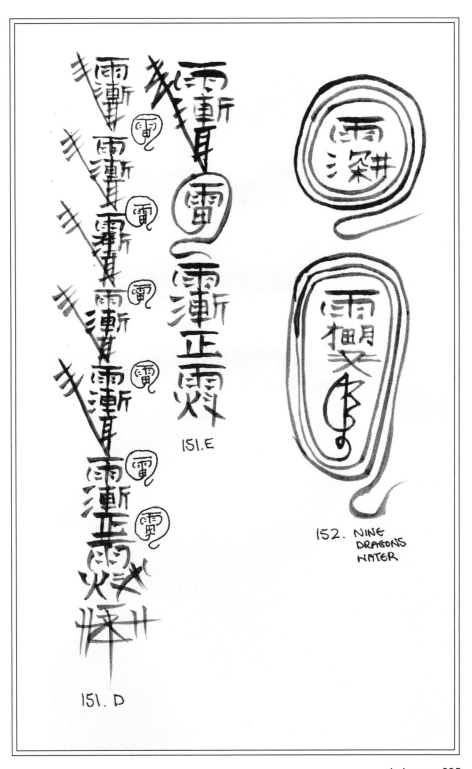

151.E

151. D

152. NINE DRAGONS WATER

Li Jun Bing Ma (Plum Troops and Horses) come,
The Lord of Profound Heaven Master (Zhen Wu Zushi),
Hua Tuo Zushi, Pu'an Zushi, Liyuan Zushi, Puti Zushi,
Damo Zushi, Liu Tou Zushi, Yin Tou Zushi, Jiu Long Dafu
Mu Jin Zushi, Jiulong Pusa shall all generate
the water method.
The first swallow is copper and iron,
The second swallow the magic,
The third swallow the Nine Dragons
descend into the deep pond,
The copper nail becomes water,
The iron nail becomes ash,
The bone becomes water,
A thousand nails become water,
Ten thousand nails become ash,
In the East is the Dragon,
In the West a Phoenix.

Nine Dragon Buddha creates this water method,
First reversing the copper and iron,
Second the steel retreats,
Third the Nine Dragons enter the deep pond,
Thirty two are sealed,
Seventy two ailments and pains are cured,
If there is blood, then bleeding stops,
Guanyin Bodhisattva comes to stop the issue of blood,
Medicine King Bodhisattva comes to halt the pain,
Guanyin sits on the lotus seat,
Above the lotus seat appear all the Gods,
One hundred ghosts dare not come,

The Thunderbolt shall slay all evil influences
and they retreat a thousand miles,
I honour Taishang Laojun.
Ji Ji Ru Lu Ling.

(Talisman Fig. 153)

The Water Method enters the deep pond,
Swallowed by the Nine Dragon Fish.
I honour Taishang Laojun
Ji Ji Ru Lu Ling.
Nine Dragons Water
Illustrious Yang,
The Sun rises in the East,
This spirit water becomes the Eastern Ocean,
Chicken bone, Fish bone and Iron needles
become but dust,
The spirit water descends and becomes a bottomless lake.
I honour Taishang Laojun
Ji Ji Ru Lu Ling.

Talismann Fig. 154-5)

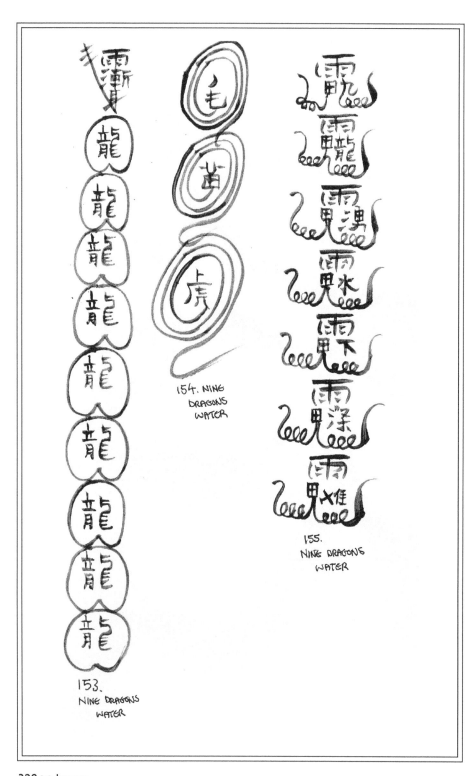

153.
NINE DRAGONS
WATER

154. NINE
DRAGONS
WATER

155.
NINE DRAGONS
WATER

161. Hua Du Zhou
Changing Poison Spell

One, Two, Three, Four, Five!
Metal, Wood, Water, Fire, Soil,
The evil is venomous,
We now release the tiger,
Releasing the ferocious tiger to bite and the venom dies,
I honour Taishang Laojun,
Ji Ji Ru Lu Ling.

Another (Spell 2)

With respect I ask Yuhuang Da Tianzun Wuyun,
Dark clouds cover my body,
Let my life receive rays of golden light
from the Precious Palace,
The ten thousand dare not manifest their power
against me,
The entire body becomes tranquil.
Qian and Kun come,
In the sky the Sun and the Moon illuminate
with their brightness,
There is an evil poison here,
Feeling the evil, the General's sword defends the heart
and the Immortal Wind disperses the evil,
The Five Thunderbolts appear in the midst,
The poison in the blood vanishes completely,
I honour Taishang Laojun,
Ji Ji Ru Lu Ling!
(Talisman Fig. 156)

162. Mi Hun Zhou
Bewitchment Spell

The Heavens unfold,
The Stars, the Sun and the Moon,
From the mouth comes green Qi and stifling black clouds,
There are thirty three Heavens and a heaven beyond heaven,
Heaven is miles outside and has the Immortal Lock
stopping the play of apes and monkeys,
Who want to walk with two feet on the cloud-ladder,
Stepping towards Heaven,
Stepping to the Underworld,
Heaven descends, the Sun returns,
The Cloud descends and the Sun is hidden.
I honour Taishang Laojun,
Ji Ji Ru Lu Ling.

(Talisman Fig. 158)

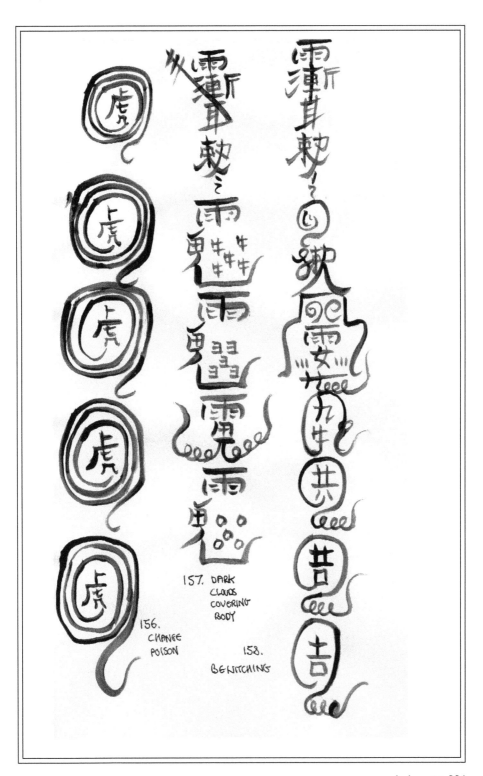

156.
CHANGE
POISON

157. DARK
CLOUDS
COVERING
BODY

158.
BEWITCHING

163. Mao'er Jue
The Cat Spell

The limbs of the cat stretch forth,
Its two eyes are like copper bells,
Standing on Tiger Mountain,
Walking and sitting on Tiger Mountain,
The Golden Silk Cat with bulging eyes,
You are concealed in the midst of the soil.
I honour Taishang Laojun.
Ji Ji Ru Lu Ling!

(Talisman Fig. 159)

Another (Spell 2)

The Ancestral Master bestowed on me the Five Tigers,
There are five rats that consume all,
The Golden Silk Cat in one mouthful swallows them all,
Tudi seizes the five rats and consumes them five miles
from the mountain,
Yes, and ten miles behind the mountain,
A thousand invocations and there are a thousand responses,
Ten thousand invocations and there are ten thousand spirits,
I honour Taishang Laojun
Ji Ji Ru Lu Ling.

(Talisman Fig. 160)

164. Ji Wen Zhou
Rid Of Mosquitoes Spell

The fifth month, the fifth day
is the Dragon Boat Festival,
Where do the swallows fly to?
Only the mosquitoes are in a place not to be found,
Forever mosquitoes are banned and cannot enter this room,
Many mosquitoes go to the green grass slopes
and can never leave there,
Laojun's Iron Fan will cause them to perish!
I honour Taishang Laojun!
Ji Ji Ru Lu Ling!

(Talisman Fig. 161)

165. Untitled
Protection Spell

With money I request the aid of Dong Fan Xian
(Dealing with Violations Immortal)
to banish and keep out evil.
He Shan Xian Shi to the incense comes,
Luban Xian Shi quickly comes.
He Ben Xian Cheng Huang Lao Ye
(Lord who gives harmony to the City Wall),
The Temples high in the mountains
and those low in the mountains,
The thousands of Buddhas and tens of thousands
of Bodhisattvas,
The Upper Assembly to the Upper,
The Lower Assembly to the lower,
The Unrighteous Gods and Evil Demons
are sealed out and cannot enter herein!
Those ghosts who hung themselves,
Ghosts who were killed,
Those who died of wounds and injuries,
Those who drowned,
Those who died at birth,
Pregnant women who died,
People of the Golden Flower Way (drowned girls),
Masters associated with ancient tombs,
Wandering Ghosts,
Baby and Child Ghosts,
Speaking red, speaking black,
All without exception are not feared

and you are sealed and forbidden to enter herein,
Roosters do not cry and dogs do not bite and whine,
Eliminate the spirits until all is clean,
Eliminate the spirits!
It is sealed!
I honour Taishang Laojun!
Ji Ji Ru Ling

(Talisman Fig. 162)

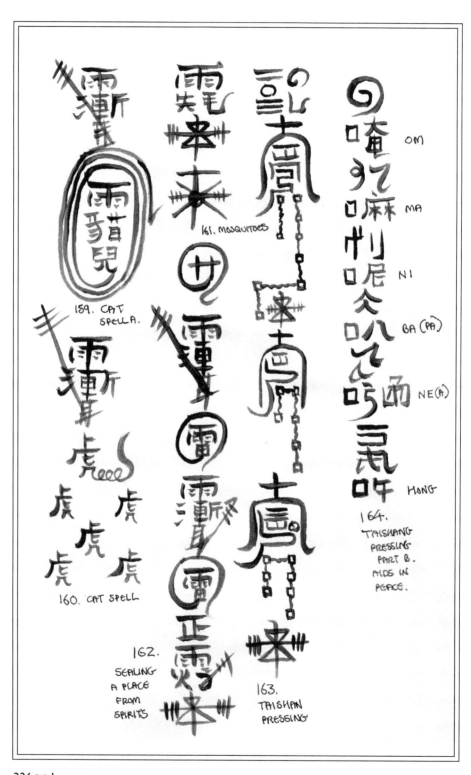

159. CAT SPELL A.

161. MOSQUITOES

160. CAT SPELL

162. SEALING A PLACE FROM SPIRITS

163. TAISHAN PRESSING

OM

MA

NI

BA (PA)

NE (A)

HONG

164. TAISHANG PRESSING PART B. AIDS IN PEACE.

166. Taishan Zhenyan
Mount Tai Dharani

Tianhuang speaks the command that moves the true
Ninth Heaven Upper Five-Coloured Auspicious Clouds,
The Auspicious Cloud that is a golden bell,
A Golden Pagoda on the left
and Kunlun Mountain on the right,
Three Mountains become a bell like pagoda
crushing all evil spirits without exception,
Reading the Command
of the Origin of Destiny Command,
The Ten thousand Gods shine brightly,
Lei Bu Guan Jiang
(Thunder Section Official General) descends,
The Five Emperors of the Three Realms
attend to the Three Purities,
The Spirit of the Three Mountains raises
the Bell Pagoda Celestial Troops and press the evil spirits,
I honour Xian Tian Chi Bei Di!
By the Six Characters Sutra that calls the Jade Emperor!
Taishan Mountain presses the demons down,
Thunder presses the demons down,
Kunlun presses the demons down.

(Talisman Fig. 163 and Fig. 164)

167. Xia Zhao Zhou
The Lower Cover Spell

This is a spell in the 'net class'. A net of magical energies is cast over a perceived evil and tightened to restrain the evil from mobilising itself against the target.

In actual spellcraft, the talisman and sometimes an actual net is strung with red thread on a bamboo hoop. These magical nets are usually eight sided to resemble both a spider web and the eight sided bagua diagram.

> The net covers the years, months, days and hours.
> Covering quickly and covering the inferior,
> Covering the evil that one might meet,
> By the Jade Emperor's command,
> The Tianshi Talisman of Destiny,
> By the Youthful Girl named Tiaolu's command,
> The Northern Emperor also has the command
> to tighten the net,
> I honour the Jade command.
> By Taishang Laojun
> Ji Ji Ru Lu Ling.

(Talisman Fig. 165)

168. Tou Shaan Yue Hai
Through Mountains And Seas Spell

This unusual spell seems to be a 'teleportation' spell in modern parlance, but in traditional Chinese Magic is called earth shrinking. That is rather than magically flying to a destination the distance between points are shrunk or brought closer.

This talisman is used with the fingernails, toenails and hair of the magician. These should be burned to ashes and used to write the talisman.

Burn the talisman and say:

The spell

The Jade Emperor Decree,
The Pre-Heaven Decree,
By the Law of the Youthful Girl Tiao Lu,
Pass quickly the rocks of mountains
when we meet mountains, the mountains open.
Meeting with the earth and the earth cracks,
Meeting wood and we pass through it,
Meeting rocks I become an axe,
Meeting metal it melts away,
Meeting fire it hardens,
True spirit descends,
Water and Soil approach the axe,
My Sword Finger shall become an axe.
I honour the Jade command!
Taishang Sanshan Jiu Hou Immortal Lord.
Ji Ji Ru u Ling.

(Talisman Fig. 166)

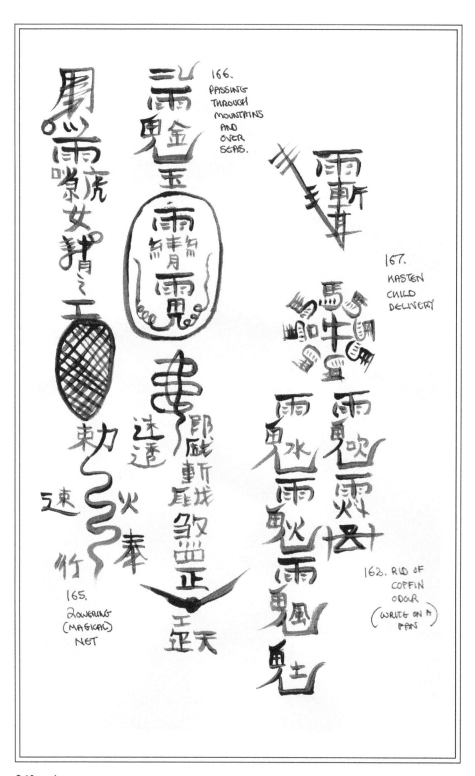

166.
PASSING
THROUGH
MOUNTAINS
AND
OVER
SEAS.

167.
KASTEN
CHILD
DELIVERY

165.
LOWERING
(MAGICAL)
NET

168. RID OF
COFFIN
ODOUR
(WRITE ON A)
FAN

169. Bu Gang Fa
Stepping Method

The magician treads the Pace of the Pre-Heaven Bagua. This step is given next in a rather cryptic form which I shall leave to the ingenium of the reader.

Tai Yi Bian. The High is mutable.
Tai Su Bian. The Simple High changes.
Tai Chu Bian. The Great Origin Changes.
Tai Shi Bian. The Great Beginning Changes.
Tai Ji Bian The Great Ultimate Changes.
Tai Ji Bian Jin Guang! Golden Light!
The Twenty Eight Mansions of Light!
The Twenty-Four Forms of Qi!
Xun Palace, Flying Cloud has five steps.
Kan Palace, Rushing Waves has six steps.
Gen Palace, Blocking Ghosts has seven steps.
Qian Palace opens the Gates of Heaven.
Flying Snow sweeps away the evil spirits.
Ghosts and demons flee.
Sending troops to suppress evil magic
The Assembly of Imperial Thunder Troops step forth.
The Pre-Heaven Bagua command slays
and ZHEN dissolves the forms of the dead.
Kun Palace closes the gates of the Underworld.
Dui Palace leads a powerful army.
Ji Ji Ru Lu Ling!
The Central Palace breaks the host of demons and ghosts.
The Ten Commanders support the Celestial Ding Spirits.

The Palace of Li is the Wheel of Fire.
The Palace of Zhen sends forth the Ministry of Thunder.
Imprisoning Ghosts and the Gods are startled.
Yuan Shuai sends forth the troops!
O the Eight Diagrams of the Taiji embrace
the ten thousand forms,
The Treasured Power meets the soul of the evil master
and his spirit flees,
Covering demons and disintegrating their forms,
When it meets ghosts and spirits they become dust.
I honour the Jade Command and cover the demons
and sweep away all evil!
Ji Ji Ru Lu Ling!

170. Cui Sheng Zhou
Hastening Child Delivery Spell

Inscribe the talisman using cinnabar ink. The spell is said three times and so the spirit comes. Burn the talisman to ashes and pour them into boiling water. Let the woman drink this medicine.

The Spell

O hasten the delivery of the child and let the Gods
protect the birth and its spirit,
Her bones open and the babe is developed,
her bones adapt to the shape of the infant,
Quickly her bones open, quickly they open!
Prohibiting injury to the life of the mother,
Prohibiting injury to the child,
I honour Jiu Lao Xian Zi Jun,
The Sun and Moon illuminate her entire body.
I honour Taishang Laojun!
Ji Ji Ru Lu Ling

(Talisman Fig. 167)

171. Ji Chou Jue
Ridding Of A Foul Odour

This spell is used to rid of the offensive smell of a body lying in wait before burial. There are accounts of this spell being used frequently even into modern times. Generally the sorcerer will be equipped with a fan and 'wave' the malodorous air from the coffin as he chants the spell and burns the talisman shown.

The Spell

The Ancestral Master is before the mouth of a pool,
There is a pond, a bath, a pit,
In that pond is a dragon with nine heads
and eighteen tails,
It cannot eat a thousand things,
Eating only in this mortal world the water of corpses,
One wave of the fan, two waves of the fan,
A thousand miles.
Three waves of the fan and a fourth,
A thousand miles.
Five waves of the fan, and five times five,
Two thousand and fifty miles the fan sends
from the dwelling of the living,
For a thousand years the stinking smell is forbidden!
I honour Taishang Laojun.
Ji Ji Ru Lu Ling.

(Talisman Fig. 168)

172. Ni Shan Zhou
The Spell Of Mud Mountain

This spell is unique to the Luban calls upon a being known as the Mud Mountain Master, seemingly to block the way of evil magic, perhaps by combining the powers of water and soil, two of the elements of Chinese cosmology.

The Spell

I reverently request the Mud Mountain Master,
Nishan Fawang Shen,
The Mud Mountain General
and King who wears on his head a golden crown,
Eyes emitting a hundred rays of light of the essence
of mud,
In the day he patrols the world
and at night he is in the Underworld,
the Yin Realm with Divine Troops.
A thousand million Yang Warriors rise,
Yin troops rise and arrive at the entrance of the cave.
I bow to and request the Mud Mountain Dharma King
to quickly descend in his chariot,
The chariot is accompanied by a hundred regiments
of mud on roads of oil and water
which become a mountain of white mud.
The mud sea path that never opens.
I honour the Mud Mountain Master!
Ji Ji Ru Lu Ling.

(Talisman Fig.169)

173. Kai Xue Zhou
Opening Blood Spell

This spell causes blood to flow, not for nefarious reasons but to encourage bleeding for medical purging or perhaps to stimulate a difficult menstruation.

The Spell

Laojun rides the ox above the Gate of Heaven,
Releasing the Yangtze River water to flow,
A dark stream of water flows on the earth,
Yan Wang Jun sees the stream,
I honour Taishang Laojun!
Ji Ji Ru Lu Ling.

(Trace the sign over the wound or womb)
(Talisman Fig. 170)

170. BLOOD FLOWS

171. BLOOD STOPPED

172. BLOOD STAUNCHED

173. DISPEL FILTH

174. SEND TROOPS

169. MUD MOUNTAIN

174. Zhi Xue Zhou
Stop Bleeding Spell

The Spell

I sincerely ask Li Laojun to aid me in this mortal world,
To close this blood-gate with an iron plate,
With a copper plate,
Close the blood stream of living water,
I ask Laojun who rides the ox to shut off
the Yangtze River water so it does not flow,
A copper plate shuts it and the Yangtze flows backwards,
Close it and the sea water retreats,
Striking the water, it flows backwards.
I honour Taishang Laojun.
Ji Ji Ru Lu Ling!

(Talisman Fig. 171)

175. Bi Xue Zhou
Closing Blood Spell

The Spell

I Ming Tian Zi will shut and cause to flow backwards
the Yangtze River and the Great Sea of Blood
using but a single character.
The evil master's life is severed.
Advancing forth I dispel and extinguish him.
I request the six stars of the Southern Dipper
and the seven stars of the Big Dipper.
I honour Taishang Laojun!
Ji Ji Ru Lu Ling!

(Talisman Fig. 172)

176. Untitled
Dispelling Evil Spirits Spell

The Spell

Heaven Spirit, Earth Spirit,

Taishang aids me and rescues the people of Earth,

If there are demons or calamities that harm living beings,

The Thunderbolt shall crack and transform them into dust.

If we meet a demon it is slain, a spirit shall be blocked,
a ghost shall be cut.

Shang Di bears the command and you cannot remain
or tamper with the hun soul,

Those spirits who disobey, those ghosts who dare to act,

The Commander will come and all evil shall be extinguished,

Ghosts will be cut quickly and extinguished like a flame,

Great fortune and great prosperity come.

I honour the Jade Command of Taishang Laojun!

Ji Ji Ru Lu Ling!

(Talisman Fig. 173)

177. Fang Bing Zhou
Sending Troops Spell

This is an important class of spell used in sending familiar spirits towards a given task, often to dispel evil, punish the wicked, obtain desired goals and so forth.

Generally such spirits, called 'troops' in Chinese magic are cultivated over a long period of time with meditation and by feeding with incense and talismans. Often such troops have a 'home' such as a vase or a clay or wood figurine.

The Spell

Heaven Spirit, Earth Spirit,
The Jade Master aids me in my work,
East and South, West and Northern Generals
command them.
The Ten Great Ferocious Ones quickly descend in clouds
and go forth in the five directions,
Seeking in this world the wicked.
I offer incense, to protect my body!
In three days, one day and seven days manifest
by my request.
I thank you!
I honour Yu Chi who musters the troops!
By Taishang Laojun. Ji Ji Ru Lu Ling!

(Talisman Fig. 174)

178. Jie Hui Shen Zhou
Expel Evil Spirits Spell

The Spell

O the drums of heaven beat loudly,
The Spirit Official quickly descends.
On the left ten spirit officials are dispatched.
On the right comes Deng Tian Jun who gives rise to ten
thousand thunder spirits of the Great Lei Gong.
Thunderbolts and lightning streak across the void,
Heaven casts down the Heavenly Net,
Ensnaring a hundred ghosts and spirits on the Earth below.
Prince Nezha strikes with a blade,
Qitian Dasheng, Heavenly Peng Yuanshuai,
Yang Zhan Zushi seize the evil energies.
The Four Great Celestial Kings calm the four directions,
The Eight Great Vajra Thunderbolts guard the Eight Gates,
All Gods who reside in the Eight Directions block those
roads, Great ghosts are imprisoned and boiled in water.
Lesser ghosts are burned in fire and incinerated in oil.
Skin opens and their flesh peels off.
Changing into dust.
Skin opens and flesh festers and changes into dust.
Slaying demons, eliminating evil spirits.
They all become naught but dust.
I honour Taishang Laojun.
Ji Ji Ru Lu Ling!

(Talisman Fig. 175)

179. Untitled
Five Thunders Formula

The Spell

Five Thunders three thousand Generals
Millions of Thunderbolt Troops,
Flaming light burning the world,
Demons becoming dust.
At the first thunderclap the Thunder Command rises.
At the second thunderclap the Earth General
comes with the Thunder Command.
At the third thunderclap, as quick as fire the
thunder command pursues its goal.
I honour Taishang Laojun.
Ji Ji Ru Lu Ling!

(Talisman Fig. 176)

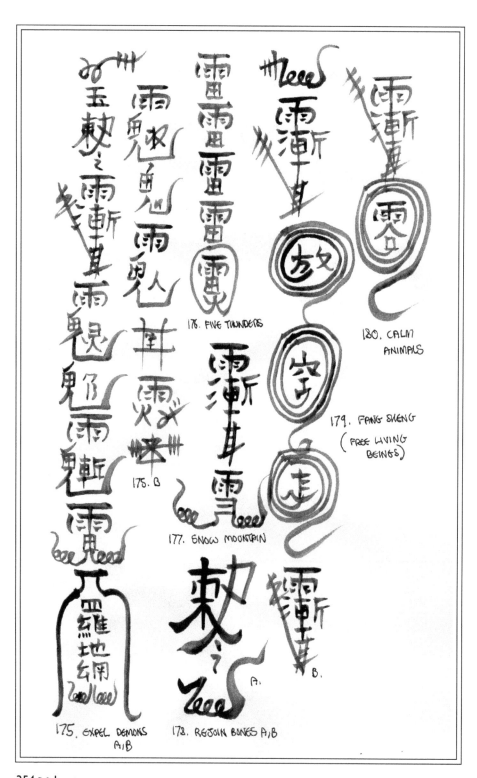

176. FIVE THUNDERS

180. CALM
ANIMALS

179. FANG SHENG
(FREE LIVING
BEINGS)

177. SNOW MOUNTAIN

175. B

A.

B.

175. EXPEL DEMONS
A, B

178. REJOIN BONES A, B

180. Untitled
The Spell Of Snow Mountain

Another Snow Mountain spell aimed at stopping the smell of corpses.

The Spell
Touding Zushi enters the door
and sees on the ground a corpse,
The Nine Oxen Immortal Master arrives,
The White Crane Immortal comes to the door,
For a thousand years water does not leak.
For ten thousand years essence does not leak.
I request it by the six Southern Dipper stars
and the seven stars of the Northern Dipper!
I honour Taishang Laojun.
Ji Ji Ru Lu Ling.

(Talisman Fig. 177)

181. Jie Gu Shui Fa
Knitting Bones Water Method

As the name implies the spell is directed at healing broken bones and other injuries. For this spell willow leaves and bark are soaked in water and the spell is said and the seal drawn over the water. The water is applied topically.

The Spell

I ask Hua Tuo, the great master who wears armour
and a helmet in a display of power,
The Three Caves Mother Xuan Nu comes in person,
The Immortals descend in person,
Virtuous men and faithful women bow and request
(show the Sword Seal Mudra)
Let Fengdao set this bone and display its power,
A thousand years the skin was broken and it now joins,
The ten thousand year wizened tree sends life,
Broken skin is rejoined,
The San Qing King's mothers passed on the secret
by word of mouth,
Broken bones rejoin,
A thousand year old willow tree,
ten thousand years water in which willow has been soaked,
Joined at the hour of Yin and grew at the hour of Mao.
I honour Taishang Laojun.
Ji Ji Ru Lu Ling!

(Draw seal over water)

Laojun bestows on me a cane,

In the Yin hour it was cut and at the Mao hour it grew,
The Dragon and Phoenix Jade Maiden Immortal Lady
calls out and the cane transforms
into the Heavenly White Ape,
The White Ape calls and it becomes river water,
In the water soaks the willow roots.
At the Yin hour it was broken and in the Mao hour it grew.
Come and intercede, grow, stay and stop the injury.
I honour Taishang Laojun.
Ji Ji Ru Lu Ling.

(Talisman Fig. 178)

182. Fang Sheng Zhou
Free Life Spell

A spell of compassion used to free captured animals or stop them being killed or hunted. Read seven times drawing the sign in the air.

The Spell

Heavenly sand, Earthly sand,
The Dragon King Lord transforms
into a magical robe and birds and beasts fly and scamper.
Fish soldiers and Shrimp Generals disappear
hiding in the sand,
The man's hand drops in command,
The Mountain God and Earth Lord capture
(those who would harm animals),
NAMO AMITABHA!

(Talisman Fig. 179)

183. Untitled
Calming Birds And Beasts

The sage before entering the mountains or wild forests casts this spell and wears the talisman to ward off dangers of wild animals.

The Spell

Guardian Mountain Spirit Official,
Calming the Mountains Spirit Official,
Great Mountain King Officer,
Mountain God Earth God,
The disciple enters the mountain.
Returning to the mountain, birds and beasts come.
Mountain Yu Huang commands the birds
and beasts to move.
I honour Taishang Laojun.
Ji Ji Ru Lu Ling.

(Talisman Fig. 180)

184. Zhan Yao Jian Jue
Slaying Demon Sword Formula

I with reverence request the Protecting Law
King Spirit Official,
Who treads on a fire-wheel to descend
into this mortal world.
The demons will be in fear as will all ghosts,
The Golden Whip with just a single lash
turns them into dust and smoke,
I request Namo Puti An Hu Fa Wei Tuo
(ie the Buddha Skanda, a warrior protector of Buddhism)
to stand at my side,
With an iron helmet and armour,
Descending by carving a way through the clouds.
OM JIA LOU!
The Precious Sword leaves its scabbard
and reaches to the stars of the Big Dipper,
I use the sword.
With one stroke I break the ghost's head,
All the demons and evil ghosts shall mourn
at the Yellow Springs (= World of the Dead),
Learning the Dao the disciple diligently cultivates and bows,
Requesting the Dharma Protector to quickly descend.
I request the Buddha to bestow this command!
Then recite Namo Amituofo (Amitabha)
one hundred times.

(Talisman Fig. 181)

185. Jian Gu Jue
Tighten The Hoop Formula

A method to punish the wicked, (see Jing Gu Zhou Fa and its relation to the Monkey King.) In essence it is a binding spell.

The Spell
The Upper Hoop of the Heavenly Palace,
The Sun and Moon become dim,
Binding the Five Mountains and Taishan crumbles,
The binding of the Five Seas and the tides surge forth,
Binding the demons and evil ghosts so they are bound like iron barrels,
A net is cast for the earth ghosts,
The disciple uses the Earth-Net and the Heaven's Net,
Up rises the great sword and five arrows to immediately capture and bring to justice the wicked.
The Jade Emperor bestows the command
to tighten this binding.
I honour Taishang Laojun!
Ji Ji Ru Lu Ling!

(Talisman Fig. 182)

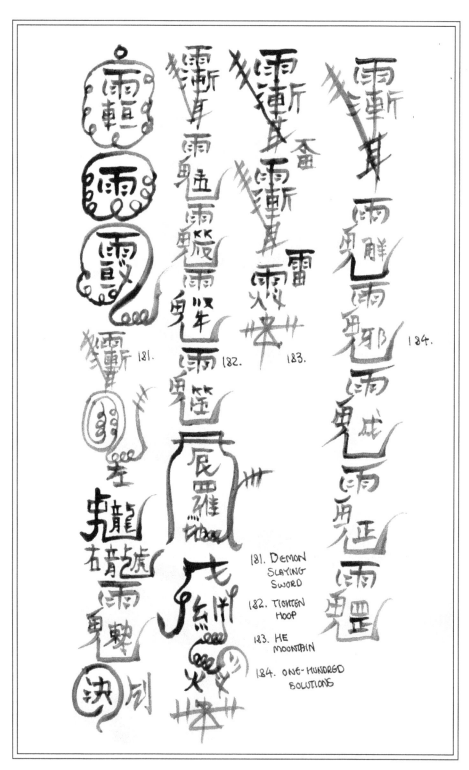

181. DEMON SLAYING SWORD

182. TIGHTEN HOOP

183. HE MOUNTAIN

184. ONE-HUNDRED SOLUTIONS

186. He Shan Zhou
He Mountain Spell

The disciple grasps the Knowing Harmony Script,
With one joining of Mountain and Water,
The Earth Veins Dragon God is harmonious.
Two harmonies of the left Azure Dragon
and the right White Tiger,
In front is the Vermillion Bird
and behind is the Black Warrior,
The Upper Harmony are the Three Doctrines
of Kongfuzi, Li Laojun and Shijiafo
(Confucius, Lao Tzu and Buddha),
The Middle Harmony Three Doctrines are
Guanyin Pusa, Zi Tong Dijun and Zhen Wu Zushi,
The Lower Harmony Three Doctrines are Chuan Zhu,
Tu Di and Yao Wang.
The Three Holy Receptacles Masters
and the Ancient Ancestors of the High Mountain Temples
and the lesser Temples of the Lower Mountains,
Thousands of Buddhas and millions of Bodhisattvas,
A thousand harmonies
and ten thousand harmonies become one harmony,
Qi is in harmony for five times five miles,
Five times five is twenty-five miles,
Green crops flourish and all the billions of works
of Tudi the Earth Lord become one harmonious qi.
All taboos are lifted!
I honour Taishang Laojun.
Ji Ji Ru Lu Ling!
(Talisman Fig. 183)

187. Bai Fa Jie
A Hundred Solutions Method

The Spell

The eyes see the Sun and the Moon become dim,
That Spirit Official Who Stamps Upon Evil Sulphurous
Spirits comes to solve and eradicate black magics.
With one dismissal changing spells into dust
by the Method of Heaven,
With a second dismissal of the Method of Earth,
Dismissing Heaven and Earth,
Dismissing the Sun and Moon,
Dismissing the year,
Dismissing the month,
My Master quickly dismisses all evil.
With a second dismissal the black magician's hands
and mouth are naught,
And the evil master's feet and body,
Dismissing the evil yellow robed monk.
Guanyin dismisses all.
Master of the Crossroads Who Release the Ox dismisses,
Jiu Tian Xuan Nu dismisses,
Pregnant Women dismiss,
The Method of Longevity dismisses,
Dishevelled hair dismisses,
Barefoot Immortal dismisses.
In Western Meishan, above the grass,
We see the ancient immortal come and he appears unaged,
The Master bestows the Divine Immortal Method,
All kinds of black magic are solved,

The first are Heavenly Methods,
the Second are Earthly Methods,
All return to Heavenly Ten Thousand solutions
and the Earthly Ten Thousand Solutions,
(ie solutions or spells that counter dark magic),
Thus all taboos are lifted!
I honour Taishang Laojun!
Ji Ji Ru Lu Ling!

Heaven is pure and Earth is spirit,
The Three August Ones and Five Lords,
The cultivation of the Dao shall succeed,
Passed down to the descendants from the Masters,
Good and evil are clearly recognised,
Those devoid of gratitude are extinguished
and their descendants are extinguished.
Taishang Laojun in the Geng-Chen Year,
in the Second Lunar Month,
on the Fifteenth Day at the Hour of Mao was born.

(Talisman Fig. 184)

Cultivation of Magick

This next series of spells are geared towards entry into and cultivation of magic, so the reader should pay great attention to this section should he want to practise the magic of the Luban.

188. Jin Ming Mi Fa
Entry To
The Profound Secret Technique

The Spell

Taiji divides the profound and the high,
The Light And Pure Teaching Heavenly Personage
can cultivate the Dao correctly,
Body and life grow correctly towards an Immortal legacy,
Three thousand years of teaching are gathered
and tens and thousands of years ancient Cinnabar and
Precious Hall give the True Oral Teaching by transmission,
I honour the Great Sage of the Ten Directions
Who Responds. (Da Sheng Shi Fang Ganying Tianzun).
Ji Ji Ru Lu Ling.

(Talisman is either drawn on yellow paper and burned or drunk
or traced over the water and drunk daily)

(Talisman Fig. 185)

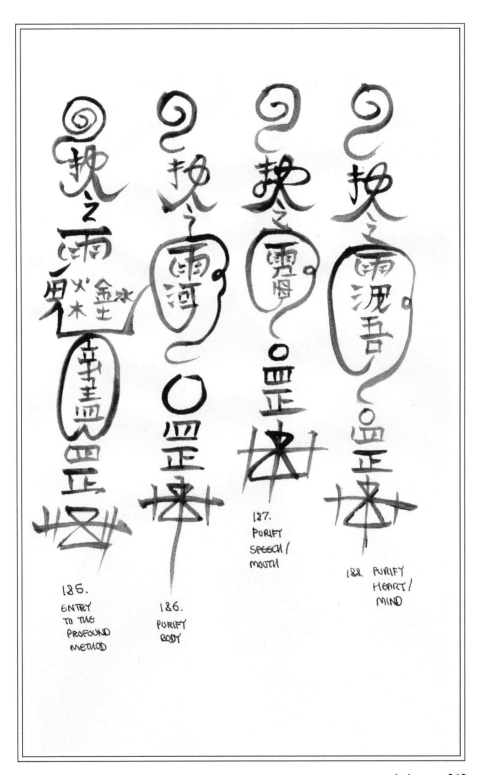

185.
ENTRY
TO THE
PROFOUND
METHOD

186.
PURIFY
BODY

187.
PURIFY
SPEECH/
MOUTH

188. PURIFY
HEART/
MIND

189 Jing Shen Shen Zhou
Purify Body Divine Spell

The Spell

Lingbao Tianzun comforts the heart of the disciple,
The Hunpo are at peace,
The Five Internal Organs guarded by the Dark Warrior.
 Azure Dragon, White Tiger are twin warriors,
Vermillion Bird and Black Warrior guard my body,
I honour Da Sheng Shi Fang Ganying Tianzun.
Ji Ji Ru Lu Ling.

(Talisman Fig. 186)

190. Jing Kou Shen Zhou.
Pure Mouth Spell

The Spell

Cinnabar Vermillion mouth spirit,
Spitting out the filth and ridding of filthy Qi,
The tongue God speaks truth
and opens command of life,
The thousand toothed god exorcises evil,
The Valiant Tiger Throat God defends the true,
The qi of the God of the heart essence,
Giving the origin of cinnabar command.

(Talisman Fig. 187)

191. Jing Xin Shen Zhou
Pure Heart Divine Spell

The three spells of purifying body, mouth and heart are clearly based on the standard versions of those spells found in the Daoist classics but also at variance and somewhat condensed. Fuller and more standardised versions can be found in my *Practical Chinese Magic* also published by Mandrake of Oxford.

The Spell

Taishang rises and the heart changes without end,
Exorcising and binding demons,
Guarding life and defending the body,
Luminous wisdom and righteousness,
Purifying the mind to tranquillity.
Three hun souls are eternal ,
And the po souls will not wander.
I honour Shifang Ganying Tianzun.
Ji Ji Ru Lu Ling!

(Talisman Fig. 188)

192. Jin Guang Shen Zhou
Spell Of The Golden Light

This version of the famous cultivation spell of the Golden Light uses a Daoist method of finger pinching or finger beating to create magical patterns on the hands. It can be compared to the Tantric idea of Nyasa, that is to divinise the body. I give both the pinyin Chinese and English due to the importance of this spell.

Tian Di Xuan Zong
(Heaven and Earth Mysterious origin)
Use the thumb to pinch the Zi point. (1)

Wan Qi Ben Gen.
The thumb presses the Chou point (2)

Guang Xiu Yi Jie
The thumb presses the Yin point (3)

Zheng Wu Shen Tong
The thumb presses the Mao point (4)

San Jie Nei Wai
The thumb pinches the middle joint of the middle finger, known in Chinese esoterica as Zhong Gong or the Central Palace. Some texts refer to it as the Yu Qing or Jade Purity. (5)

Wei Dao Du Zun
Thumb presses the upper joint of the middle finger.(6)

Ti You Jin Guang
Thumb presses the tip of the middle finger
or Wu point. (7)

(These seven gestures form the Big Dipper)
Fu Ying Wu Shen
Thumb returns to the Zi point (1)

Shi Zhi Bu Wen
Thumb to the Hai point

Ting Zhi Bu Wen
Thumb to the Xu point.

Bao Luo Tian Di
Thumb to the second joint of the ring finger.
Yang Qu Qun Sheng
Thumb to the Zhong Gong point.

Shou Chi Wan Bian
Thumb to the upper joint of the middle finger.

Shen You Guang Ming
Thumb to the tip of the middle finger.

(These seven form the Southern Dipper)
San Jie Shi Wei
Thumb returns to the Zi point

Wu Di Si Ying
Thumb to Chou point.

Wan Shen Chao Li
Thumb to Yin point.

Yi Shi Lei Ting
Thumb to the Mao point.

Gui Yao Sang Dan
Thumb to Zhong Gong.

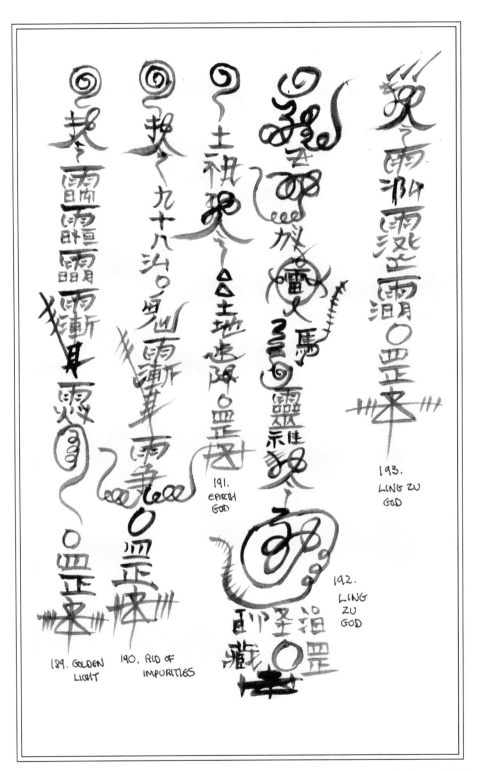

189. GOLDEN LIGHT

190. RID OF IMPURITIES

191. EARTH GOD

192. LING ZU GOD

193. LING ZU GOD

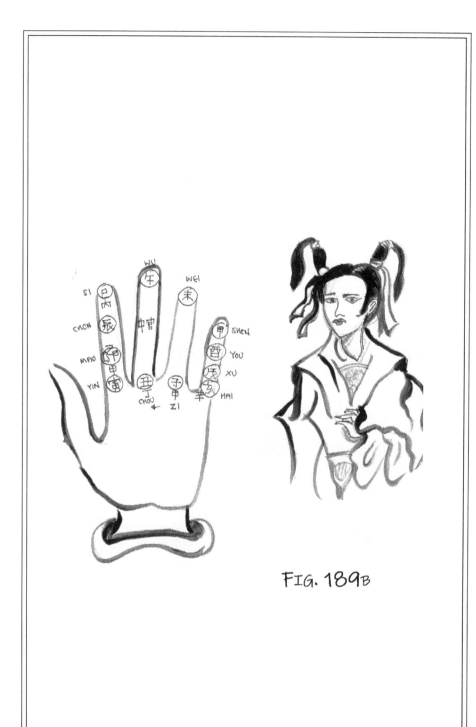

FIG. 189B

Jing Guai Wang Xing
Thumb to the second joint of the middle finger.

Nei You Pili
Thumb to the middle joint of the little finger.

Leishen Yin Ming
Thumb to the Xu point.

Dong Hui Jiao Che
Thumb to the ring finger upper joint.

Wu Qi Teng Teng
Thumb to the middle finger upper joint.

Jin Guang Su Xian
Thumb to middle finger tip.

Fu Hu Zhen Ren
Thumb to Zhong Gong.

In doing the exercise the disciple visualises a sphere of powerful and radiant golden light emanating from the dan tian area some 1-2" below the navel.

(Talisman Figs. 189 and 189b)

193. Jie Hun Shen Zhou
Ridding Of Filth Spell

The Spell

Heaven and Earth Nature,
Offensive Qi disperses,
In the midst of the cave is the profound void,
The Eight Directions powerful Gods,
Send me peace and calm.
O the Lingbao Talisman command,
Informs the Ninth Heaven.
Qian Luo Da Na! (mantric)
The Cave of the Powerful and Highest Profundity,
Slaying demons and binding evil.
Killing tens and thousands of ghosts,
The Central Mountain God Spell!
Yuanshi Wang Wen accepts and maintains the faith,
Repulsing ghosts to prolong life,
The Five Sacred Mountains press the Eight Seas.
The Demon King has his hands bound,
Slaying the inauspicious and so filth dissipates like smoke,
The Qi of the Dao is eternal.
I honour the Shiwang Ganying Tianzun.
Ji Ji Ru Lu Ling.

(Talisman Fig. 190)

194. Tudi Shen Zhou
Earth God Spell

The Spell

In this place is the Earth God,
The God knows the spirit of the place,
Having access to Heaven and reaching Earth,
Going to the Underworld and entering the depths,
Appear to me and pass on my petition,
Do not leave us,
Rendering great service today at this time,
By the Script of the Name of the Upper Purity.
I honour Shifang Ganying Tianzun.
Ji Ji Ru Lu Ling!

(Talisman Fig. 191)

195. Ling Zu Shen Zhou
Looking up to the Gods of Power

The Spell

Wei Huo Luo Jiang calls the Bringing Orders
to Heaven Spirit Official,
Leigong Fire Wheel comes,
Sending the San Qing to cut down the abominable ghosts,
Hand grasping a golden whip and rushing through
the world to seek the evil,
Wearing helmet and armour
and manifesting great spiritual power,
With green phoenix boots he shall guard my body.
From his eyes leap the fiery spirit of heaven and earth.
Carving the mark of the Three Heavenly Court Lords
of Heaven,
The Sage shall save the people of the mortal realm.
Silver toothed and phoenixed mouth General,
With three thousand tiger headed Pixiu
(Dragon dog) troops.
Rushing fire searches and the wind rushes over the world.
Piercing mountains, breaking stones and seizing evil spirits.
We entreat that rain shall spill upon this world.
Protecting the body,
The circle of light reveals meaning.
Exorcising evil spirits
and curing sickness as quick as lightning.
Stopping infectious diseases.
Vanquishing evil spirits and crowds of shouting demons.
Command the thunderbolt by the mantra

HONG.

The thunderbolt flies upwards through the clouds and mist and into space.

The demons of the Three Realms must bow.

Obstacles of the Ten Direction paths are vanquished and must accept the Dao.

I gaze upwards today and await your coming.

Bestow upon us your divine and mighty protection.

Om! Chi Ling! Suo Po He!

(Talisman Fig. 192-3)

196. Hou Zhan Gan Shi
The Prime Minister descends and comes

To deal with theft and robbery, calamity and misery.
Dealing with infectious diseases and pestilence and war.
The command is read aloud three times and the Celestial
Gods protect all from calamity and changing all to dust.
The Azure Dragon Yan Yue complies with the command
and flies down from aloft.
Slaying without rashness the crowds of demons.
I honour Han Tianzun who helps the needy
and relieves the distressed.
Emanating brightness!
Ji Ji Ru Lu Ling!
HUO LEI YIN
I revere the Heavenly Upper Fire Thunder God,
Red fire spreads throughout the heavens,
His red hair is dishevelled and he cuts the spirits
and ghosts so they leave no trace,
If there is an evil spirit that comes to harm or hinder,
The thunderbolt resounds and becomes fire.
I honour the Fire Thunder Command.
Vanquishing the demons in the Three Realms.
The Great Vanquisher on the sixth month
and twenty third day was born.
In the fifth month the Thirty Five Sages descended!

197. Ming Zhou
Underworld Spell

Next follows a series of spells concerned with the descent into the underworld, that is the land of the dead.

The Spell

The Supreme Root Sage,

The Protecting Dragon Yan Yue Thunderbolt,

Who is fond of his loyal sons,

Who loves loyal and loving people.

Venerated Supreme Lord who teaches,

Esteemed Lord who reads the spells.

Transforming the Lord's Seal to allow you to rove in the Underworld.

Returning the Yang and holding onto life,

Bringing comfort and transforming ignorance.

Explanation Of You Ming
Or Travelling In The Underworld

The disciple must master the travelling in the Underworld Talisman Method. Refine the spirit by burning it to ashes and placing them into pure water, gazing at the steam for a time and then drinking it.

Immediately descending into the Underworld he will see the deceased of the client's family up to thirty five days after their death.

Speak to the dead soul in the Underworld and ask your questions or about the year, month and day of a vow, or a rooster to be sacrificed, oil lamps, incense or papers to be given.

What is approved for the Yin Altar in terms of fulfilling

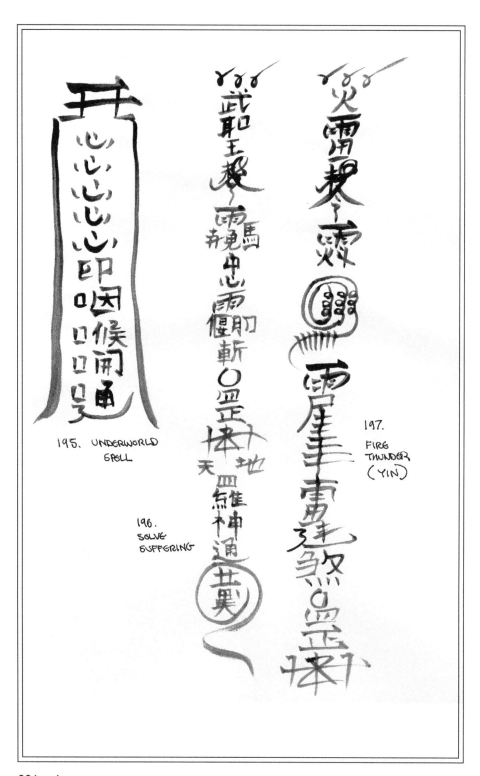

195. UNDERWORLD SPELL

196. SOLVE SUFFERING

197. FIRE THUNDER (YIN)

vows, what altar is harmonious for the good of the people?

One may be blocked or cannot pass certain doors or gates such as those of the Fifth and Sixth Halls. One can use the Ling Guan spell given previously, then use the mighty power of the Thunder Fire Seal.

If you encounter a person or entity with enmity or run into a person who has died before their time, or one who is newly deceased in the Underworld one may record their grievances and petition on behalf of that person and speak in defence of the deceased. Immediately ask Tudi to release their three and seven souls. If they are alive you can bring them back to this world.

See Appendix 3 for a clearer spell of descending to the Underworld from my own Jasper Lake Maoshan Tradition.

(Talisman Figs. 195-97)

198. Spell To Make Beans Cast To Become Warriors

The Spell

Heaven is spirit, Earth is spirit,
The Jade Emperor acts for me,
Scattering beans and there come forth warriors
whose hands grasp the Jade Emperor Command,
On the first cast (cast beans)
there are thirty-three armies of Laojun,
On the second cast,
five hundred and fifty five thousand troops
of the Mountain-Earth God,
On the third cast eight
eight troops of the Five Sea Dragon Kings,
On the fourth cast,
the ten great ferocious generals quickly descend,
On the fifth cast,
all the troops and horses quickly transform into a million
clouds that pass over the five directions of the world,
They search for the source of offered incense
and give great protection to the Zhenren
(Righteous or True Person),
Those who do not listen to the command
are banished from Heaven
and are punished by cangue in prisons,
I honour Yuhuang,
Casting beans to become troops,
I honour Taishang Hunyuan.
Mu Jin Zushi!

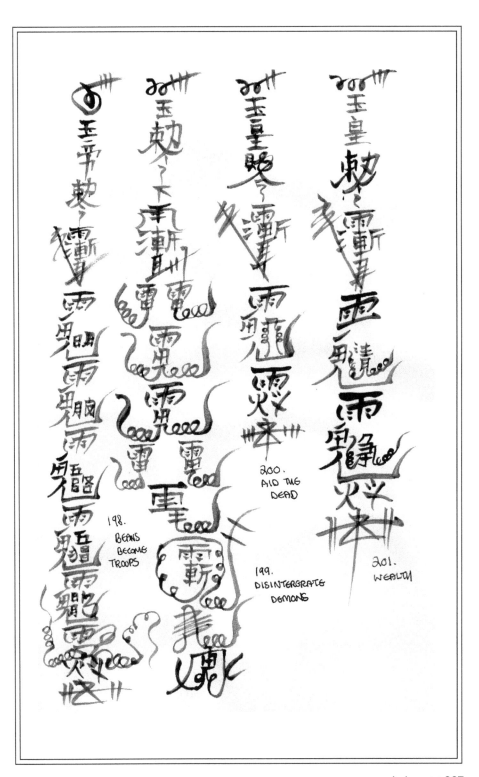

198.
BEANS
BECOME
TROOPS

199.
DISINTERGRATE
DEMONS

200.
AID THE
DEAD

201.
WEALTH

Ji Ji Ru Lu Ling!
(Talisman Fig.198)

The Spell

Lightning glitters and sparkles,
The Heavenly drum beats and the Jade Emperor Command
acts to allow me to subdue evil spirits,
On the left is Deng Yuan Shuai the Commander
of the Thirty Six Thunder Generals,
On the right is Tuo Ta Li Tian Wang
the bearer of the Pagoda,
Before me is Nezha Immortal Feng Jiang,
Behind me are the Eight Great
Diamond Thunderbolt Lords who shall follow me,
I act to stop the demons and evil spirits, I behead them.
Celestial Troops, Earthly Generals shall return
to the Court of Heaven,
The Jade Emperor commands you to slay demons
and eliminate evil spirits,
I honour Taishang Hunyuan Mu Jin Zushi,
Ji Ji Ru Lu Ling!

(Talisman Fig.199)

You can use this spell so you transform in the eyes of evil forces:

My spirit is not an extraordinary spirit,
I am Hunyuan Lao Zu Shen
who comes to the Great Person,
My hand grasping the Jade Emperor Seal,
The Underworld opens
and the ignorant people are pardoned,

The sea of suffering retreats,
The Jade Emperor bestows the order that quickly opens it.
I honour Taishang Hunyuan Mu Jin Zushi.
Ji Ji Ru Lu Ling!

(Talisman Fig. 200)

199. Untitled
Money Spell

The eyes gaze upwards to the blue sky,
Zuben Er Shi is present,
His hand holding the Jade Emperor Seal,
Opening the heart that he comes
to transform circumstances,
Changing it to the Earth Treasury millions of gold
and millions of silver,
The black pen is poised above the paper.
I honour Taishang Hunyuan Mu Jin Zushi,
Ji Ji Ru Lu Ling!

(Talisman Fig. 201)

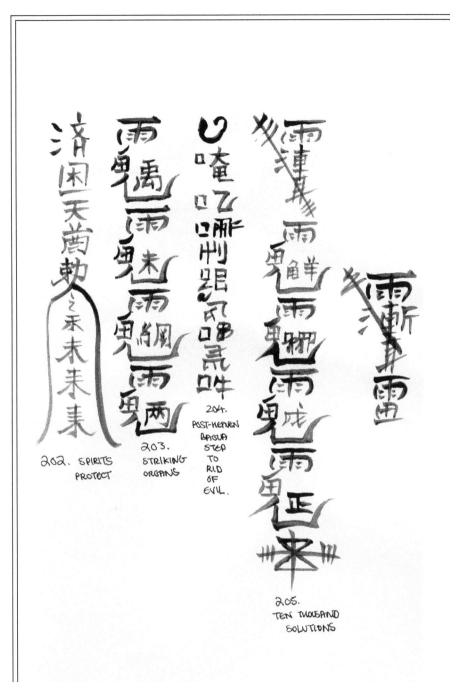

202. SPIRITS
PROTECT

203.
STRIKING
ORGANS

204.
POST-HEAVEN
BAGUA
STEP
TO
RID
OF
EVIL.

205.
TEN THOUSAND
SOLUTIONS

200. Protection Spell

All spirits protect the affairs of the people,
Save The Afflicted Celestial Worthy,
Let the spirits protect the affairs of the people who pass
on to you their wishes and desires.
Quickly O Hong Ren Ji Kun Tianzun lu ling!

(Talisman Fig. 202)

201. Untitled
Attacking Spell

Tianshi command sends the hand that makes insane
the head,
The sword enters the intestines of the belly
and seeks the five solid organs and the six hollow organs,
With this fur all the hairs avenge with death.
Ji Ji Ru Lu Ling.

(Talisman Fig. 203)

202. Ta Hou Tian Bagua Jue Bu Gang Fa
Treading The Post-Heaven Bagua Formula

I reverently request Wuji Taiji Lord,
The Bagua Master quickly descends,
The Celestial Troops and Earth Generals protect my body,
The Liu Ding and Liu Jia follow me,
I act and the Heavenly Net and Earthly Net are requested,
Qian Yuan Heng Li!
Spirit is present and the Five hundred Fierce Thunders
together resound,
Demons and evil ghosts become dust,
The Bagua calms all and brings longevity,
The Bagua calms the home and the home is at peace,
The Jade Command is given and evil is neutralised
by the Six Characters Classic!
Om Mani Padme Hong!
I honour Taishang Laojun.
Ji Ji Ru Lu Ling!

(Talisman Fig. 204)

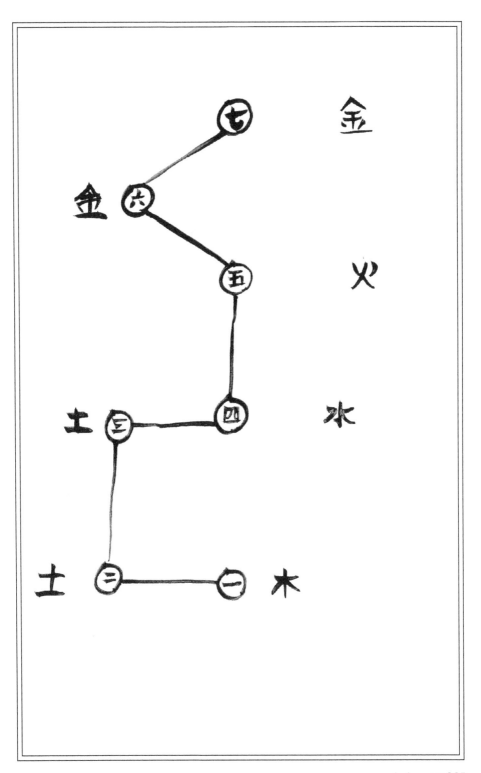

203. Taiyi Zhenren Ta Bagua Jue Bu Gang Fa
Taiyi Steps The Bagua Spell

1. KAN Palace sends forth gushing waves.
2. XUN Palace the wind sweeps away demons.
3. ZHEN Palace the thunderbolt resounds.
4. GEN Palace blocks the Ghost Road.
5. Central Palace, the Sun, Moon and Stars.
6. QIAN Palace Qian Yuan Heng Li!
7. DUI Palace the Lake of the Heroic Army.
8. KUN Palace closes Difu.
9. LI Palace fire burns the ghosts and spirits.
10. Break ghosts and demons now!!
11. The Jade Emperor promptly commands
the Celestial Generals to guard my body,
To slay ghosts and uproot demons to cast them
thousands of miles away,
Tranquility quickly comes to the house
and there is calm and peace.
All people have longevity.
I honour Yu Chi Taishang Laojun,
Ji Ji Ru Lu Ling.

204. Untitled
Stepping The Stars
Of The Sevenfold Big Dipper

White Qi of Hundun (Primordial Creation) guards my body,
The step of Yu both creates and destroys ,
I ascend to the brightness (also righteousness),
Heaven answers,
Earth returns by the Step of the Big Dipper,
Light but strong I tread the Dipper of the Nine Spirits,
Hand grasping the Seven Star Demon Vanquishing Sword,
All calamities perish and people have longevity.
I have eternal virtue and tranquillity.

Stepping The Seven Stars Spell

Stepping the Seven Stars,
Step by step we generate,
In Heaven above are Three Wonders,
Sun, Moon and the Stars,
Liu Ding and Liu Jia protect my body,
The Twenty Eight Palaces are distributed
on my left and right,
Celestial Troops and Earth Generals follow me,
Demons see me and flee a thousand miles,
Demons meet me and their forms are disintegrated,
I honour the Jade Emperor's True Command,
Slaying demons and vanquishing evil
so that they become dust.

Ji Ji Ru Lu Ling!
Wan Fa Jue

Ten Thousand Solutions Method

My spirit is not an extraordinary spirit,
I am Mu Jin Er Shen Ren,
On the left are the Five Thunders Generals
numbering three thousand,
On the right are the Six Doors eighty thousand troops,
Above my head in the blue sky the Sun and Moon
become dim,
Treading in the five directions
and uncovering the gods of the earth,
Thunder roves through the Land Under Heaven
and patrols the world,
Coming to the midst of this house to dispel black magic,
My body manifests a hundred thousand ways of power,
A thousand methods,
ten thousand methods by which I can act,
Seventy two transformations follow from my actions,
My Master today dispels all evil from this place
and all is at peace!
I honour Taishang Hunyuan Mu Jin Zushi,
Ji Ji Ru Lu Ling!

(Talisman Fig. 205)

205. Xiu Lian Qing Shen
Cultivating The Invoking Of Gods

Burning one stick (of incense)
yellow clouds cover the midst of Heaven,
Burning two sticks and a purple cloud
covers the Earth below,
Burning three sticks and in all the ten directions
the disciples are devout.
Bowing I ask Hunyuan Laozu who was born
in the First Month, 19th Day and in the Yin hour.
The Jade Emperor was born in the Bingwu year
in the First Month, Ninth Day at the Wu Hour.
Wang Mu Niangniang,
Taishang Laojun born in the Gengchen Year,
Second Month, Fifteenth Day at the Mao Hour.
Yuanshi Tianzun, Tong Tian Jiaozhu, Jiang Taigong,
Guanyin Dashi born on the Second Month
and Nineteenth day.
Wu Sheng Dijun born on the Sixth Month
on the Twenty third Day,
Hufa Ling Guan and the Ten Kings shall follow,
Buddha was born on the Fourth Month on the eighth day.
A thousand thousand Buddhas,
Millions of Bodhisattvas, Celestial Troops and Earth
Generals, Liu Ding and Liu Jia, the Four Great Celestial
Kings, the Eight Great Diamond Thunderbolt Gods
born on the Sixth Month on the Sixteenth Day,
The Thirty Six Thunder Deng Marshal,
Xin Tian Hu Shizhe Zhen Tian Jun,
Pang Jian Gou, Bi Ma Guan, Zhao Kang, Tian Cui Liu,

Tao Gao Deng Xian, Weng Wang Marshal, Zhao Jiangjun, Wen Taibao, Zhao Si Shi, Yang Wang Shi Chen Jiangjun, Gong Cao, Tudi, Marshal Mu, Marshal Jin, Marshal Huo, Marshal Tu, Hua Tou Zushi, Yao Wang Sheng, Cai Yao Tongzi, Lian Dan Immortal Teacher, Master Zhenwu, Master Pu'an, Master Li Yuan, Master Puti, Master Damo, Master Liu Tou, Master Gang Tou, Master Immortal Luban who was born in the Xu Year, on the First Month, on the twentieth day at the hour of Xu, Mysterious Lady Xuan Nu, Master Xue Shan, Master Ni Shan, Immortal Jiu Tian Ying, Meng Ji Pu Hua Tianzun, Lingbao Tianzun, Marshal Shi Da Dou Chang, Jiang Kang E, Meng Wei Wen, Li Tie Liu Yang, Emperor San Huang, Immortal Master Dong Zhong, Immortal Master Qi Shui Bao Fan,

Immortal Master Feng Jin He Shan, Immortal Li Zhen, Nine Dragon Buddha, Five Directions Jie Di Hong Ren, Master Ji Kun Tianzun, Five Seas Dragon King, Master Mu Jin, Sun Moon Star Heavenly Gate, Tudi Chuan Zhu,

O the Genius Loci Tudi Spirit is requested to attend to this incense altar and accept true incense as evidence of the essential unity with the devout disciple, the disciple requests all the Masters before and behind to pass on the teaching, kindly teacher, we bow our heads at the incense burner as we request, O we bow and request Yin Chuan Teacher to pass on and explain and answer our queries so that the Magical Method prospers,

Xing Dong Shang Qing, Dong Ming Yi, Yang Hou Quan, Hong Yong Jiu, Yang Chuan Shi, Shi Zhong Da, Ji Wu Ying, Gao Yu Hua Deng Xing, Shun Lu Xing, Jun Chen Ren, Xin Tang Xing, Cheng Chen Tong, Shun Wu Ming, Zhong Chuan Du, Enshi Yang Hou Qian,

I bow and ask the Masters to descend as if on horses,
I request that you descend to and attend to this altar
of incense and accept this show of solidarity,
Come! I bow and request all the generations of Masters,
Tian Di Jun Qin, Zhi Fa Guan, Si Guan Caishen,
Niu Da Shi, Guanyin Da Shi, Wu Dai Wang Ren,
Descend to the seat of prosperity.
Tudi Yue, De Rui Qing Furen, Meishan Master,
Xi Shu Ling Tan, Wufang Wudi, Zhen Lai Long Jun,
Leave your homes on the mountains,
come from the mountain caves and come to us
from the twenty-four directions so they all
become prosperous.
On my left the Dragon God called the Azure Dragon,
On my right is the White Tiger,
Before me is the Vermillion Bird,
Behind me is the Dark Warrior,
Dipan Yezhu, All you ancient ancestors, Zhaocai Tongzi,
Jin Bao Lang Jun, Men Shen Er Jiang, Wuyuan Tongzi, Di Shui
Lang Jun, Zao Wang Fu Jun, Li Shi Furen, Ban Chai Tongzi,
Lian Shui Lang Jun,

Please attend to this altar and accept this incense as a true
and great proof of solidarity.

206. Ji Lian Qing Shi Pai Zuo
The Cultivation Rite Of Requesting The Masters To Be Seated

When the disciple has established an altar in his home and requests Gods, Ancestors, Masters and other spiritual beings to stay in his home, there is an initial period when such entities are said to be 'unsettled' and must be encouraged to remain. This ritual is aimed at settling the Gods and spirits in the home.

> I chant the High Seat of the Gods
> Invocation Immortal Sutra,
> All Gods are tranquil in this place,
> Secure and tranquil are the ten thousand Gods,
> The Masters of the Three Doctrines are at their stations,
> All the Gods descend,
> San Huang ascend to their places and Wu Di is tranquil,
> A thousand troops are on the left,
> Ten thousand Generals are on the right,
> The Masters gather and arrive,
> All points of the compass are tranquil,
> Guarding the room of the altar,
> Bestowing us with good fortune,
> A thousand invocations and there area thousand answers,
> Ten thousand invocations
> and there are ten thousand responses,
> Demons are cast aside and devils hidden are revealed,

There comes longevity, prolonging life, converting all to the Path of Dao, the family home is auspicious, those Gods who do not help us and those spirits who cannot take responsibility shall go.

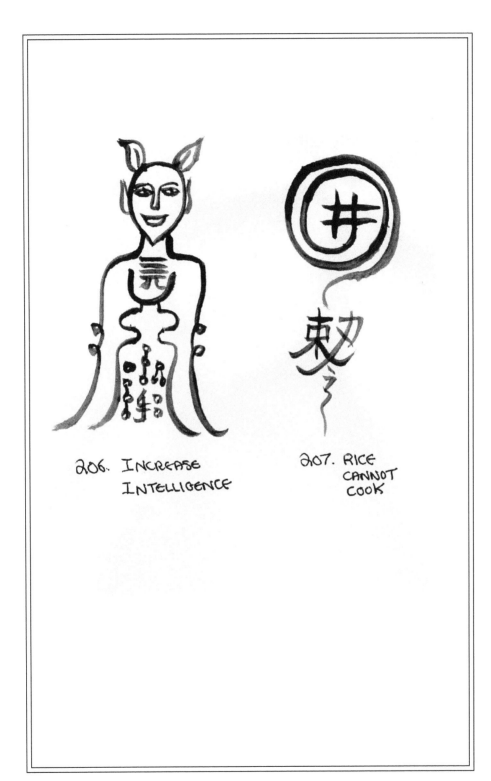

206. INCREASE
INTELLIGENCE

207. RICE
CANNOT
COOK

I honour Tai Hunyuan
Lao Tzu,
Mu Jin Immortal Master!

Ji Ji Ru Lu Ling!

Book IV
A Compendium Of Spells

207. Kai Yuan Fa
Opening Foolishness

The meaning here is to dispel foolishness and ignorance and increase intelligence. In China academic intelligence and the passing of rigorous exams was highly important to ascend in social status.

Heavenly Mother and Earthly Grandson,
Four Girls and Three Spirits,
Southern Dipper Six Officials,
Northern Dipper Seven Stars,
Twenty Eight Mansions that gave birth to ignorance,
Foolishness, Foolishness, Confusion are driven back,
Driven from the seven apertures of the head,
Drive away the uneasy essence!

This method can be used both on males and females. Each month, as well as the spell compound a medicine of purple calamus, three earthworms and with the ashes of the talisman shown. Drink and intelligence and cunning will come without fail.

(Talisman Fig. 206)

208. Ya Ying Zhi Ren Fa
Pressing The Shadow
To Curse A Person

The stonemason lays down the stone at midday as the person passes by or is present. At the moment the sun casts his or her shadow, push down the square stone. Their shadow is pressed under the stone.

In 120 days it becomes a headache and at the zi hour there comes giddiness and a trance like state.

When the Sun is present there is illness but when the sun sets they feel better. The solution is to remove the 'shadow stone' and boil it in water with some soil.

209. Ye Wen Geng Niu Fa
Hear Cattle At Night Method

If a client is not grateful for the work you have done and there are arguments, obtain two old worn out ink markers.

Use white paper to cut out a paper man and point the mouth with the blood of a chicken.

Place the paper doll on the rear of the large roof beam but in the middle.

Use the two old ink sticks to form a cross to support the figure.

The home owner will at night hear sounds that seem to be someone ploughing fields, shouting and ox bellowing.

The solution is to burn the doll and ink markers.

210. Zhufan Bu Shu Fa
Spell So Rice Cannot Be Cooked

You want a certain woman to have difficulties cooking rice. Get three feet of straw rope and bind it around your waist and chant the spell:

Heaven is Pu'an, Earth is Pu'an,
A thousand troops and millions of Divine Generals.
I honour Taishang Laojun.
Ji Ji Ru Lu Ling.

Then draw the sign.

(Talisman Fig. 207)

211. Ding Ren Fa
Nailing A Person

On the fifth month, on the fifth day at the hour of Wu (That is a fire month, fire day and fire hour for extreme Yang energies), go to an open field where there are no people.

Kneel down facing the Sun and say the spell forty nine times and inhale the Solar Qi once and then blow once above shoulder height forty nine times.

After this you should bathe the whole body.

Use cinnabar to draw the talisman and again say the spell forty nine times. Wear the talisman.

The Spell

Fixing Heaven, Fixing Earth,
First fixing Heaven, Earth, Sun and Moon,
Second fixing, Mountains and rivers and seas dry up,
Third fixing,Taishan is broken.
Fourth fixing, the bones of the person's body pass away.
I honour Taishang Laojun.
Ji Ji Ru Lu Ling!

When cultivating this method use the (Fig. 208) Three Mountain Hand Seal. After forty nine days of practising it, recite the spell and draw breath from over your left shoulder in the direction of the target person and that person will be fixed.

When restraining, use (Fig. 208) Three Mountain Hand Seal as above. Burn the Sun and Moon talisman for the sentence

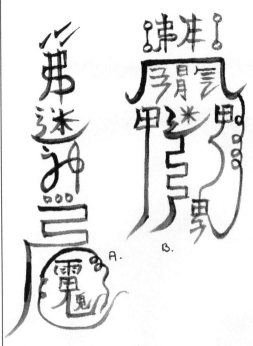

208. FIXING A PERSON

    A. CULTIVATION

    B. SOLAR QI

    C. RIVERS AND SEAS

    D. THREE MOUNTAINS

209. CUT A DRESS

beginning 'First fixing...' and the Rivers and Seas talisman for the sentence beginning 'Second Fixing'.

210.
BEAUTY
UNDRESSES

211. BEAUTY
UNDRESSES
(SEDUCTION)

212. The Three Mountain Hand Seal Method:

Hold out the left hand palm up, let your thumb touch Zi, Hai, Xu , You, Shen, Wu, then to the Jade Palace then to Wu. Suddenly close the fist as if to grasp Qi. Then in order extend the index, little finger and finally the thumb.

(Talisman Fig. 208)

213. Meiren Tuo Yi Fa
The Beauty Strips
Off Her Clothes

To enact this method make a small dress with yellow paper, adding details with chicken blood mixed with a drop of your own blood from your finger. Go to your altar, bow, burning incense and say the spell:

Fuyi! The hand holds the Golden Knife
and red cinnabar gathers,
Ten people see me and nine people are sad,
I honour Laojun who sits at the mouth of the cave,
The beautiful girl takes off her clothes
and is watched by the noble Lords.
Ji Ji Ru Lu Ling!

Later you can burn the dress near a woman and she will be confused with passion and strip off her clothes. The solution is to bite three times on the corner of your robes or clothes and write the command sign and the girl will dress again.

(Talisman Fig. 209, 210)

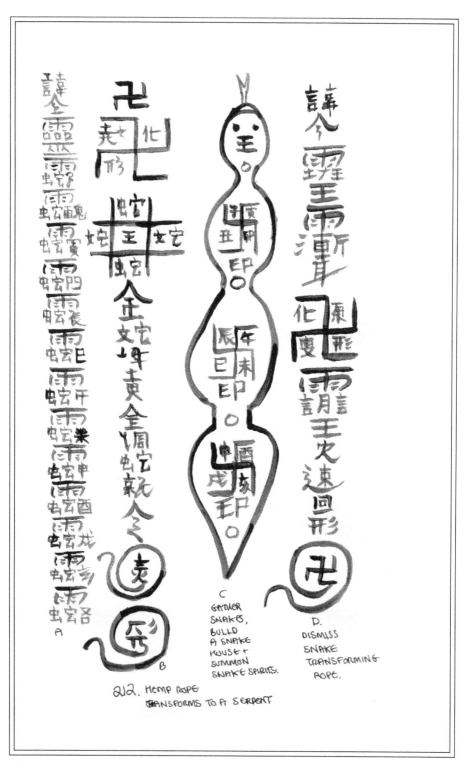

C
GATHER
SNAKES,
BUILD
A SNAKE
HOUSE +
SUMMON
SNAKE SPIRITS.

D.
DISMISS
SNAKE
TRANSFORMING
ROPE.

A

B

212. HEMP ROPE
TRANSFORMS TO A SERPENT

214. Mei You Tuo Yi Fa
The Beauty Strips Off Her Clothes

The sword finger is used to draw the characters above the soft copper coins. Soft copper coins are a species of spirit money in the form of copper foil discs.

The Spell:

Great Cloud Mountain,
Great Cloud Mountain Immortal Waves Cave God,
Dark Female Immortal is above your body
enchanting your three souls and seven spirits,
Losing your modesty and feeling lust, dazed and bewitched,
Lusting and bewitched so that your body follows my desire,
You wish to go east but you go west when I will it,
Commanding you to take off your clothes,
take off your clothes! Strip quickly I command!
I honour Sanshan Jiu Hou Immortal Master!

(Talisman Fig. 211)

215. Caosheng Bian She Fa
Transforming A Hemp Rope
Into A Serpent

Heaven purity and Earth Spirit,
Immortal Luban changes to a serpent form,
The Dao moves and the soul changes its bodily form,
Yin, Mao transforms the bodily form,
Chen, Si transforms the body.
Wu, Wei transforms to a serpent form.
Shen, You transforms and it comes slithering.
Xu, Hai the golden serpent!
This serpent is not an extraordinary serpent
Zhenwu generates the Golden Snake!
I honour Taishang Laojun!
Ji Ji Ru Lu Ling!

(Talisman Fig. 212)

216. Bi Jian Fa
Avoiding The Arrow Method

With confidence, I who am named ......request the Celestial Immortal Cave of Ming Shan to come to this altar that is in this mortal world. Great calamities as arrows shoot do not reach their mark.

(Talisman Fig. 213)

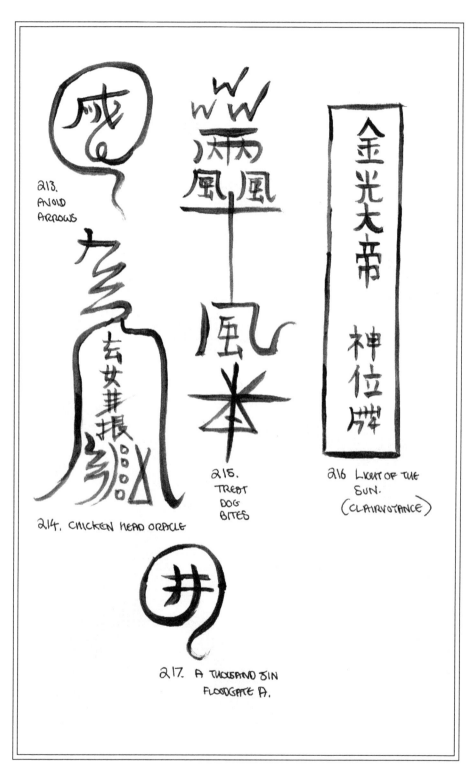

213. AVOID ARROWS

214. CHICKEN HEAD ORACLE

215. TREAT DOG BITES

216 LIGHT OF THE SUN. (CLAIRVOYANCE)

217. A THOUSAND JIN FLOODGATE A.

217. Jitou Tou
The Chicken Head Oracle

Begin this spell at a place where no one can hear you, and let it be a quiet place. Obtain a white rooster with a red beak and red legs if possible, but it can never be black. At the Hour of Wu, read out the spell and cut off the chicken's head and use cinnabar powder to plug its mouth.

Every day at Hai, Mao and Wei hours chanting the spell three times and burn three Tong Shen Fu talismans. Also have incense and candles and cultivate this for thirty five days.

The Spell
Chicken Head Tongzi, Chicken Head Spirit,
I today request you to come to this altar
and attend to me even if there is no altar,
Report to me all that is good or bad,
If the good or ill fortune is not reported
then Jiu Tian Xuan Nu herself will illuminate this method.
I honour Taishang Laojun
Ji Ji Ru Lu Ling!

At some point one will begin to hear a sound like an infant, usually after 45 days. In 100 days it can speak of matters. Do the ceremony often chanting the spell seven times while your hand is in the Sword Hand Seal.

The Spell
High Chicken Head, Chicken Head Official,
I today request you to become a divine general,
In the four seasons there will be a ritual done
on your behalf,

Make known to me the auspicious and the inauspicious,
I request it from Jiu Tian Xuan Nu.
Ji Ji Ru Lu Ling!

For the spell
(Talisman Fig. 214)

218. Qimen Cang Shen Fa
Qimen Hiding Body Method

When going outdoors tread the Ding Bu step (T-shaped step) and read the spell at each step you take on the seven stars.

The Spell

Treading the stars and stepping
the Dipper Path of the Seven Spirits,
Heaven is a circle and Earth is a square,
O I am stepping the Seven Stars.
Filling my form with the two Qis of Hundun,
Ascending to the brightness,
The horse step quickly acts!

The horse step is made by means of the left foot. Before a journey, one wishes to use the Qimen to seek an auspicious door, gaze into the distance towards the auspicious door and tread this step and say the spell.

219. Qu Cao Fa
Gathering The Auspicious Grass Powder

In each of the months, in this order obtain three or twelve stems of grass.

Hai, Zi, Chou, Yin, Mao, Chen, Si, Wu, Wei, Shen, You, Xu.

Before picking the grass perform the Qimen Hiding Body Spell and Step as given previously. Put the tongue on the roof of your mouth and say the spell as follows:

Qian Yuan Heng Li Zhen!
The Sun and Moon hide my form,
The Northern Dipper covers my body,
A hundred stalks of grass conceal my form in the grass
at the roadside,
People cannot see me and ghosts are not aware
of my presence,
I honour Taishang Laojun,
Ji Ji Ru Lu Ling.

The best directions are as follows:
SPRING: East and West
SUMMER: South
AUTUMN: West
WINTER: North

220. Making Use Of Hiding The Body

When reading the spell the right hand is held in the hand seal of the sword and the left hand is held over the heart. Inhale three breaths of Solar Qi and blow on your palm. Turn around and do not speak.

On Metal days use a bamboo leaf upon water.

On Fire days use red flowers.

Water days use straw upon the head.

On Soil and Wood days use straw as well.

For Metal begin at the hour of Ji.

For Fire begin at the hour of Yin.

For Wood begin at the hour of Hai.

For Water begin at the hour of Shen.

The Spell of Hiding the body is thus:

One spirit enters the Greedy Wolf,

Second, spirit enters the Giant Door and is hidden,

Third, Ghosts and Gods are enthroned,

Fourth, the spirit serves Wen Qu,

Fifth, the spirit is in the place of Lian Zhen,

Sixth spirit is in Wu Qu,

Seventh, spirit is concealed in Po Jun.

The san hun spirits cannot be seen.

The Upper Hall of the Jade Emperor comes to my incense,

My form and my body transform into the God Zhenwu,

On my left is the Azure Dragon,

On my right is the White Tiger,

Around my body there is a luminous light,

Ten thousand parts are now divine.

I honour Taishang Laojun,

Ji Ji Ru Lu Ling.

221. Feng Gou Yao Ren Fa
Dealing With The Bite Of A Rabid Dog

From a wall facing south take soil from its upper part and put it in a bowl and add water that has not touched the earth. That is rain water that you have caught in an earthenware bowl. Place the bowl in the direction of the Sun at the place of your altar and have a lamp or candle lit. Your right hand is in the sword seal and the left in Three Mountains seal holding the bowl. Using the sword seal fingertips write the talismanic seal shown over the water. In the four corners write over the bowl the character of zi, (?), as you write each Zi character chant:

> First I write a small point,
> I read a small point,
> Qian and Kun are great.
> Second I write a circle,
> I read the horizontal of cinnabar,
> The Sun and Moon grow.
> Third I write in the four corners,
> The treasure of the south,
> Ten thousand feet deep.
> Fourth I write and it returns.
> I Buddha sit at the centre.

This is chanted three times. Then use mud formed in the bowl to cover the wound.

(Talisman Fig. 215)

218. THOUSAND
JIN
FLOODGATE
B.

219.
DISMISS
FLOODGATE

220.
SPELL OF
SNOW
MOUNTAIN

221. CAST
ILLUSIONS

222. CAUSE
INSANITY

222. Untitled
Sunlight Illumination Method

In a clean room that is peaceful, have a paiwei tablet on the altar. The right hand is in the Sword Seal. Have a young child sat on a chair and with the left hand write between the eyebrows the following characters:

光 Guang, Light   红 Hong, Red

Then read the spell and the child will see the spirits, find lost articles and so on.

The Spell:
Son of Heaven the Essence of Light,
Earthly ground and Spiritual light,
The twelve disciples manifest the light of divinity,
720,000 dragon eyes,
If you do not come,
The Chief of the Thunder Court
will not tolerate your disobedience,
O Dong Wang Gong and Xi Wang Mu.
Today I sprinkle these eyes with dew,
Green brightness (Qing Qing Ming Ming),
The aged shall have longevity,
The disciple is consecrated (Kai guang),
The eyes see and the ears hear,
Southern Dipper Six Officials,
Northern Dipper Seven Stars.
The Great Golden Light Emperor!
Taishang Laojun!
Ji Ji Ru Lu Ling!
(Talisman Fig. 216)

223. Qian Jin Zha
The Floodgate Of A Thousand Jin

Use the right hand to form the Sword Seal and use it to write on the left palm the forbidden word character. No matter how much the people try to lift the coffin once you have touched it with your left hand, they cannot lift it. Recite the spell when touching the coffin:

The Spell:
First change, one thousand jin,
Second change, two thousand jin,
Third change, three thousand jin,
Fourth change, four thousand jin,
The changing arises
and there are a hundred and eight thousand jin,
A thousand men cannot lift it,
Ten thousand men cannot lift it,
Not afraid of the evil magical methods
the Master makes it immoveable,
Not afraid of the nine thousand creations, it is motionless.

A strong and powerful method to cause spirits and evil gods to retreat is to use the forbidden word and say:

The Spell:
First, retreat one thousand miles,
Second retreat two thousand miles,
Retreat one hundred and eighty thousand miles,
Gods do not come near,
Ghosts do not come near,
Retreat to the Ninth Heaven in the midst of the clouds!

(Talisman Figs. 218 and 219)

If you wish that a certain person's domestic animals do not prosper, use this method to cause their swine to waste away. The swine will be in turmoil, excreting in the pen, reluctant to eat and sleep and will not grow meat. Use an old knife and put it in the pig pen beneath a rock and silently say:

The Spell:
Outside the Three Heavenly Doors,
Vast and Mighty,
Dragon and Tiger King descend,
Carrying catastrophe and misfortune!
The hand draws the 'Well' symbol.

The solution to the above spell is to burn incense and light a candle. Remove the rock and knife from the pen and use black ink to write the Seal of the Purple Palace.

224. Xue Shan Ling
The Snow Mountain Command

For thirty nine days you shall cultivate it by placing your middle finger into cold water or ice. That is one has a bowl of ice or ice in water in which you hold your finger as you recite the spell.

The Spell

Snow upon the mountain, Snow upon the mountain,
Snow carried off the mountain,
Snow carried off the mountain,
Before us is Snow Laojun,
His head wears the Snow Hat
and he cries 'le!' the sound of the spirit of water,
Respect my command for my method
is done with diligence,
O celestial brightness of the Southern Dipper,
And you Northern Dipper stars.
Ji Ji Ru Lu Ling.

(Talisman Fig. 220)

225. A Healing Spell
Water of Heaven, Water of Earth

Little Buddha who holds in his hand an iron lotus,
Lower Heavenly Water Person,
Upper Heavenly Water Person,
Water Horse Water General.
A mouthful of hot Qi from the heart,
A mouthful of water Qi quickly descends technique,
Water, the Water Gods come,
Chilled water, meeting with the wound to disperse the injury,
Meeting flowing blood it stops it,
I ask it to be so!

226. Fu Zhong Zhong Du She Fa
Poisonous Serpent
Enters The Belly Method

This spell can put in the belly of an opponent a long snake. The cultivation is similar to the Tighten the Golden Hoop Method.

To work this method form with your left hand the Laojun Hand Seal and above a cup of water chant the spell seven times and give it to the opponent without them knowing.

The Spell

I the Buddha face before an onion,
Peeling nine times nine to make eighty-one layers,
On the left the peelings go to the Azure Dragon,
On the right the peelings draw in the poisonous serpent,
A poisonous serpent goes to enter your belly,
It grows to fifty-six zhang long,
Slowly moving and breaking the intestines,
You shall indeed die.
I honour Taishang Laojun,
Huo Ji Ru Lu Ling!

227. Luan Gu Fa
Disordering The Bones Technique

The right hand forms the hand seal of Er Lang (The Child Official). The thumb shall press the middle finger and the ring finger, the other fingers straighten upwards naturally. Make the hand seal stamp the floor twice and say the spell seven times:

> Heaven causes the bones to upheave,
> Earth causes the bones to upheave,
> From the Western Heaven the Buddha
> comes to trouble your bones,
> First disordering the head and the head is paralysed,
> Second, disordering the bones and the body softens,
> All the bones of your body are troubled and immoveable.
> I honour Taishang Laojun,
> Ji Ji Ru Lu Ling.

228. Du Nei Zhong Shui Lian Fa
A Water Lotus Forms
In The Belly Technique

This method will plant in the lower belly of the enemy a water lotus. Step the Big Dipper while the right hand makes the Er Lang hand seal. Then chant the spell seven times.

The Spell

Heaven implements this technique,
Earth implements this technique,
From the Western Heaven the Buddha
comes to implement this technique,
Neither using the divine method nor the ghost method,
Only the Method of the Water Lotus,
Blooming behind the heart and before the heart,
A great shout as the pain in the belly
becomes hard to endure.
I honour Taishang Laojun!
Ji Ji Ru Lu Ling.

229. Laojun Bai Bu Duan Chang Sha
Laojun One Hundred Steps Breaks The Intestines Killing Method

In this method a person cannot leave a room in one hundred steps. To cultivate this method, you step the Big Dipper with the left hand in the Laojun hand seal. After applying this law the person cannot walk a hundred paces or he will be stricken with and die from belly pain.

The Spell

Iron gives birth to steel,
Steel protects iron,
The steel chain goes to the place of Laojun's burner,
Tempering it for forty-nine days,
It can hold the steel chain and cultivate it,
Once accomplished it can grind the seven seas
and the waters of the eight rivers,
The steel chain is aroused to become
the truly renowned steel chain,
A steel chain becomes a flying dragon that whips its tail,
The steel chain falls to the earth
and the tiger turns its body,
Pushing aside teeth and prying open the mouth,
The twelve links of the steel chain enter the belly
to cut the large intestine,
To cut the small intestine, to cut the five
and six internal organs.
You cannot walk a hundred steps.
I honour Taishang Laojun
Ji Ji Ru Lu Ling!

230. Zhi Ren Fa
Making Person Method

This is a method to capture the soul of a person, a Chinese method of controlling and bewitching a person. The Zhi Ren Fa skills are many, such as the Mi Hun Dafa (Bewitch the Soul Technique) and here we shall introduce one such method.

Do not use it casually for this is the method of Fetching the Human Soul (Qu Ren Hunpo). Write on paper the full name and date of birth (ba zi) on paper and have the braided hair of a woman about a foot long and arrange it in a circle on the floor. Put the paper in the centre and point the paper with the blood of a rooster.

Then suddenly pierce the paper with a knife. You can also use a portrait or cut the paper into a paper doll except you can never pierce the heart. Then recite the Bring Soul Spell seven times:

Heaven is Pu'an, Earth is Pu'an,

Earth has a thousand troops,

Ten thousand times ten thousand Divine Generals come.

I honour Taishang Laojun

Ji Ji Ru Lu Ling!

One should do all the above in a quiet room to avoid distracting noise and have a Taishang Laojun Shenwei (a spirit tablet devoted to Taishang Laojun).

Do at the Hour of Zi and chant the spell seven times daily over a period of twenty-one days. Others cannot see.

231. Gou Hun Fa
Hooking The Soul Method

The capturing the soul technique is a dark method of the netherworld. Using two dishes or shallow basins.

Both eyes are open and the whole body is relaxed, breathing deeply nine times.

Have the left hand in the Laojun hand seal.

This is done by having the left hand palm up, the index finger stands upwards, the thumb presses the root of the index finger at the point of Yin. The little finger is bent behind the ring finger.

The ring finger forcefully holds the middle finger and the middle finger is bent to the centre of the palm.

Place this hand seal on the left knee and the right hand is opened naturally and placed on the right hand.

The Spell

In the first seizing, Heaven arrives,
In the second seizing, Earth arrives,
In the third seizing, seize the person named…,
Their soul arrives,
Tightly and firmly grip them,
The gripping slowly arrives,
If you do not come then the Kitchen God
and Door Gods together come to lift them and seize them,
First seizing, there is darkness and confusion,
Second seizing, there is weakness,
Third seizing and in several days you can crawl
but you cannot rise up!
I honour Taishang Laojun!

Huo Ji Ru Lu Ling!

老尹诀
(TAI SHANG)
LAOTUN JUE

Prepare in advance a five inch long and two inch wide rectangular peach wood tablet and paint on one side the evil person's full name and their accurate birth date.

Then hold the peach tablet in your left hand and say the Gou Hun Dafa Zhou (Hooking Soul Great Method Spell given above).

Say the spell once through and blow a mouthful of qi in the direction of the peachwood tablet. Then with red thread wrap around the tablet, read the spell again, then another circle of twine around the tablet and so on for forty-nine times.

Next you place the tablet underneath a table leg ... the heavier the table the better. If the person is weak you only need to do this only once but for a person strong with yang qi you will need to do the spell on seven consecutive days.

The best time to do the spell is at 3am or 5am.

If the soul of the person is hooked in a severe way they will waste away and become emaciated.

If you are merciful you can remove the tablet from under the table and the spell is dissipated.

Anymore than 100 days and they shall surely die.

(Talisman Fig. 224)

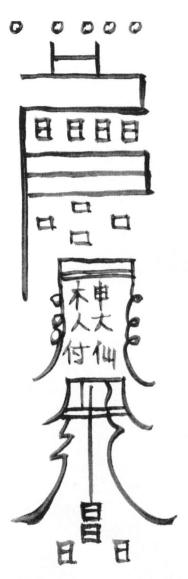

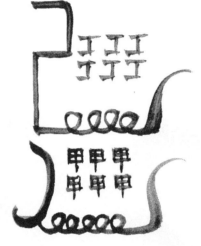

224. HOOK SOUL.

223. BLACKENED EYES
     FIXING TECHNIQUE

232. Hei Yan Ding Shen Fa
Blackened Eyes Fixing Body Method

The Blackened Eyes Fixing Body Technique is a spell that is infamous and dreaded in Chinese magical culture. The sorcerer aimed at pinning the life forces of the target which manifested as a vague, trance-like state, loss of appetite, bodily aches and pains and eventually wasting.

With the emaciation the eyes sink into the skull and hence the name 'blackened eyes'.

Two of the talismans shown were drawn and burned daily, the Big Dipper step is trod while the hand is in the Big Dipper Hand Seal to cultivate this method.

It is best done on the first or fifteenth day of the first lunar month or on the fifth day of the fifth lunar month.

The Spell
Heaven is in chaos, Earth is dark,
The Sun and Moon are darkened,
HE! Black clouds obscure them,
I ask the Southern Dipper Six Officials,
I ask the Seven Stars of the Northern Dipper,
I honour Taishang Laojun,
Ji Ji Ru Lu Ling!

(Talisman Fig. 223)

233. Zhao Yan Fa
Covering The Eyes Method

This method will dim or blur a person's sight so they cannot distinguish between the real or the unreal.

The 'Rivers and Mountains' conjurers use it so people cannot see their tricks.

To practise this method step the Big Dipper Step with the left hand in the hand seal of Laojun, and the right hand adopts the Sword Seal and points to the person or people you wish to influence magically. Recite the spell and draw the magical glyph seven times with the Sword Seal.

Recite the Spell seven times:
Blue Stone Mountain, Orchid Stone Mountain,
Stone Mountain,
The mountain turns upside down and splits,
Four little ghosts barr the road,
The Mountain God and Earth God block the road,
Seizing yellow soil to obscure their eyes!
I honour Taishang Laojun,
Ji Ji Ru Lu Ling!

(Talisman Fig. 221)

234. Wan Bing Feng
Ten Thousand Sicknesses And Insanities

If a person repairs a house and uses ink and tea to draw this seal on the doors, windows or best of all the central beam, then a month later their home will have sickness and they cannot even leave the bed to eat.

The solution is to say the Spell of Dismissal:

Heavenly Emperor, Earthly Emperor, Emperor of Man,
I request you to descend from the Hall of Prosperity,
The disciple honours you and requests that there will be
a recovery from the illness and a return to yang.
I honour Taishang Laojun.
Ji Ji Ru Lu Ling!

(Talisman Fig. 222)

235. Taishang Laojun Kun Xian Sheng Fa The Immortal Binding Rope Technique Of Taishang Laojun

This method is best done on the second lunar month on the fifteenth day and at the hour of Zi.

Before the rites of cultivation one should bathe and rinse out the mouth and burn incense.

Obtain three hemp strings that you shall twine together as you read the Twelve Divine Generals Spell. Read one sentence and twist to entwine the three strands to make a rope.

Note that the twelve generals are associated with the twelve months in a year of the Chinese calendar:

1st. Deng Ming, Water and Hai

2nd He Kui, Soil and Xu

3rd Cong Kui, Metal and You

4th Chuan Song, Metal and Shen

5th Xiao Ji, Soil,Wei

6th Sheng Guang, Fire, Wu

7th Tai Yi, Fire,Si

8th Tian Gong, Soil, Chen

9th Tai Chang, Wood,Mao

10th Gong Cao, Wood, Yin

11th Da Ji, Soil, Chou

12th Shen Hou, Shui, Zi

Spell Of The Twelve Generals
For Making The Rope

Taigong Taiyi who transmits the holy light of auspiciousness, The Big Dipper Chong Kui to which we ascend to the bright spirit that is there,

Then the great Gong Cao, Tai Chong, Tian Gong, Tai Yi, Sheng Guang, Xiao Ji, Chuan Song, Cong Kui, He Kui, Deng Ming and Shen Hou!

After the making of the rope by twisting the three strands of it, then in the second lunar month upon the 23rd day, again chant the spell of the Twelve Generals and dye the rope to a red colour. The rope is finished.

With this rope you can bind evil spirits and demons and remove them.

Perhaps the patient is fierce and ferocious, demonic, evil, or even charming and bewitching, or having lost their mind they are weeping, laughing and speaking.

The Master of the Method should grasp the rope and read the Spell of the Immortal Binding Rope. Evil spirits or demons will find it nigh impossible to escape and in fact the more it tries to writhe and jump the more entangled it becomes, the more taut the rope until it begs piteously. The Master should ask the demon its purpose in clear terms, its power and its name. Be careful not to release it too soon for demons are deceptive and clever.

236. Kun Xian Sheng Zhou
Immortal Binding Rope Spell

Spirits are dispelled, scattered and bound,
People have longevity and are bound,
First binding, ghosts become dust,
Spirits who are not true and are demons.
Second binding, poisonous horned fire official gods.
Third binding, Evil Fox Immortals and Yellow Weasels.
Fourth binding, The White Tiger spirit of broken temples,
Fifth binding, The five ways river spirits,
Sixth binding,
Pressing the Ancient Tree Spirits who cause pain,
Seventh binding, The drowned and hung ghosts,
Eight binding, Spirits lodging in the Temple Hall,
Ninth binding, Jiu Tian Xuan Nu comes to aid,
Tenth binding, To the Ten Palaces of the King
of the Underworld.
Cannot disobey the high binding,
Cannot disobey the low binding,
Calling the High Mountain Great Court Assembly of Gods,
Binding the spirits of the lesser Low Mountain Temples,
Binding the Immortal Willow Spirit,
I honour Taishang Laojun,
Ji Ji Ru Lu Ling.

Talisman 225

237. Zhu Ye Bian Yu Fa
A Bamboo Leaf
Becomes A Fish Technique

The Spell:
Buddha Mountain in the midst of the Black Bamboo Forest,
There in the forest is the Lotus Flower Pond and within it
is spirit fish among many spirit fish.
The root of the bamboo shoot is high,
Thus we create the spirit fish
and cultivate them in this water,
Raising the spirit fish to be golden and nine cun long,
See how they swim in lines in the midst of the water,
Using this water to manifest spiritual power,
Within golden Qi light sparkles within as the heart
of Guanyin enters the pond to aid in this cultivation,
I today speak the True Method and to my command
rise up the forms of fish,
I today create you and cultivate spirit
and follow you in the river,
Seven characters transform your form,
I sincerely ask you to pass the ways of longevity to all living
beings and allow a successful cultivation,
My seven characters descend quickly
and the transformation begins.
Listen to my command and transform
into the form of a fish!
I honour Taishang Laojun,
Ji Ji Ru Lu Ling.

Secondary Spell:

A great river of three thousand miles,
A small journey through eight hundred doors,
Wind and water aid in the journey,
The pure water of the rivers go to the Four Seas,
Come to the flowing water and act!

(Talisman Fig. 225)

Appendix 1
The Luban Ruler

Who Was Luban?

Luban is a rather mysterious character in Chinese history. From a western point of view we could say he is like a Western Daedelus, an inventor, a master craftsman, woodworker and builder.

Lu Ban (Chinese: 鲁班) (507–440 BC) was a Chinese carpenter, engineer, philosopher, inventor, military thinker, statesman and contemporary of Mozi. He was born in the State of Lu and is the patron saint of Chinese builders and contractors. He was born in a renowned family during the Spring and Autumn Period (770 BC–426 BC) when China was suffering from the chaos of civil wars between kingdoms. His original name was Gongshu Yizhi (Chinese: 公输依智). He was also known as Gongshu Ban (公输班), but he was more commonly known as Lu Ban.

According to tradition, he was responsible for several inventions as seen on Mozi chapter 49 and 50:

– Cloud ladder – a mobile counterweighted siege ladder.

– Grappling hooks and ram – boat implements used during naval warfare.

– Wooden bird – a non-powered flying wooden bird which could stay in the air for three days, and had been suggested to be a proto-kite.

There were also other inventions contributed to him, such as a lifting implement for burial, a wooden horse carriage and coachman, and some other woodworking which can be seen from various texts. These inventions led Lu Ban to be acknowledged as a master craftsman.

However, Luban was also credited with an esoteric and magical knowledge which makes sense, since Luban was a builder. In ancient times, to build tombs, temples and houses would require an enormous knowledge of FengShui. In order to place buildings correctly and engineer them to the esoteric principles of understanding Qi flow. Thus the Luban Ruler came into being.

The luban ruler is used in measuring all things correctly. Whether it is the height of a statue, the length of a magical instrument, the dimensions of an altar, a house and its furniture and so on.

It is one of the frequently forgotten tools of the Feng Shui master in modern feng shui where the focus tends to only be on the luopan or feng shui compass.

In ancient times the luban ruler would have used string or wood to measure out Chinese inches. Thankfully today we can buy a convenient one in the form of a builder's tape measure that is in fact more durable and accurate.

Using A Luban Ruler

The Luban ruler **魯班尺**, Luban Chi, is also sometimes known as the Scholar's Ruler **文公尺** or Wen Gong Chi.

At first glance it may appear to be an ordinary tape measure. Indeed millions of Chinese and Japanese may use it as such without realising its real significance.

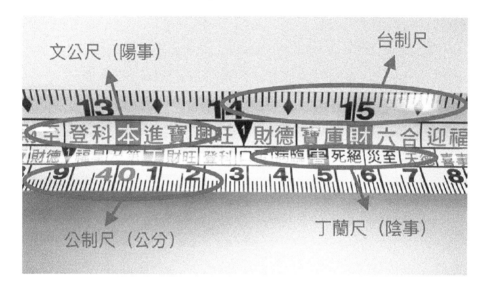

The first thing to take into account is that the Luban Ruler is divided into two halves. Look at the photograph above that shows a section of the Luban ruler.

You can immediately see the difference in that the ruler is divided into four sections.

The top half, using Chinese inches, is the Yang side and is used in Yang Zhai fengshui. That is, the Feng Shui that is used in the houses of the living.

The lower half using fractions of Chinese inches is for Yin

Zhai Feng Shui, the feng shui of the Houses of the Dead, that is tombs.

In the centre you can see words in ,of course, Chinese. The red letters are auspicious, and the black ones inauspicious.

The Luban ruler was originally created by Luban in the Spring and Autumn Period, and over time the various factors of Feng Shui were added to it by the Masters.

Ancient craftsmen were highly aware of feng shui and the fact that measurement is equal to vibration. There is a correspondence between length in space and energy. Sometimes this energy is good and sometimes not so good.

This knowledge was codified on the luban ruler to ensure that when building a house or temple the best frequencies were crystallised within its layout and structure.

The writing on the inside is based on the five characters of:

Birth … Sheng 生

Old Age … Lao 老

Sickness … Bing 病

Death … Si 死

Suffering … Ku 苦

These five are the foundation of the Luban ruler and are further divided by eight further principles:

1. Cai or Wealth 財 The ability or capability to gain, keep and attract wealth.

2. Bing or Sickness 病 Indicates the calamity(zai) of disease or sickness and is obviously unfavourable.

3. Li is one of the names of the Trigrams 離 but also refers to the Six Relations, Liu Qin 六親, Father, Mother, Elder Brother, Younger Brother, Wife and Children and their separation from each other.

4. Yi means Justice or righteousness. 義 ? This principle refers to whether we accord with righteous behaviour, moral standards and do good deeds.

5. Guan means Official 官 It is a neutral term referring to our career, our fortune as an 'official'.

6. Jie means to be robbed or plundered. 劫 Obviously this is never fortunate and means we have lost property by coercion or force.

7. Hai means harm or damage. 害. As the name implies, it's a condition or influence that damages property, career and so forth. It indicates conflict.

8. Ben or Root. 本. Indicates the starting point of a given vibration, the beginning or start of something.
These characters are then combined with the following to give a more precise reading on the Luban Ruler as follows:

1. **財** Cai, or Wealth is indeed highly fortunate and indicates a vibration where wealth can enter the home or Temple. Often this is the measurement wanted in designing an altar, a temple or even office furniture and placement for a business.

2. **財德** Cai De, can means Wealth and Virtue. Again a highly auspicious vibrationary measurement that speaks for itself. This is especially good for the family home and temples and measuring Taoist or Buddhist images and tools.

3. **寶庫** Bao Ku literally means Treasury or Storehouse of Wealth. Initiates in a Daoist lineage will have a deep understanding of the concept of the Bao Ku as being tied to merit and virtue and the riches which manifest in life. This is more about the ability to save wealth.

4. **六合** Liu He or the Six Harmonies is an auspicious measurement referring to the harmony and tranquillity between the Four Directions, Heaven and Earth.

5. **迎福** Ying Fu or Blessings. Happiness and joy, so very positive for a home.

6. **病** Bing, sickness. Obviously it indicates a measured frequency that can potentially bring sickness or disease.

7. **退財** Yui Cai means Money Returns. Negative in that it indicates a loss of wealth and damage and loss of assets.

8. **公事** Gong Shi, Official Matters. Refers to matters such as lawsuits, legal problems and other matters that bring the attention of the authorities.

9. **牢執** Lao Zhi, prison and confinement. Punishment.

10. **孤寡** Gu Gua, widowhood. Obviously has a negative connotation. Death of a spouse or loneliness and trouble in relationships.

11. **離** Li , Separation is highly inauspicious for the family relationships. Indicating a fateful or even a forceful separation of the 'six relatives' in a family.

12. **長庫** Chang Ku, is an ancient term for prison. Punishment and/or isolation and depression.

13. **劫財** Jie Kai, Looting meaning loss of wealth and assets.

14. **官鬼** Guan Gui, Official Ghost. This measured frequency indicates troubles coming from the authorities. A bad relationship with police, government and councils for example.

15. **失脫** Shi Tuo. Loss. Loss of assets and loss in relationships via separation.

16. **義** Yi, Righteousness. Highly auspicious frequency. Philanthropy, gaining of merit and virtue.

17. **添丁** Tian Ding Means 'Add to the Family', it is a good frequency for couples who want a child. Hence this measurement can be used in the bedroom.

18. **益利** Yi Li means Profit. An excellent measurement for businesses and merchants.

19. **貴子** Gui Zi, Noble. A measurement to attract rich clients or sponsors and for promoting one's children to become 'noble' and to have a successful career.

20. **大吉** Da Ji. Great Fortune is a highly auspicious frequency.

21. **官** Guan. Official. Referring to the actions of authorities. Good for those in office, not so good for those who are not officials.

22. **順科** Shun Ke. One of the best measurements for students and scholars and for passing examinations.

23. **橫財** Heng Cai. A sudden windfall of unexpected wealth. Ideal for some furniture in a business premise, for gamblers and so on.

24. **進益** Jin Yi. Benefit or Progress. Auspicious for advancing in any project or life matter.

25. **富貴** Fu Gui literally means Rich and Expensive. Attracting riches and executive power. A good one, say for a manager's office or an altar to the Gods of Wealth.

26. **劫** Jie, Robbery. Loss , coercion, crime. Obviously not a positive frequency.

27. **死別** Si bie. Death. Must never be used. If you find this in examining a home, action is needed.

28. **退口** Tui Kou, literally means retreat, but refers to the harmony of filial piety. Good relationships between parents and children.

29. **離鄉** Li Xiang, means to be far from home. Refers to being uprooted from one's home or having to have extended trips to far away places. Generally inauspicious for family integrity.

30. **財失** Cai Shi. Loss of wealth and assets.

31. **害** Hai or Harm, is very inauspicious in all matters.

32. **災至** Zai Zhi, Disaster, especially those having to do with water. Very inauspicious to those living near water with risk of flooding, poor Water Feng Shui situations and of course in measurements on water vessels.

33. **死絕** Si Jue, Death so very inauspicious.

34. **病臨** Bing Lin. Illness and disease, not a good measurement especially for homes, temples and clinical practices.

35. **口舌** Kou She, Breath or tongue, encourages gossip, disputes and back-bitng.

36. **本** Ben, the Root, auspicious.

37. **財至** Cai Zhi, Wealth and profits come.

38. **登科** Deng Ke, Excellent for scholars and examinations.

39. **進寶** Jin Bao, Treasure Enters. Attracting wealth and riches.

40. **興旺** Xing Wang. Prosperity, another good measurement for the same.

In using the Luban Ruler, a good rule of thumb is black is bad and red is good.

However serious Feng Shui practitioners and fangshi masters will need to be far more specific.

The Luban ruler is used in two ways:

The first is in building, making or choosing a home or furniture, which also includes statues for your altar.

The second is when you are assessing a home or business for potential energetic pathologies.

In general we can summarise:

– For homes Daji characters are best.

– For businesses the wealth characters are best.

– For Temples or altar rooms the characters of righteousness and virtue are best.

For government offices, police etc, the Official characters are best.

The ruler can be used to measure both the dimensions of things and measurements between things, i.e. the distance.

The Luban Ruler is best used with the Feng Shui Compass (Luopan) to establish correct directions to relate them to measurements.

For your own Altar Room, use the Luban Ruler to find the Wealth point. To do this measure from the ceiling to the floor to find a suitable height for the altar and from wall to altar position.

From the Altar to the end of the room the distance should be 2.5 as much as the height of the Altar.

Remember to consider the Left (Azure Dragon) and right (white tiger)!

Appendix 2
The Twelve Earthly Branches

The 12 Earthly Branches or Dizhi, will be much more familiar to the western reader as you will know them as the Twelve Animals of the Chinese Zodiac. The Earthly Branches give their name in combination with the Heavenly Stems to hours, days, months and years. Thus we can speak of the year of the Metal Pig. The Heavenly stem gives the Element and the Branch the zodiacal animal quality. This system allows the occultist, diviner or medical practitioner to analyse the general occult forces at play in any given hour, day or year. At its simplest this may be the consultation of a Chinese Almanac, at an advanced level, it requires methods such as Qimen Dun Jia or astrology.

When we say Chinese Zodiac it has a completely different meaning to that of the Western Zodiac. The western zodiac is based on observations of the movement of the Sun along the plane of the ecliptic, i.e. in its apparent orbit around the earth. This takes about a year and this is divided into twelve sections which make up the signs of the zodiac. The ancient Chinese astrologers took as their cosmic base the orbit of Jupiter rather than that of the Sun, which rounded off takes around twelve years. Each year is assigned one of the twelve earthly branches. We combine these with the Heavenly branches to arrive at a calendrical system we call Ganzhi.

Table of the Twelve Branches.

Combine the Heavenly Stems and the Earthly Branches and we have a complete calendar that has a cycle of sixty years or 12 multiplied by 5. Thus we can give an energetic value for each year. 2020, the year I am writing this book, for example, is a Yang Year governed by the Metal Rat. This is important knowledge for the occultist and healer.

The Twelve Earthly Branches are also assigned to the hand for use in Taoist magical hand seals as you will see later in the practical magical section of this book.

An interesting concept in Asian culture is that when a person reaches 60 years of age one cycle of the sexagenary cycle has passed, and so 60 is considered the Second Birth is an auspicious year. A special celebration is held and red clothes and vests are worn. The red clothes are the same as those worn by newly born infants. 60 is, therefore, the time of renewal and birth into the higher octave of one's cycle.

Unfortunate ages are said to be 24 and 41 for men and 18 and 32 for women.

Chinese Name	Animal	Time Period	Season	Direction	Element and polarity
Zi	Rat	11pm-1am	Winter	North	Yang Water
Chou	Ox	1 am-3am	Winter	Northeast	Yin Water
Yin	Tiger	3 am-5am	Spring	Northeast	Yang Wood
Mao	Hare/Rabbit	5 am-7am	Spring	East	Yin Wood
Chen	Dragon	7am-9am	Spring	Southeast	Yang Wood
Si	Snake	9am-11am	Summer	Southeast	Yin Fire
Wu	Horse	11am-1pm	Summer	South	Yang Fire
Wei	Sheep	1pm-3pm	Summer	Southwest	Yin Fire
Shen	Monkey	3pm-5pm	Autumn	Southwest	Yang Metal
You	Rooster	5pm-7pm	Autumn	West	Yin Metal
Xu	Dog	7pm-9pm	Autumn	Northwest	Yang Metal
Hai	Boar/Pig	9pm-11pm	Winter	Northwest	Yin Water

子 Zi. Rat. 丑 Chou. Ox. 寅 Yin. Tiger.

卯 Mao. Hare. 辰 Chen. Dragon. 巳 Si. Snake.

午 Wu. Horse. 未 Wei. Sheep. 申 Shen. Monkey.

酉 You. Rooster. 戌 Xu. Dog. 亥 Hai. Pig.

Table Of The Heavenly Stems

NAME IN CHINESE	ELEMENT	POLARITY
JIA	WOOD	YANG
YI	WOOD	YIN
BING	FIRE	YANG
DING	FIRE	YIN
WU	SOIL	YANG
JI	SOIL	YIN
GENG	METAL	YANG
XIN	METAL	YIN
REN	WATER	YANG
GUI	WATER	YIN

Jia
Yang Wood.

Yi.
Yin. Wood.

Bing.
Yang Fire.

Ding.
Yin Fire.

Wu.
Yang Earth.

Ji.
Yin Earth.

Geng.
Yang Metal.

Xin.
Yin Metal.

Ren.
Yang Water.

Gui
Yin Water.

Appendix 3
Journey To The Underworld

Though the text of the Luban has a spell for descending to the Underworld it is not entirely clear, so I have decided to reveal one of the methods used in the Jasper Lake Maoshan system to which I owe my own initiation.

Essentially the idea is to send one's own soul to the Underworld to rescue the souls of others or garner information from the dead. Some will also take on this journey for personal gnosis.

In Maoshan we call this the Xia Yin Mi Fa or Descend to Yin Secret Technique. Needless to say one should be very careful in its use and for this reason this is usually done in pairs. That is one takes the role of the medium and another as the magician who invokes and takes care of the medium's safety.

Items to be prepared a white cloth, several pieces of rough straw paper (cao zhi).

The straw paper should not be the usual imperial yellow used in many talismans but white or beige.

On the white cloth draw in red ink the design shown in the diagram and on the sheets you will be drawing the talisman of Yin Descent or Jiang Tong Fu representing the Child Spirit who will guide the medium to the Underworld or Yin World.

Steps

1. To prepare for Yin Descent, have a quiet room and a single

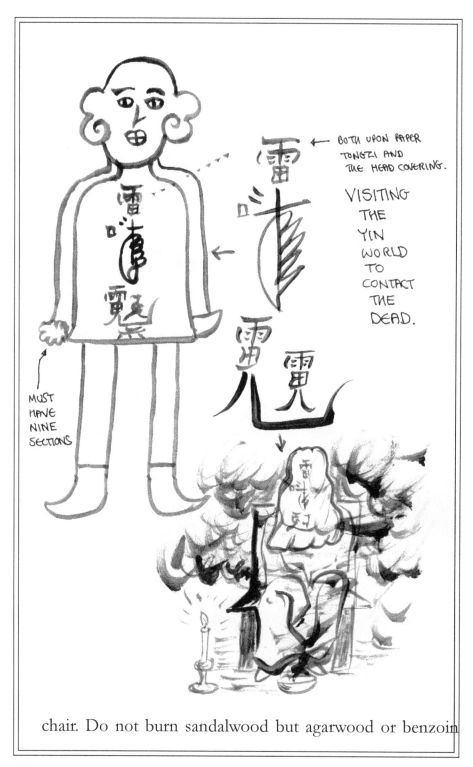

chair. Do not burn sandalwood but agarwood or benzoin

incense. A single candle, white in colour is used.

2. The magician at the threshold of the door recites the Qing Shen Zhou (Request Spirits Spell) and burns some silver spirit money. This money is a yellow sheet with a silver foil square in the centre. Do not use gold money. Burn three sheets. Repeat the spell three times and each time burning three sheets of silver cut spirit money.

QING SHEN ZHOU
The sun is sinking and the night is Yin,
Request the Immortal Auntie to carry the Yang Soul beyond,
Carry the Yang Soul to return to the Road to Yin,
Over the Naihe Bridge,
The hands sway and the feet sway,
Over the Naihe stream
(the river separating the Yang World from the Yin World),
The hands are hooked and the feet are hooked,
Fourth Sister Zhang opens the Flower Door,
Seventh Sister Zhang carries the disciple
to the Flower Garden,
Pulling the flowers and trees
and the roots of golden flowers,
I who am in the mortal world see the people of the flowers,
Quickly come, come! Come early, Come early!
Do not come at dusk or late at night!
(ie do not tarry, in Chinese euphemism).

3. On the straw paper the magician now draws three Descending Child Talismans (Jiang Tong Fu) (see figure).

On the white cloth use the Sword Seal finger to trace over the painted sigil to energise it with protective qi.

4. Light three agarwood or benzoin incense sticks. Put the cloth over the head of the seated medium to cover the face. Burn the talismans at the feet of the medium who should be aligned with the Ghost Gate, that is, to the North East.

5. Keep repeating the Shen Zhou Spell until the medium is unconscious or in trance. The average time in which the medium will be gone is around two hours.

The magician will call back the medium by calling at the chest of the medium and pat them on the back three times saying 'Hua Lai, Hua Lai, Hua Lai' (Return, Return, Return) and also request them to return to the earth and call their name.

Initially they will be sleepy on return, may have temporary amnesia and have bodily aches.

Notes: Xia Yin is a long process with lots of chanting so be prepared. Do not write the paper dolls haphazardly, take your time.

Women make the best mediums as men have a heavier Yang. The First and Fifteenth days of the lunar month are best. Keep the light to a minimum, the darker the better.

In the picture below you can see the practitioner descending to the Yin World with a veil of face cloth in position so the medium is ready to project the soul across the Naihe Bridge.

The face cloth suggests the cloth placed over the faces of the dead lying in wait before burial.

Going Further

For further information on the Jasper Lake Maoshan School please contact lanyards71@gmail.com or visit our website:

https://maoshantemple.com/

Index of Spells

Index

Printed in the USA
CPSIA information can be obtained
at www.ICGtesting.com
LVHW051306211123
764224LV00048B/1444/J